Let's Grandparent

Activity Guide
for Young Grandchildren

Let's Grandparent

*Activity Guide
for Young Grandchildren*

by
JoAn Vaughan

INFORMATION AGE PUBLISHING, INC.
Charlotte, NC • www.infoagepub.com

Library of Congress Cataloging-in-Publication Data

Vaughan, JoAn.
  Let's grandparent : activity guide for young grandchildren / by JoAn
Vaughan.
     p. cm.
  Includes bibliographical references and index.
  ISBN 978-1-60752-025-2 (pbk.) – ISBN 978-1-60752-026-9 (hardcover)
  1. Grandparent and child. 2. Creative activities and seat work. I.
Title.
  HQ759.9.V38 2009
  649'.51–dc22

                                                          2008046565

Printed in the United States of America

To my grandchildren—
Jake, Jenna, Emerson, Alex, and Amy

Contents

Introduction

Let's Begin

Merging Personal and Professional Experiences

Perhaps it was the incessant rain that cast a gloom over my spirits, but as I listened to my grandchildren vehemently arguing over whose turn it was to push Thomas the Tank Engine through the tunnel, I pondered, "What

Let's Grandparent: Activity Guide for Young Grandchildren, pages ix–xi can I do to make my new role as grandparent more fun and meaningful?" It was then that the latent preschool teacher emerged to exclaim, "Let's make play dough." As we stirred up a gooey batch and turned it into snakes and cakes, the sun came out and I declared it the perfect day for a puddle-jumping walk. Now I look forward to each visit with my grandchildren so I can try out a new activity. They greet me at the door with the excited refrain, "What are we going to do today?"

I have the good fortune of having five young and energetic grandchildren. Three live right next door to me. They challenge me constantly to come up with new activities to do with them. Unfortunately, my other two grandchildren live on the opposite coast. Here the challenge is to find ways to stay connected across the miles.

In my new role as grandparent I have drawn upon the knowledge and experience of a long career in early childhood education. My PhD program in Child and Family Development at the University of Missouri emphasized the importance of the family in the child's formative years. During my 30 years in the Education Department at Stephens College, Columbia, Missouri, I worked at various times as preschool and kindergarten teacher, college professor, director of the Stephens College Lab School, director of teacher education, and chair of the department. I taught courses in child development, early childhood education, and family studies. Most recently I have taught child development, sociology of the family, and psychology courses in the Psychology Department at Menlo College, Atherton, California.

My professional career as an early childhood educator has provided me with a repertoire of fun and educational experiences to share with my grandchildren as well as a better understanding of their behaviors and feelings. I have written this book so that other grandparents might benefit as I have from knowledge about child development and early childhood education.

This book focuses on those crucial early years when grandchildren are most open to new relationships, yet they sometimes may puzzle, alarm, or exasperate us with their unexpected behavior. In it, I share developmental insights and strategies that can make time with grandchildren more personally fulfilling and educationally relevant to their development.

Acknowledgments

My friends and family provided their generous support and assistance in the writing of this book. My sister, Laura Berns, PhD, gave major organizational, editing, and anecdotal input. My husband, Ed Vaughan, PhD, enthusiastically supported me throughout the process with ideas and editing suggestions. My oldest son, Joe Vaughan, provided valuable insights about the organization and presentation of the book. Many grandparents shared their ideas, including Rosemary Walden, Phoebe Rastorfer, Tom and Susan Gray, Nancy Newbill, John Lange, Jenny Myers, Sonja Griffiths, and Karen Newborn.

Steve Vaughan, Liu Quanjing, Laura Vaughan, and Mark Lange, who have given their children abundant love and exemplary parenting, generously let me kid-test these activities with my grandchildren, including some that left them splattered with paint or dripping with water. The enthusiastic participation of my grandchildren—Jake, Jenna, Emerson, Alex, and Amy—made writing this book such a pleasurable experience.

My brother-in-law, Charles Mahan, MD, a retired obstetrician and public health professional with a lifelong avocation as a cartoonist, created all the cartoons for this book. The cover is by Desk-Tech Graphic Design. The front cover photo is from Jupiterimages (www.comstock.com). Laura Vaughan took the photos on the back cover, while Jeff and Mellissa Klein at J and M Photography provided editing assistance. Rick Pfeiffer provided professional editing for the text. I especially thank George Johnson and the staff at Information Age Publishing for their work in bringing this book to completion.

1

Let's Grandparent

Learning New Grandparenting Skills

Nine years ago I held my first grandchild in my arms, instantly bonding to this one-day-old miracle, and knew that something special was beginning. Recently, I held my tiny fifth grandchild and again felt this special

1

joy. My satisfaction with this new role of grandparent has continued to grow with every hug, laugh, and adventure we have shared.

I know, however, that I am not the only grandparent with the cutest and funniest and most talented grandchild ever. I know because I have only to mention a word or two about my grandchildren before a friend will interrupt me to describe how her Alex at 18 months can already say "Go Gators!" or how Cassie at 3 can already "read" *Goodnight, Moon*. I know because I can barely say the word *grandchild* before someone is pulling out a photo of David in the bathtub or Maggie eating chocolate cake. Indeed, it's because I'm not alone in my delight that I'm writing this book for you, my fellow grandparents.

What's a Grandparent?

The answer to this question isn't as simple as it might seem. In the past, a grandparent was usually respected as an authority in the family, but the role did not necessarily involve strong bonds of intimacy with numerous grandchildren. Grandparents often lived close to their grandchildren. The grandmother might help with childcare, but grandfathers typically remained more distant, rarely becoming involved. Many seniors were financially dependent upon their children, and poor health often limited what they could do.

Today, that traditional family pattern is rapidly changing in our urbanized and mobile society. Some changes make it more difficult to spend time with our grandchildren. Grandparents are more likely to live across the country rather than around the corner, and both grandmothers and grandfathers often continue to be employed. Other changes, though, are more positive. We typically live longer and have better health than seniors of earlier generations and thus can be energetic companions of our grandchildren. In addition, we are more likely to have enough money so that we can afford frequent trips, even when they require a boarding pass. Since the number of children per family has decreased, most of us have fewer grandchildren, a change that allows us to develop a more intense relationship with each grandchild. Since both parents may be working themselves, they especially appreciate the individual attention we can provide to each grandchild.

These societal changes create the opportunity to develop new grandparenting roles. Grandparents generally opt for leaving the tough work of parenting to parents, saying "Been there, done that." They want to supplement the parents' efforts, not take over major responsibilities. Today many grandparents want instead to concentrate on developing a strong, loving relationship. They want to have fun with their grandchildren by sharing satisfying activities. They may also want to enhance their grandchildren's learning. Fortunately, these roles are compatible. Having fun together lays a foundation for developing close emotional ties, and learning takes place as a natural outcome of informal play, especially when grandparents select appropriate activities.

What Are the Benefits?

For a child, a warm, intimate relationship with a grandparent has many benefits. Grandparents who think a child is extraordinary and talented build self-confidence. They can provide a relaxed interlude, a counterbalance to the child's often demanding schedule of structured activities and the pressure to achieve. They can appreciate their grandchild in the here and now and value the special pleasures of the childhood years, rather than focusing so strongly on the child's future development. In addition, time away from parents can paradoxically improve the parent–child relationship, as parents are refreshed by a respite from constant childcare.

When there are several children in the family, grandparents can provide what the child may crave most: private time when she does not need to compete with a brother or sister for attention and has someone who will listen intently to her, play *just* with her, and take her on special trips. This desire for personal attention is evident in a story of a friend who spends most Tuesdays with her 5-year-old grandson. Recently, when she went to pick him up, he ran over to his infant sister and, as he jumped up and down, told her: "It's Tuesday! That's Grammy's day for me! You're too little. When you're big, maybe you can have a special day, too!"

We grandparents also benefit. Young children are definitely on a different timetable from that of grown-ups; they enjoy what they are doing right now instead of focusing on a distant goal. Taking this perspective can help us slow down and savor the present, experiencing it fully. We can again experience the curiosity and sense of wonder of a young child as we explore together a world containing so many new things: the roly-poly tightening into a ball, the ice cube melting in our hand, or the puppy lapping up water. For some of us, this time spent with a grandchild is a chance to recapture the past, when our own children were young; for others, it is an opportunity to enjoy something we missed with our own children, when we may have been too involved with the demands of a career or the constant care of several children. A generation ago, it was far less common for fathers to take an active part in childcare, and now, at this later stage in life, many men may seize the opportunity to become involved with their grandchildren.

One of the great joys of time spent with grandchildren is seeing them develop and learn new things. Their refreshing excitement as they develop new competencies and their persistence in the face of difficulties is a great model for all of us. The spontaneity and humor that emerge from a fresh, young mind is its own reward. In addition, a close relationship with your grandchild can fill your life with new meaning at a time when you may be experiencing the disconnected feelings of retirement or the loss of friends or a spouse. In addition, it can make you healthier, as well as happier.

Where Do I Start?

Trying to understand your grandchild is a good place to start. Begin by observing her activities and listening closely to what she says. Give her your undivided attention. It is best to spend some time with just the two of you together, without parents, other grandparents or siblings around to dilute the one-on-one focus. Enjoy her unique personality and current developmental level, giving her that unconditional love that every child wants.

Your understanding will be enhanced if you can put what you observe about your grandchild into a developmental framework. You need to know what she is currently able to do and what will be her next achievements. With this knowledge you can more accurately interpret what she says and does and then respond in appropriate ways. You will be able to provide pleasurable experiences that challenge and instruct without being frustrating or boring, experiences that are neither too difficult nor too easy. If your grandchild has special needs, it is doubly important that you carefully observe her abilities and provide stimulating experiences that encourage her to progress to the next step in her development. Later in this chapter, I will provide you with concepts useful in understanding how children learn, and I will call your attention to developmental issues within each subsequent chapter.

What Should I Do with My Grandchild?

Much of the time, you may simply want to join your grandchild in whatever she is doing at the moment. You can help a toddler put on her clothes or a 4-year-old brush her teeth. You can keep the 1-year-old supplied with Cheerios while she sits in her highchair at breakfast or help the 3-year-old spread peanut butter on toast. You can talk to your grandchild about whatever interests her right now, whether it be her toy cars, her tyrannosaurus costume, or her swimming class. You can help her find the next piece in the puzzle, play a game of *Candyland*, or kick a soccer ball.

In addition, you will want to plan activities to do with your grandchild, as these add zest to your time together. But which ones, you may wonder, should you do? First of all, it is crucial to match activities to her developmental level. What works magically at one age can be a disaster at another. At Halloween, 1-year-old Alexandra was only interested in exploring the neighbor's yard and climbing up steps, whereas her 4-year-old sister delighted in the pretend game of being a princess in high heels and glitter and at the chance to knock on doors in the neighborhood. Similarly, your 6-year-old grandson may have a great time at the baseball game, but his 3-year-old sister only gets restless and irritable. In contrast, your toddler may delight in simply patting and poking play dough, but the 5-year-old will be bored quickly with this and may start throwing it at her sister unless you can help her see the possibility of making pizza or kitties out of it. This book, with activities linked to the age of the child, provides help in finding activities that are a good fit.

As you plan, consider your grandchild's interests. These are usually easy to figure out simply by observing her play and her conversations. Her parents are, of course, an excellent source for supplementing what you have learned. Build upon her interests. Since my grandson was so passionate about trains, we read books about trains, worked train puzzles, played train board games, drew train tracks, and road on trains. It would be great if you could become enthusiastic about her interests. I have found that there is always more to learn about sea creatures and construction equipment.

Another important consideration is your own interests. You will enjoy your time with your grandchild more if you are sharing something that you especially enjoy. Your enthusiasm will rub off on her. So, how do you spend your leisure time? Is it reading, hiking, playing the guitar, surfing the Internet, cooking, gardening, or bird watching? The trick is to find how your interests can fit with what is developmentally appropriate for your grandchild. You can't expect a 4-year-old to follow a recipe for sugar cookies, but she can help add the icing and sprinkles. Your toddler grandchild may not be ready to plant seeds, but she may enjoy digging in the dirt with a shovel. For a successful match, start with the basic knowledge of child development presented in this book, add some careful grandkid watching, and finish with your ingenuity and imagination.

Here are some examples to get you started. Since my favorite leisure activity is reading, each week I select a few new children's books from the library to share with my grandchildren. Nothing gives me a greater thrill than seeing them totally engrossed in a story, and then asking me to read it again and again and again.

An avid nature lover, Grandma Susan always lets whichever grandchild is visiting help her feed the birds. All the grandchildren helped her nurse an injured bird they found in their backyard back to health. She has found that grandson Steve especially likes to help her dig in the garden. Her husband Tom, the family's gourmet cook, has the younger boys help with making cookies, while their older sister is assistant chef for homemade bread.

My cousin Rosemary found ways to share her interest in music and art with her very young grandson. When he was just a few months old, he was attentive to the classical music that she played as they spent time together each morning, and he loved watching the Baby Van Gogh video. When he was barely 3, she found strategies to make even attending a symphony a successful experience; front row seats at a morning concert allowed him to see the instruments up close at a time of day when he was well rested.

How Does a Child Learn?

This section presents key developmental concepts that are especially useful in understanding young children. Application of these concepts can help you decide what to do with your grandchild and serve as your road map on your journey together. Your understanding of why she behaves as she does also provides an added intellectual dimension that can deepen your pleasure in your relationship. Although these concepts may not be new to you, a review in the context of a new grandchild may be useful.

Interaction between Nature and Nurture

Which is more important in human development, nature or nurture? The genetic makeup of the child or the experiences she has during her life? Is a child born to become a basketball star, a Nobel laureate, or a concert pianist? Or were there experiences at home or school that account for this achievement? Conversely, do the roots of the problems that confront us, whether they are addictions, obesity, or mental illness, lie in our genes or in our life experiences? The answers to questions such as these matter to us as a society and personally as grandparents, who would like to see our grandchildren reach their full potential.

The debate continues, but there is agreement that nature and nurture interact to determine what the child will become. We know that the tiny, helpless newborn is already programmed to become a full-grown, independent adult, but we also know that maturation alone is not enough. Her experiences in her home and wider world also shape her development. As grandparents, perhaps the best we can do is to provide rich and varied opportunities for our grandchild and follow her lead in the activities she wants to pursue.

Temperament

Innate behavioral tendencies, such as activity level, intensity of reaction, and adaptability, are present even in newborns and influence how a child responds to her environment. Such temperamental differences may explain why the younger sibling of your mellow, compliant grandchild is intense, moody, and difficult to please, in spite of having the same parents who use similar childrearing practices. The grandmother of 2-year-old triplets told me that she was surprised at the major differences in personality and developmental rates. As grandparents, we need to recognize that we can't change the quiet 5-year-old who loves to play alone with her dolls into a loquacious child who recruits whoever is at the playground to play house with her. But you can join her in dressing up her dolls or taking them on a neighborhood stroll. You can enjoy her for who she is.

Sensitive Periods

Recent research shows that the brain is most responsive to certain kinds of learning at specific times in its development. There are special windows of opportunity when, for instance, the brain is primed to make sense of visual images or to process language. If unused, neural pathways are pruned (inactivated), making it more difficult to recapture learning missed during this sensitive period. Later, the window does not slam shut, but it gets harder to squeeze through. The most striking example is how easily children can learn several languages in their early years but how hard it is for seniors to learn a new language. Many believe that early exposure to musical experiences facilitates optimal musical, and perhaps even mathematical, ability.

We shouldn't, however, jump to the conclusion that more or earlier experiences are necessarily better. Introducing learning that is far beyond the child's current ability only results in frustration or, at best, rote learning. Many parents and grandparents are so eager to see that a child doesn't miss any opportunity that they mistakenly fill up her schedule with so many art, music, and gym classes that she has little time left for spontaneous, open-ended play. What your young grandchild needs is not a regiment of structured lessons, but a typical home environment with responsive people and opportunities to explore at her own pace.

Same Sequence, Different Rates

Children typically go through the same sequence of abilities in their development. This biological unfolding is most evident in motor development, as the child proceeds from rolling over to sitting up to crawling to walking, but it also holds true for language, cognitive, and social development. She needs to coo and babble before she can say that first word, to count before she can add, and to scribble before she can draw. However, each child will follow her own timetable, moving at her own rate. Your first grandchild may walk before she is a year old but say her first word at 14 months, whereas your second grandchild may say half a dozen words by her first birthday but wait until she is 15 months to walk. Although parents and grandparents often look at these different patterns for clues to the future, the timing of development does not in fact predict which child will be smarter or better in language or sports later in life.

Stages of Development

Many developmental theories use the concept of stages to emphasize that development proceeds more like a series of steps than a smooth diagonal line. These theories stress that children are not miniature adults; they perceive, learn, and interact in their own uniquely different ways, depending on their stage of development. Rather than gradually and consistently adding new learning, children instead experience dramatic changes in abilities or understanding in which they suddenly surge ahead to a new level of development. They then enter a plateau period in which they consolidate this new insight before they are ready to take another dramatic step forward to the next stage of development.

According to Erik Erikson, who is especially remembered for his delineation of psychosocial stages, each stage of social development offers a unique challenge to resolve. During the first year, the infant needs to develop a sense of trust that others will provide for her basic needs. During the next 2 years, a sense of autonomy becomes most important: She is learning to be self-sufficient and self-directed in such basic activities as talking, toileting, and exploring her environment. Between ages 3 and 6, the major task is developing independence and initiative: She becomes more goal directed and wants to begin and complete her own activities. From 7 to 11 the emphasis is on the development of industry; she strives to be competent and productive in mastering new skills.

Piaget, a major pioneer of cognitive theory, described stages of cognitive development. The child processes information and uses it in qualitatively different ways at each stage. During the sensorimotor period from birth to 2 years, the infant uses her senses and motor abilities to understand the world. During the preoperational stage from 2 to 6 years, the child uses symbolic thinking, develops her imagination, and uses language as a significant means of self-expression. It is not until the stage of concrete operations from 7 to 11 years that the child applies logical principles to her understanding of experiences. More recent research, which has had the advantage of better technology and more diverse samples, has brought into question some details of his findings, but the basic premise of how children learn is still generally considered valid.

Constructivism

Drawing on Piaget's theory of cognitive development, we have come to understand that we cannot teach mathematical and logical knowledge directly. The child must "reinvent" these concepts by trying things out for herself and repeating these experiments over and over again. The infant learns cause and effect through making things happen. When she pushes a button, she hears music; when she vocalizes, interesting faces appear. Similarly, the preschooler will only gradually understand the concepts of numbers, addition, and subtraction. The best way to foster true learning is to use these concepts in meaningful, authentic situations, not in artificial skill-building lessons. You will do more to teach your grandchild the concept of subtraction by having her count how many cookies are left after she gives two to her sister than by drilling her in abstractions such as $5 - 2 = 3$.

Learning through Play

During these early years, your grandchild learns best through play, which is intrinsically motivating, enjoyable, and freely chosen. There is no need for tangible rewards or even praise. Children are programmed to engage their environment and play, play, play. The goal is not to produce something, but to experience the pure pleasure of doing the activity. Children often concentrate intensely when they play, in the process developing new skills and understandings.

Child-Centered Approach

The focus is on your grandchild. This means respecting her interests and allowing her to make her own discoveries. You ask questions that arouse her curiosity and then support her in finding answers on her own. You provide opportunities for in-depth exploration, keeping curiosity and the love of learning for its own sake alive and healthy.

You can encourage a longer attention span and stronger focus by letting your grandchild stay with an activity for as long as she wants. You can talk with her about the activity and add some props or play along with her, but let her determine the direction. You want to be responsive to what she is doing by naming things, describing what she is doing, and suggesting ways that she can expand on her play. For example, as you sit with your 2-year-old grandchild in the sandbox, provide a running commentary, "You are loading the dump truck with the cool, damp sand and driving it away. I am making a road with the bulldozer." She may decide to drive her truck on your road, borrow the bulldozer, or continue with her filling and dumping.

Guided Participation in the Zone of Proximal Development

The concepts developed by Vygotsky early in the 20th century have only recently been applied to early childhood education in the United States. He emphasized that most learning occurs in the zone of proximal development, which is the range of skills that a learner can master with assistance but not yet do independently. To optimize learning, this may mean simplifying the task, providing cues, or suggesting appropriate strategies. You can suggest touching each car as she counts them or starting the zipper but letting her pull it up. Coaches in the first stage of Little League baseball provide us with an excellent model in their practice of having players hit the ball off a tee, because they know that hitting a pitched ball is too difficult and discouraging at first. As your grandchild gains in competence, she can increasingly complete more of the task, until she does it all independently.

Problem of the Match

There is a real art to determining when a child is ready to try a task and how much assistance to provide. Introduce it too soon and the child will be frustrated and quickly lose interest. Provide a task that she can already do and she will not be challenged to learn, but if you provide too much assistance, she may become too passive and feel incompetent. When Jake and Jenna watched me sewing up a doll with protruding stuffing, they immediately wanted to learn to sew. I pictured us sitting on the couch with our sewing project and imagined them quickly frustrated as the thread became tangled and the needle pricked their fingers. Before dispiritedly abandoning the task, Jenna might grumble, "I'm doing my best, but it's not good enough." Next I considered sewing cards—weaving shoelaces through precut holes around a square or triangle—but quickly rejected this idea too. It might hold the interest of a younger child, but my 4- and 6-year-old grandchildren would give it scarcely a glance, saying,

"We want to *make* something. That's baby stuff." The right match turned out to be beginning sewing kits, featuring precut animal shapes, oversized needles, and precut holes. Although Jake could do most of the sewing independently, Jenna needed help in figuring out whether to "go up or down" through the holes. Still, she felt good about her efforts, commenting, "I'm good at thinking."

Multiple Intelligences

Howard Gardner, an American psychologist who has recently done extensive research in educational psychology, raises our awareness that there are many facets to intelligence, including logical–mathematical, linguistic, bodily–kinesthetic, musical, spatial, interpersonal, intrapersonal, and naturalist skills. This perspective helps us value the unique strengths of each grandchild. They are each "smart" in their own way.

Attachment

In the 1970s Mary Ainsworth did extensive research on the concept of attachment, an enduring emotional tie formed between the infant and her primary caregivers. Fortunately, your grandchild comes into the world primed to seek the strong emotional attachment that she needs. Even as a newborn she will stare at your face and, before long, respond with a winning smile. When she is a little older, she may cry when her mother leaves or run to hide in her father's lap when a stranger appears, her anxiety evidence of her attachment. It was disconcerting when I returned from a vacation only to find that 10-month-old Emerson cried and reached for his mother when I picked him up. Fortunately, after viewing me from the safe haven of his mother's arms, we soon resumed our friendly relationship.

Strong emotional attachments often develop between grandparents and their grandchildren. What an advantage for a child to have a long continuing attachment to another grown-up! And what an advantage for the grandparent who shares this ardent affection! I am amazed by the intensity of my feelings for my own grandchildren. Just one week with newborn Alex and I was trying to figure out how soon I could fly back across the country to see him again.

Modeling

Social learning theory points out that children learn through imitating the behaviors of others. They particularly choose as models those powerful, nurturing adults to whom they are attached. "Actions speak louder than words" and "Practice what you preach" are especially true with young children. They will imitate not just what you are consciously trying to teach, but all those other, not so admirable words and actions. During a long weekend in which my sister Laura was visiting her son's family, her daughter-in-law Lisa noted that 3-year-old Cassie had started to preface each activity, whether it was fitting in another puzzle piece or selecting a color of paint, with a distinct *hmmmn. Now where did she pick that up?* Lisa wondered. A few minutes later, as my sister Laura paused to select her salad dressing, all those around the table heard an *hmmm* and knew they had found the culprit. So proceed with caution! Along with your behaviors, they are also absorbing your attitudes, values, and feelings.

Hands-On Learning

Not only does actions speak louder than words, actions *teach* better than words. For optimal learning, young children need to touch, try out, and mess around. The toddler learns *through* by crawling though the tunnel and *under* by sitting under the chair. Only after the preschooler picks an apple from a tree, finds the seeds inside, and plants them in dirt does she truly understand how a seed is different from a pebble. Addition makes sense to the 5-year-old when he counts his cars and trucks to find out how many vehicles he has.

Whole-Child Approach

All aspects of a child's development are interrelated. For example, a child with good language skills does better in developing peer relationships. The child that is emotionally stable usually focuses better on academic tasks at school. We need to avoid overstressing one aspect of development as more important than others. A well-rounded child with many interests and competencies is the goal. Grandparents can encourage their grandchildren to do things in areas they may be neglecting, such as active play, art projects, or reading/writing experiences.

What Blocks the Way?

Once you have determined the kind of relationship you want and have begun to understand what makes your grandchild tick, you are on your way to taking your journey together. Often, though, obstacles block your way.

One major obstacle is distance. If you and your grandchild live hundreds or even thousands of miles apart, your times together will necessarily be limited. In subsequent chapters I address ways to make the most of your times together and to keep connected when you are far apart, along with other special tips for long-distance grandparents. For now, I would only suggest making your trips a priority. For instance, my sister Laura, who lives in Florida while her grandchildren live in Missouri, decided that she wanted to visit at least every 2 months, and so she puts her next visit on her calendar well in advance before she starts scheduling other commitments.

Another obstacle, even for those who live near their grandchildren, is squeezing time with each grandchild into an already busy schedule. Maybe you can find ways to include your grandchild in your current activities, whether that means taking her along on your bike ride, letting her help with the yard work, or going out for a meal together. Most grandparents, perhaps aware of the quick passage of time and with memories of lost opportunities, do somehow find time for their grandchildren, even if it means bumping it up to priority status.

Having a rocky relationship with your own children or their spouses can make for an especially bumpy ride. If your grandchild is growing up in a single-parent or blended family, it may complicate matters even more. Yet this may make it all the more important for your grandchild to have a consistent relationship with you. In any case, many families find that their shared delight in a child brings them closer together. It can be the impetus that improves your relationship. If you view your role as supporting the parents, not criticizing or attempting to change their behaviors, it can go a long way toward creating harmony. When the parents see how your relationship benefits their child, they are more likely to encourage frequent contact. It may take all of your patience and skill to improve your relationship, but the payoff is well worth the effort.

Throughout this book I stress the advantage of time spent alone with a single grandchild. Yet, for many grandparents, finding this one-on-one time may be the most persistent obstacle. For many of us, one reason we take care of our grandchildren is to help out our own children, something that continues to be important to us even when our children are adults. We stay with the grandchildren in part so that our own children can have time for themselves, whether it allows the parents to go out to a movie or to take a trip to Paris, whether it be as primary caregiver while parents are at work or simply to fill in during school holidays. It gives us pleasure to know that we are helping.

With the first grandchild in a family, all is usually fine, but with the second or third, all of your time with grandchildren may be taken up in the caregiver role. You may find that you can barely manage to feed the baby, supervise the baths, and wipe up the spills. You are too exhausted to read

Curious George one more time or to clean up after more finger painting, much less plan a trip to the zoo.

If this is happening to you, it may be time to reassess. I believe that having this one-on-one time has many benefits both for you and your grandchild. You might begin by talking with the children's parents about your wish to have more time with only one grandchild and discuss possible ways to do it, perhaps by concentrating on one child while the others are in preschool or at a babysitter's, perhaps by having one child visit in your home for a day or more. When 10-month-old Emerson stayed with me while his family went on an overnight camping trip, I was able to focus solely on him and plan activities that fit his schedule and interests.

You may be able to arrange time alone by having your own spouse take over responsibility for a different grandchild. Often one grandparent is more enthusiastic about getting involved, but you may encourage your reluctant partner if you suggest activities that he or she enjoys, perhaps watching a softball game at a city park or going to the carwash and then to MacDonald's. Or you might go together on a trip to the pumpkin farm, but once there each of you stays with one child.

I know that even with your best efforts many of these obstacles are not going to totally disappear. Life is full of compromises, but I am confident that given ingenuity and determination you will be able to find a way to spend time with your grandchild and develop the relationship that you want.

How Can I Use This Book?

After reading this introductory chapter, you may want to explore what looks most interesting to you in the chapters that follow. Each concentrates on one type of activity, such as cooking, taking trips, or celebrating holidays, and the activities are grouped by age. This should make it easy to find appropriate things to do with your grandchild.

These activities are meant as a guide to get you started and to spark your own original ideas. I suggest that you experiment with a variety of activities to see what works best and repeat those successful experiences frequently. Children like the sense of mastery that comes from reading the same story, playing the same game, or doing the same puzzle over and over and over. They often look forward to having the same pleasant experiences each time they are with their grandparents. My sister Carolyn, for instance, told me that her grandchildren especially liked to pick oranges off their tree and squeeze out the juice and usually requested going for a walk to a nearby park each time they came for a visit. If you have an unsuccessful experience, don't cross it off the list for good. Evaluate what went wrong and how you might modify it to make it easier, more challenging, or more appropriate to your grandchild's abilities and interests.

Try a variety of activities. Your grandchild may gravitate toward a few types of activities and neglect others, but to achieve well-rounded development, encourage her to have frequent experiences that foster all areas of development—physical, social, verbal, academic, and creative. Use your grandchild's current interests to jump-start participation in new types of activities. To encourage my 3-year-old grandson to draw, I drew roads on paper for his ubiquitous cars to drive over, then handed him the markers for adding his own marks. If your granddaughter loves kitties but not books, perhaps books filled with photos of cats will tweak her interest. A trip to a new playground with water sprinklers or a giant spiral slide will get your TV junkie up and active.

Use the age categories for activities as a general guide about age-appropriateness. They provide a sequence of easy to more difficult activities. They are listed under the youngest ages at which children typically can engage in them successfully, but most children will enjoy and profit from them even when they are older. So don't dismiss activities presented for a younger age because you think your older grandchild will not find them interesting or challenging. I think it is better to err on the side of selecting an easier activity and then increase the complexity when you discover your grandchild can profit from a greater challenge.

Children with developmental challenges can follow a similar sequence of activities. Go by developmental age, not chronological age, in making your selections. For children with physical challenges, you may need to adapt activities and provide additional help.

In most chapters I distinguish between activities that are Old Faithfuls or New Twists. Old Faithfuls are basic everyday activities that merit frequent repetitions. You will probably want to repeat them many times and have them available on short notice. When you want to try something different, select an activity in the New Twists section. These typically add the enticement of novelty, but take a bit more equipment and planning.

My cousin Rosemary shared the following story about her 3-year-old grandson. It illustrates many ideas discussed in this chapter—picking up on the child's interests, finding a developmentally appropriate activity related to her interests, and repeating the activity frequently. But most of all it reveals the joy and humor that grandparenting brings.

> Michael has been enthralled and almost obsessed with trucks since he was 18 months. . . . We have a UPS station in Peachtree City where all the UPS trucks gather in late afternoon and early evening. . . . Michael and I often go out there and drive around the building slowly, checking out all the trucks and the packages on the conveyor belts. . . . He has been reciting "The Lord's Prayer" for a few months. A couple nights ago he told his mother, "Mommy, whenever I say "deliver us from evil," I think of UPS delivery trucks."

2

Let's Do Art

Moving from Scribbles to Narrative Art

With crayons and paper scattered all over the kitchen table, 7-year-old Jake ignored the chaos of dinner preparations and his noisy siblings as he focused intently on adding the finishing touches to his futuristic spaceship—

Let's Grandparent: Activity Guide for Young Grandchildren, pages 17–32
Copyright © 2008 by Information Age Publishing

some fiery red emissions, an astronaut at the controls. When I asked where the spaceship was going, he drew Saturn with its rings, a red Mars, and a comet with a long, yellow tail. As he drew, he gave a running commentary about the astronaut's adventures, complete with a booming blast-off. While he was explaining the comings and goings of his spaceship, I pondered where his artistic abilities had come from and where they were headed.

Snapshot of Development

Artistic development evolves through clearly defined stages. Purely sensory/ motor movements evolve into early scribbles. Next come simple shapes and designs, which in time come to represent suns, houses, and people. Then isolated figures on the page become organized scenes, often ones that tell a story. Unfortunately, as children get older, the originality and spontaneity of these efforts all too often gets submerged under self-critical striving for realistic depiction. Sometimes, with encouragement, it may resurface and blossom in the mature artist.

Why Try It?

As a grandparent I take special pleasure in observing and nurturing this artistic progression. I can explore my long-dormant creative side as we work with clay or experiment with paint. Sometimes I capture the perspective of my grandchildren: total immersion in the pleasure of the process without too much concern for the finished product.

The bonuses for your grandchild are many. Along with all the fun, he develops his creative and aesthetic side and hones fine motor skills. He can express his personal experiences and fantasies in ways that are concrete and compelling, even when he cannot articulate them with words. As he conceptualizes what he wants to express, he thinks more deeply and clearly about his world.

Tips for Art Activities

Support Free Exploration

Let your grandchild discover the possibilities of the materials in his own way, making his own creative decisions. He needs frequent opportunities and ample time to explore the many uses and properties of the materials. He focuses on the process, the pure pleasure of doing the activity, without feeling the need to make an acceptable finished product. We grandparents should avoid imposing our goal-oriented viewpoint on our grandchildren.

Case in point, one afternoon my grandchildren enthusiastically painted rocks and sticks collected on a walk and helped me make play dough, but I was the one who wanted to "complete" the project by assembling everything into a centerpiece for their table.

Support with Words

Without being too intrusive, you can encourage your grandchild to work more diligently on art projects and to try more challenging ones. Be an attentive observer, and talk with him as he works. Comments should be mostly descriptive: "You are using lots of red and green" or "You made lines all over the page." Make any evaluative comments quite specific ("I like the way you worked so carefully on your picture") rather than global ("What a pretty picture!"). Saying "Tell me about your picture," lets your grandchild provide the interpretation of his work. This avoids such faux pas as telling him you like the apple tree only to find out that the "trunk" is actually a boy's legs and the "apples" his eyes and mouth!

Model with Caution

It is fun to use the art materials along with your grandchild. Unobtrusively, model ways to extend and vary the experience. Choose possibilities just one step ahead of where he is—enough to challenge him but within the range of what he is capable of doing. Roll the play dough into a ball, or prick it with toothpicks. Experiment with mixing colors to get just that right shade of forest green. But what if he asks you to draw a car or dog? It's hard to refuse but probably better if you encourage him to make his own attempt.

Provide Technical Help

Your grandchild may want to experiment and create in ways that tax his fine motor abilities. So do provide any technical assistance requested. When Jake ran out of space when drawing a Tyrannosaurus Rex, I helped him tape on another piece of paper so that he could add a long, scaly tail. When he wanted a door in his cardboard spaceship, he drew it and I cut it out. The trick is to lend a helping hand that enables the project to move forward without taking it over.

Organize for Easy Access

Time spent upfront in assembling supplies pays off in quick and easy preparation. Stock up on a variety of art supplies: construction paper, paints, brushes, markers, crayons, pipe cleaners, glitter, modeling clay, stickers, string, glue, and tissue paper. Your trash becomes treasure, as you see creative ways to use cardboard tubes, Styrofoam, greeting cards, oatmeal boxes, and catalogs. Add such common household items as dried pasta, glue, and food coloring and you are ready for most art experiences. A crafts store is the best place to find materials for special projects like making plaster of Paris handprints or experimenting with potter's clay. Store these art supplies together for easy access right near your typical space for doing art projects.

Minimize the Mess

There is no denying that art projects can be messy. It helps to make the limits about where and how to use the materials very clear to your grandchild ("You can paint on the paper, not on the chair"). Then supervise closely and redirect any transgressions. To cut down on cleanup time, put down multiple layers of newspaper on the working space. For the inevitable paint or glue spill, just peel off the top layer, leaving another protective layer beneath. An unobtrusive way to limit the quantity used (and spilled) is to downsize the containers and utensils. Pour glue from the large bottle into a small paper cup with a Q-tip as an applicator and put glitter in a spice jar with small holes for sprinkling. An old adult shirt buttoned in the back minimizes paint on clothes. When weather permits, set up the materials on a child-sized table outside.

Make Cleaning Up Fun

Involve your grandchild in the cleanup. Soapy sponges and absorbent bath towels add to the fun. A bigger challenge is getting your grandchild clean without major collateral damage. To avoid drips of paint down the hall and smears all over the bathroom fixtures, start with a preliminary wipe-off or quick hand rinsing in a basin before a more thorough washing in the bathroom. On one occasion as my grandchildren washed off multiple layers of paint, they delighted in seeing the water change from yellow to green to brown. When I pointed out to Jake that he had missed the paint on his nose, he replied, "My eyes can't see my face." A look in the mirror brought a smile and quick cleanup.

Do It Again

Provide multiple opportunities to use the same materials. Each time, your grandchild can discover new possibilities and develop useful techniques. When introducing something new, allow ample time to explore its properties before using it for a specific purpose. The first time Jake used a single-hole punch, just punching multiple holes in paper was challenging enough. Later, he used it for making tree ornaments and snowflakes. Similarly, the first few times your grandchild uses clay, focus on learning its properties and the special techniques for working with it. Making an object to keep can come later.

Save It

Start a collection of artwork for each grandchild and add to it over the years. Saving their work affirms how much you value their efforts. Note the child's name, date, and an explanatory comment on the back of each piece. I particularly like to document the development of drawing. Jake's folder includes an early drawing of random lines that he labeled train tracks and recent realistic scenes of helicopters, sailboats, and fire trucks. While his drawing ability has taken off, the transportation theme remains consistent.

Display It

Hang up your grandchild's art work in a prominent place. This is yet another way to let him know you value his efforts. A few magnets are all you need to hang the most recent masterpiece on the refrigerator. For high visibility, tape pictures to your front door. Remember to hang them at your grandchild's eye level. Emerson was so taken with his brother's car picture hung on my refrigerator that he made his first attempt at drawing a car all by himself.

Activities

The ideas for art experiences suggested later in this chapter include *Old Faithfuls* and *New Twists*. **Old Faithfuls** are basic everyday activities that merit frequent repetitions. Quick and easy to set up with readily available materials, they encourage open-ended artistic exploration. When you want to do something different, try an activity in the **New Twists** section. These add the enticement of novelty, yield an interesting finished product, but take a bit more equipment and planning,

One- and Two-Year-Olds

Developmental Insights

No section for infants? During the first year infants explore extensively with their hands and enjoy sensory experiences, but they are not ready to focus on creating something. They are more likely to taste the markers than draw with them. Play dough is just another object to swipe off the highchair tray. So stick with manipulative toys and sensory materials and hold the art experiences for later.

A toddler begins by exploring the sensory and motor possibilities of art materials. He likes the feel of the wet, slippery fingerpaint. He pounds and pokes the play dough. Then he becomes more intentional in his efforts. He notices the colored marks that he made on the paper and tries to make them all over the page. He observes the hole his finger made in the play dough and pokes more holes. He grasps the paintbrush or marker in his fist and makes broad, sweeping motions with his whole arm and upper body, not just his hand. Therefore, he works best when he has ample space and can stand up to fully utilize these large muscles when drawing or painting.

His early efforts with crayons and markers are not "just scribbling." They are an important first step toward drawing and writing, fostering hand control and conscious efforts of placement and form. Between the ages of 2 and 3 these scribbles evolve into simple shapes such as circles, rectangles, and crosses. Since the simple symmetrical shapes that your grandchild creates are easy to remember and aesthetically pleasing, he intentionally repeats them.

Toddlers do have a short attention span, so be resigned to the fact that your grandchild is probably not going to stay with your carefully planned task for very long. He may get distracted but then come back later to do it again. So, when possible, leave materials out for awhile and encourage him to use them a second time.

Old Faithfuls

Make Your Mark: Watercolor markers are easy for toddlers to hold and don't require as much control and pressure as crayons or pencils. Since they still have a penchant for putting everything in their mouths, do be sure to provide only the nontoxic ones. Your grandchild can use these on a whiteboard or large sheet of paper. You can demonstrate making lines, circles, and dots and encourage him in his early efforts. Provide these materials frequently, but do supervise closely. A toddler is just as likely to decorate the wall or couch as the paper you provided! My granddaughter especially liked coloring on herself. I allowed this even though it did mean a through scrubbing before her parents returned.

WHAT YOU NEED: *watercolor markers, large sheets of paper or a whiteboard*

Chalk it Up: Another easy drawing experience is to use large, thick pieces of chalk. Dip the chalk in water for brighter colors and draw on a large piece of paper. Or take it outside and draw on the sidewalk, driveway, and stone walls.

WHAT YOU NEED: *chalk, water, bowl, paper*

Paint It Pretty: The ideal setup for painting is a low easel with a tray for holding three or four paint containers, each with its own large brush. Use washable tempera paints and clip a large piece of paper to the easel. Rocks, sticks, dried pasta, or plastic toys are also fun to paint.

WHAT YOU NEED: *paint containers, large brushes, washable tempera paints, easel*

Stamp It Out: Your grandchild can make prints with big, easy-to-grasp objects. Put thick tempera paint in shallow bowls. Then dip blocks, cookie cutters, a potato masher, or plastic lids into the paint and make prints on a large piece of paper. I like to demonstrate how to print with the objects and guide my grandchild's hand to make the first print, but then let him use the objects however he likes. Toddlers often prefer to use the objects more for painting than printing.

WHAT YOU NEED: *tempera paint, shallow bowls, large sheets of paper; blocks, cookie cutters, potato masher, or plastic lids*

Paste-a-Plate: A good early pasting experience is gluing items on a paper plate. Set out an assortment of items, such as buttons, ribbons, pasta spirals, pom-poms, and feathers. Put a small amount of glue in a shallow container and add a pasting brush. Show your grandchild how to put a dot of glue on the paper plate and then place the item on top of it. Or he can dip the item in the glue and then place it on the plate. The first time I tried this with my 16-month-old grandson he mostly wanted to play with the jewels and beads, and the next time he focused on dumping out the glue. It was not until he was 2 that he began deliberately pasting items on the plate. Instead of a paper plate you can use a one- foot square of cardboard or any heavyweight paper that is sturdy enough to hold these bigger items.

WHAT YOU NEED: *paper plates, glue, glue brush, shallow container; buttons, ribbons, pasta spirals, pom-poms or feathers*

Poke and Pound: Ready-made play dough is a good choice for toddlers. Its inexpensive, comes in many bright colors, and stores well. Playing along with your grandchild, pound with your fists, squeeze and roll with your whole hand, and poke objects to make impressions, all efforts he can imitate. Save making objects for when he is older.

WHAT YOU NEED: *ready-made play dough*

New Twists

Fingerpainting: Don't be fooled by the label. This is usually a whole hand, whole arm, even whole body experience. Admittedly it's about as messy as it can get. So be sure to protect the area with newspaper, cover your grandchild with a smock, and have a soapy bucket of warm water handy for washing up afterward. Instead of painting on paper, place several spoonfuls of paint on a large tray or shallow pan and have your grandchild paint directly on it. He can then poke, stroke, and explore the paint for as long as he wishes. When I put yellow and blue on the tray, my granddaughter was amazed to discover that she had made green. To encourage similar discoveries try yellow and red, red and blue, or white and red. To save a picture, take an imprint by gently laying a piece of paper over the creation. If you prefer painting directly on paper, select a heavy, glossy paper that will not become saturated and tear too easily.

You can buy fingerpaint, or make your own with this simple recipe: Mix 1 cup cornstarch with 1 cup cold water. Then add 3 cups hot water and work out all lumps. Cook over medium heat, stirring constantly, until mixture is clear and thick (about 1 minute). Remove from heat and add 1 tablespoon glycerin. Divide into small jars and add a different color of powdered tempera paint or food coloring to each, stirring together thoroughly. Store extra fingerpaint in the refrigerator for several weeks.

WHAT YOU NEED: *child's waterproof smock, tray, fingerpainting paper; purchased fingerpaint or cornstarch, water, glycerin, tempera paint or food coloring, saucepan, small jars*

Sandy Sprinkles: Your grandchild can make pictures that sparkle by using colored sand. To color sand, add a squirt of undiluted food coloring to a half cup of sand and stir thoroughly. Add more drops of food coloring, as needed, to produce a rich color. Make three or four colors of sand and put each in a plastic container with large holes, such as a cheese shaker or spice container. Then have your grandchild use a large paintbrush to spread glue on a paper plate. Next, he can sprinkle colored sand over the paper. When the glue is dry, gently shake off any excess sand before hanging.

WHAT YOU NEED: *sand, food coloring, containers with large holes, paintbrush, glue*

No Paste/No Problem: When making collages, you can skip the glue problem altogether by using contact paper. Remove the backing from a 2-foot square of white or clear contact paper. Tape it onto the table with the sticky side up. Then provide items (e.g., ribbon, pom-poms, feathers, beads, and foil rolled into balls) that are big enough for toddler fingers but light enough to stay stuck when you hang up the collage.

WHAT YOU NEED: *contact paper, tape; ribbon, pom-poms, feathers, beads, foil*

Making Tracks: Your grandchild can use small toy vehicles to create interesting patterns on a large sheet of paper. Pour a small amount of tempera paint in a shallow container. Place a toy car or truck in the paint and roll it along the paper. Tractor tires make especially interesting prints. This was the first painting experience that I did with my first grandson, because he went everywhere with several toy cars clutched in his hands. He was fascinated when he ran his vehicles through the paint and then back and forth on the paper to make tracks.

WHAT YOU NEED: *toy vehicles, paper, tempera paint, shallow container*

Barefoot Fun: Making footprints with paint is a memorable experience. The best place to do this is outside on the sidewalk. Put a small amount of paint in an 8 × 8-inch cake pan. Spread out a 12 × 24-inch piece of construction paper on the ground in front of it. Hold your grandchild's hand as he steps barefoot into the paint and then takes a few steps on the paper. You could also suggest doing handprints on the paper.

WHAT YOU NEED: *cake pan, construction paper*

Three- and Four-Year-Olds

Developmental Insights

As fine motor skills develop, your grandchild no longer draws with his whole arm but relies on smaller movements of his wrist and fingers. As a result, his ability to draw or paint what he wants takes a leap forward. He can make snips with scissors at age 3 and cut on a line at age 4. Cognitive advances also expand options for art experiences. A longer attention span and better understanding of the task means he can do more complex projects. He helps mix up the play dough before playing with it and paints with watercolors over his crayon drawing.

Three-year-olds begin to combine simple shapes and lines, creating interesting designs. Children's drawings throughout the world share similar designs, such as mandalas (circles or squares with crosses through them) or suns (circles with rays extending out on all sides).

Representative art may begin when your 3- or 4-year-old grandchild unintentionally creates an image that reminds him or you of some real object. Soon he is deliberately making this image and labeling it a person, house, or tree. When Jenna discovered that a circle with marks inside could be a face with eyes and a mouth, she drew face after face, naming each after someone in her family. When older brother Jake was busy drawing sharks and other sea creatures, 4-year-old Jenna discovered with delight she had made an octopus, though it looked suspiciously like the "sun" found so universally in children's early drawings.

Innate aesthetic principles, such as symmetry and balance, guide this early drawing. A hand may be a circle with six "fingers" because this symmetrical figure emerged from previous "suns." Stereotyped models or drawing instruction may interfere with this natural process. At this stage a child draws similar objects over and over. Four-year-old Sydney filled her page with many "suns" of varying size and color. She will expand her repertoire as she masters her favorites.

It is not only in drawing or painting that your grandchild shifts to representative art. The lump of play dough becomes a snake or bowl and the circles and squares are pasted together to create a house or truck. At the beach 3-year-old Emerson drew an oval in the sand with his shovel and turned it into a car by adding two wheels.

Old Faithfuls

Medley of Markers: One of the easiest and most valuable art experiences is drawing, so provide regular opportunities with a variety of drawing tools. A new box of crayons is sure to encourage an enthusiastic drawing session. Or provide washable markers, preferred by many children because of their brilliant colors and ease of use. Try colored chalk on a chalkboard or on the sidewalk. Dip the chalk in water to produce brighter colors. Your grandchild may also like to draw with pencils and pens because these are what grown-ups use.

WHAT YOU NEED: *paper; markers, crayons, or chalk*

Painting Big and Bold: Big brushes, tempera paints, and large sheets of paper invite experimenting with broad strokes and color combinations. Expand upon earlier tempera painting experiences by providing a full range of vivid colors, including black, brown, and white, each with its own brush to minimize inadvertent mixing of colors. Using an easel minimizes spills and makes whole arm movement easier. Your grandchild may want to draw bold figures or fill every inch of the paper with color. Rainbows, suns, and faces are favorite themes for many children.

WHAT YOU NEED: *paintbrushes, tempera paint, plastic paint cups, large sheets of paper*

Rorschach Test: When you have the paint out, try this fun variation. Fold a piece of paper in half. Unfold and put a blob of paint on the fold. Fold the paper again and use fingers to spread the paint by pressing and rubbing over the outside of the paper. Unfold to see the mirror image design. Use your imagination to describe what it is, and write this label under the painting.

WHAT YOU NEED: *paper, paint, marker*

Watercolors: These provide a different painting experience from tempera paints. A major attraction is the ease of blending colors on the paper. Another advantage is that it's easy to set up in a small space. Just one small brush, a 9 × 12-inch sheet of paper, and a glass of water is all it takes. Wet each color with an eyedropper before beginning to paint. So the colors don't get muddy, encourage your grandchild to wash off his brush when he changes to a different color.

WHAT YOU NEED: *watercolor set, small paintbrush, glass, water*

Make-and-Play Dough: Since this quick and easy play dough recipe requires no cooking, it is easy to involve your grandchild in making it. Combine 3 tablespoons vegetable oil, 1 cup hot water, and a few drops of food coloring. Stir in 2 cups flour and 1 cup salt. Knead until smooth. If you want to keep it for a few weeks, add 4 teaspoons cream of tartar and store in a closed container in the refrigerator.

My grandchildren enjoy sprinkling extra flour on the dough and working it in with rolling pins and their hands. Extend the play by adding plastic knives and forks, cookie cutters, buttons, straws, or doll dishes. Make simple objects, such as snakes, balls, bowls, or pizza.

WHAT YOU NEED: *vegetable oil, water, food coloring, flour, salt, mixing bowl and spoon; cream of tartar (optional)*

Cut-and-Paste Projects: Provide an assortment of items for pasting, such as fabric, feathers, sequins, yarn, ribbons, pom-poms, gift wrap, tissue paper, and pasta pieces. Keep this collection together in one box for easy access. Since it's all too easy to squirt out prodigious amounts of glue from a bottle, put a little glue in a disposable cup with a pasting brush or Q-tip as an applicator. When your grandchild is able to cut with scissors, encourage him to cut out pictures from magazines or to cut paper into the desired sizes and shapes.

WHAT YOU NEED: *paste or glue, disposable cup, pasting brush, scissors; fabric, feathers, sequins, yarn, ribbon, pom-poms, gift wrap, tissue paper, or pasta pieces*

New Twists

Marvelous Marbles: Make interesting designs with paint and marbles. Put a piece of paper in the bottom of a 9 × 14-inch cake pan. Dilute tempera paint with a little water and put two or three spoonfuls, each a different color, in separate places on the paper. Then have your grandchild drop several marbles in the pan and roll them through the paint by tipping the box in different directions. Talk about the tracks the marbles are making and how to make them run in many different directions.

WHAT YOU NEED: *large cake pan, paper, marbles, tempera paint*

Make-a-Mosaic: Take you grandchild on a treasure hunt for pebbles, sticks, leaves, and pods. Then have him poke them into a big ball of homemade play dough that you flatten on a paper plate. Add paint and glitter for a festive look. Set on the family dinner table to inspire comments and conversation.

WHAT YOU NEED: *play dough, paper plate, tempera paint, glitter; pebbles, sticks, leaves, or pods*

Spongy Splotches: Use scissors to cut kitchen sponges into squares, circles, and triangles. Put slightly diluted tempera paint on a paper plate, using sep arate plates for two or three colors. Wet the sponges, but squeeze out excess moisture. Dip a sponge in the paint and then press on paper several times to make interesting designs. Repeat with different colors and shapes. Demonstrate the technique, but let your grandchild use the sponges in his own way. Younger children often prefer to use the sponges like a brush, instead of a stamp. My granddaughter liked to make her designs on white tissue paper, using holiday colors and shapes. Then she used it for wrapping gifts.

WHAT YOU NEED: *scissors, sponges, tempera paint, paper plates, paper*

It's Me!: Obtain a 2½ × 4-foot piece of heavy wrapping paper. Have your grandchild lie on his back with his arms and legs spread out. Trace an outline of his body with a marker. Then he can draw his face and clothes on the outline of his body. Cut it out and hang it up with the feet touching the floor. This way your grandchild can stand beside it and compare it to his actual body size. When asked how he had made this giant person, my grandson replied, "Grandma captured me." Do this each year near your grandchild's birthday for a record of both physical and artistic development. Just before her fifth birthday I again did this project with Jenna. She painstakingly painted every inch of her body in a rainbow of colors. To limit the amount of paint on the floor, we saved the cutting out until after the paint had dried.

WHAT YOU NEED: *heavy wrapping paper, markers, scissors, tempera paint*

Fruit and Veggie Prints: Use fresh fruits and vegetables to print unique patterns. To create stamp pads, put kitchen sponges in saucers and saturate each with tempera paint. Cut an apple, orange, potato, carrot, green pepper, kiwi, or star fruit in half and use the flat inside part for making the print. Show your grandchild how to press the fruit or veggie onto the sponge and then use it to make a print on construction paper. For an especially interesting effect, cover an ear of corn with paint and roll it on the paper.

WHAT YOU NEED: *fresh fruit or vegetables, sponges, saucers, tempera paint, paper*

Spaghetti Squiggles: Cook and drain spaghetti. Mix a half cup of water with a quarter teaspoon of food coloring in a bowl. Make two or three colors in separate bowls. Add a half cup of spaghetti to each bowl, let stand a few minutes, and drain. Let your grandchild arrange the colored spaghetti in intricate designs on heavy paper or cardboard. The starch in the spaghetti sticks it to the paper as it dries.

WHAT YOU NEED: *spaghetti, food coloring, bowls, heavy paper or cardboard*

Five- to Eight-Year-Olds

Developmental Insights

As your grandchild stands at the threshold of school, his artistic expression flowers. Your 5-year-old grandchild replaces the seemingly random placement of figures on the page with an organized scene. For example, my granddaughter drew two people holding hands in the center of the page, placed their feet squarely in green grass along the bottom and shaded in a line of blue across the top for the sky, commenting, "The little one is me and the big one is you." Combining the pleasures of art and storytelling, your grandchild may accompany his artwork with a verbal storyline about his recent sled ride down a snowy hillside or an action-packed fantasy about dueling spaceships.

Old Faithfuls

Creating Colors: When you bring out the tempera paints, add the challenge of creating new colors. Assemble red, blue, yellow, black, and white tempera paint, large sheets of paper, a container of water, and a brush. Encourage your grandchild to experiment with mixing these colors on a paper plate or small cardboard square, creating just the color he wants. Ask "How can we make lime green? shocking pink? burgundy?" Rather than using the paint to draw outlines of figures, encourage your grandchild to paint solid shapes and backgrounds.

WHAT YOU NEED: *tempera paint, water, cups, brushes, paper plates, paper*

Create-and-Bake Play Dough: Your grandchild may be interested in making objects to keep. This recipe produces soft, pliable dough for making objects. When baked, it hardens into a durable finished product. Mix 2 cups salt with 2½ cups boiling water. Stir the salt solution into 4 cups flour. Knead on a floured board until smooth. After it has cooled, shape into objects. Those molded from one piece of dough are not as prone to break, but the preferred method for most children is adding small pieces together to form the object. To minimize breakage, moisten the pieces where they are joined. Bake in the oven at 250 degrees for an hour or more. After completely cool, your grandchild can use tempera paint to enhance his creations.

My 5-year-old granddaughter frequently asked to make this play dough. She especially liked to make kitties, along with all their bowls, beds, and balls.

WHAT YOU NEED: *salt, water, flour, mixing bowl and spoon, oven, tempera paint*

Collage with a Theme: Help your grandchild locate and cut out magazine pictures that focus on a theme, such as food, animals, families, toys, or vehicles. Have him cut the pictures in interesting shapes and paste them in an overlapping mosaic on a large sheet of construction paper.

WHAT YOU NEED: *magazines, scissors, paste, construction paper*

Play with Clay: Clay provides a very different experience from play dough. You may want to start with a modeling clay kit, complete with tools and many colors of clay. For more extensive projects buy premixed clay from a crafts store. As you work together, you can demonstrate simple techniques, such as slicing off a piece of clay with a string and making it slippery with water for joining and smoothing pieces. Let it air-dry overnight before decorating with tempera paint.

WHAT YOU NEED: *clay, string, bowl, water, carving/shaping tools*

Working with Wood: Before your grandchild is ready to make objects, he needs to experiment with sawing a piece of wood, hammering nails into a board, and using a screwdriver. Real tools, but ones that are small and lightweight, are best. Provide a supply of soft wood and nails with large heads. A piece of plywood on a picnic table can substitute for a workbench. A simple first project could be that ubiquitous airplane made by nailing several narrow pieces of wood together.

WHAT YOU NEED: *soft wood, hammer, nails, screwdriver, screws*

New Twists

Arches and Spirals: Your grandchild can create an interesting structure with strips of construction paper fastened to a cardboard base. Show him how to make loops, steps, spirals, bridges, towers, arches, and tunnels with the strips. Fasten them to the cardboard and each other with a combination of glue, tape, and staples. He can interconnect the paper strip objects in imaginative ways.

WHAT YOU NEED: *strips of construction paper, cardboard, glue, tape, staples*

Under the Sea Scene: Suggest that your grandchild use crayons to draw an underwater scene on white paper. It could include sharks, turtles, jellyfish, coral, or seaweed. Then make a light wash from diluted blue watercolors or food coloring. Use the wash to paint over the picture and create a delightful underwater scene. Likewise, create "a dark and gloomy night" by drawing scary ghosts and goblins and then painting over them with a dilute wash made from black watercolor paint.

WHAT YOU NEED: *crayons, white paper, paintbrush, watercolors or food coloring*

Twist and Twirl: Have your grandchild put three or four balls of clay on a paper plate. Then he can anchor brightly colored pipe cleaners in each and twist them together to create an impressive sculpture. For a finishing touch add tinsel, beads, or yarn.

WHAT YOU NEED: *clay, paper plate, pipe cleaners; tinsel, beads, or yarn*

Fun with Folding: Your grandchild is probably an expert at folding and flying paper airplanes. Add to his repertoire of paper toys with a boat that floats, a pirate hat, and a cootie catcher. Good books for beginners with simple projects and detailed directions are *Planes and Other Flying Things* or *Easy Origami.* Another good source for directions and origami ideas is the website *www.paperfolding.com.*

Use origami paper or cut your own 6-inch squares from lightweight paper. Choose a few objects with simple, minimal folds. Make the object first so that your grandchild can see what he is trying to make. Then have him sit next to you as you simultaneously complete each fold. Once the folding is done, he has the extra pleasure of playing with the toy he has made.

WHAT YOU NEED: *origami paper, directions for making objects*

Cartons to Castles: Set out a generous supply of small- to medium-size cardboard boxes. Round salt and oatmeal boxes are especially appealing. Include craft sticks and tubing from paper towel and toilet tissue. Have your grandchild attach these items to a 2 × 3-foot cardboard base. To attach them securely, first glue the pieces and then hold them together with masking tape until the glue dries. He can design a complex, interconnecting structure that may end up being a castle, highway system, or space station. When thoroughly dry, use tempera paint to add details and color.

WHAT YOU NEED: *cardboard boxes, craft sticks, cardboard tubing, cardboard, glue, masking tape, tempera paint*

Creating with Papier-Mâche: A major delight when working with papier-mâché is the slippery, slimy feeling as you dip paper into the paste and smear it on the mold. A simple recipe for making the paste is to mix equal parts of flour and water and then add more water until it has the consistency of thick glue. Tear newspaper into strips about 1-inch wide by 6 inches long. An easy initial project is to use an inflated balloon as a mold. Dip newspaper strips into the paste and spread over the balloon, covering it completely. Hang the balloon up and let it dry overnight. Then pop and remove the balloon. The last step is to paint the papier-mâché ball, perhaps making a smiling face, dinosaur egg, or beach ball.

WHAT YOU NEED: *flour, water, newspaper, balloon, string, tempera paint*

3

Let's Talk

Enhancing with Fingerplays, Stories, and Rhymes

My grandchildren begged me to tell them "one more story." Jenna wanted it to be about a fairy, kitty, and unicorn, while Jake wanted a 16-wheeler, bulldozer, and Reddy, the racing car star. While I pondered the formidable task of weaving these disparate characters together into a coherent story, my grandchildren proceeded to provide an elaborate storyline. Just when I thought I was off the hook, Jake abruptly declared, "Now tell the story." I protested that they had already told it, but he insisted, "You need to add all the details." Fortunately, with their frequent prompts, I rose to the challenge and completed the complex, meandering storyline.

Why Try It?

Fostering such complex and imaginative use of language is fun and easy. Having a conversation or playing language games can happen spontaneously, for most require little time and only you and your grandchild. Talking with your grandchild is the best way to build strong emotional bonds. As she becomes more proficient in language, talking together about her interests and feelings lays the foundation for a strong, intimate relationship. Because language is so closely tied to thinking and interacting with others, as you foster her language development, you also strengthen her social, emotional, and cognitive development.

Snapshot of Development

Language seems to emerge with magical ease from the newborn's coos and cries. Linguists offer differing explanations for this remarkable achievement. Some focus on how children imitate what they hear and receive reinforcement for their responses. This is certainly important in learning vocabulary. Think, for instance, of the excitement generated when the child first says, "dada" or "mama." Other linguists point to an innate human ability to acquire language with little effort, the brain apparently hardwired for language. They note in particular that children learn grammar (e.g., word order, plurals, verb tenses) rapidly. They apply the rules of grammar intuitively without direct instruction, sometimes in ways they have not heard. This rule learning is apparent, for example, when the child overgeneralizes the rule for forming the past tense, saying, "I drinked it" or for forming plurals, saying "mouses." Still other linguists emphasize the social context. We are social beings, and language gives us the power to communicate and connect to others.

Despite the controversy over how language develops, we seem intuitively to know how to foster its development. We talk to our grandchildren long before they can understand our words; we support their language efforts and modify our speech to match their developmental level. They don't need intensive language stimulation or special lessons and techniques—

just a typical language-rich environment with someone to talk to them and be responsive to their efforts.

Tips for Talking

Although language learning is easy for our grandchildren, it still takes skill and patience to have clear and meaningful conversations with them. One grandchild rambles on incessantly, but you can't decipher what she so ardently tries to tell you. Another averts her eyes and refuses to respond to your most impassioned queries. Yes, it can be frustrating to converse with a young child, but it's well worth the extra effort. The more you connect through talk, the more you develop a close rapport. In the process you are helping your grandchild build a rich vocabulary, fluency, and confidence in her ability to express her thoughts and feelings. As an added bonus, grandparents find these interactions yield humorous and entertaining stories to share along with their wallet full of grandchild photos.

Be an Active Listener

To overcome communication hurdles, let your grandchild know how much you want to understand her. Getting down on her level and maintaining eye contact lets her know she has your undivided attention. I usually sit on the floor or beside my grandchild on the couch. Then, keeping in mind the adage about why we were given two ears and only one mouth, I let her do most of the talking.

Work at really understanding what your grandchild is saying and feeling. We all appreciate a good listener, one who truly wants to understand our point of view and is interested in whatever we are doing or feeling. It takes even more skillful and patient listening with a young child, coupled with careful observing as well. If you are not sure whether you understand her words or feelings, ask whether you have interpreted correctly, for example, "Do you want a different cracker? A graham cracker or a soda cracker?" or "I think you are frustrated that your block tower fell over again." Hopefully, she will be able to tell you whether you understand correctly.

Tune into Actions

Her facial expressions, gestures, and other body language convey her thoughts and feelings better than words alone. One-year-old Emerson could not tell me I was his trusted friend, but when he toddled over to where I sat on the floor and gave me a big hug, I got the message. When Jenna lay quietly on the couch with her face buried in a pillow, her behavior expressed her feelings more eloquently than words that her brother was getting all the attention.

My sister Laura had a similar experience. She had asked Alex if she could sit next to her in a booth at Starbucks. But with 2-year-old independence, Alex answered with an emphatic "No!" Her older sister Cassie generously offered, "Grandma, you can sit next to me." As they munched cookies, Alex was unusually quiet. Then she abandoned her snowflake cookie to come over and give her grandmother a big hug. No words could equal this silent but eloquent apology.

Tailor Language to Grandchild's Age

Modify your language to match your grandchild's language abilities. The trick is to strike a balance between making it simple enough for her to understand and still provide a challenging language model. Usually we do this without much conscious effort. With my 1-year-old grandson I found I used shorter sentences, spoke more slowly, and used mostly concrete words, especially those he knew. But with my 5-year-old grandchild, I found that I was using all the rich vocabulary and complex syntax of adult speech.

Teach a Second Language

If you are fluent in a language other than English, give your grandchild the precious gift of learning a second language the easy, natural way. Beginning in infancy, use this second language every time you talk to her. She will absorb it along with her native language and intuitively know to use it when talking with you.

Activities

You can enrich the basic language learning that happens in ordinary conversations with planned activities. Those suggested in this chapter include *Old Faithfuls* and *New Twists*. **Old Faithfuls** are basic everyday activities. Easy to do at a moment's notice, they engender a comforting familiarity. *New Twists* take more planning and special equipment. They also include ways to document your grandchild's language development.

The First Year

Developmental Insights

Although your grandchild is not talking yet, she still finds abundant ways to communicate with you and is developing a repertoire of sounds. Even in the first months of life she makes a variety of crying and cooing sounds. By 4 months her sounds become more varied and deliberate. She delights you with her laughs, gurgles, and squeals. By 6 or 7 months she begins to babble, repeating sounds such as *mama* or *nana.*

Don't be surprised if you find yourself using infant-directed speech (motherese), which is delivered in short, simple sentences spoken with more intonation and a higher pitch than typical speech. Parents and grandparents worldwide adopt this special speech with babies. It's what your grandchild is programmed to prefer, and right from the beginning you are going to do whatever it takes to elicit eye contact and a big smile. It doesn't matter what you talk about; just keep up a running commentary of whatever comes to mind. I usually find myself talking about what we are seeing and doing, as I rock, diaper, or play with my grandchild. She may not understand my words yet, but she is listening and learning about language. Practice turn-taking "conversations." When she coos or babbles, give a verbal response, and then wait for her to respond.

Gestures are an early avenue for communication. Even before she is talking, she understands many simple words and communicates with gestures, such as raising her arms for you to pick her up. Older infants can learn to imitate actions associated with specific words. Waving *bye-bye* is the classic example. Wave and say *bye-bye* over and over again. Then praise the slightest imitation efforts. Teach her other gesture–language pairs, such *as pat-a-cake, peek-a-boo,* or your own inventions.

During the second half of the first year you can teach her words by frequently pointing to and repeating the names of familiar objects, people or actions, such as *ball, milk, uppy, bye-bye,* and definitely *Grandma or Granddad.* If she utters a sound remotely close to the word, you will, of course, reinforce this effort with smiles and cheers. This breakthrough development of making the sound–object connection and producing her first words usually occurs around the end of the first year.

Some children entertain themselves with jargon, chattering away using nonsense utterances with all the inflections and intonation of adult speech. At 10 months my grandson was the loudest and most expressive "talker" in the house. If only we knew his language!

Old Faithfuls

Sing-Along: During daily routines—going to bed, taking a walk or getting a diaper change—make a practice of singing a special song to her—a traditional lullaby, a bouncy children's tune, or your favorite song. Don't let your ability to carry a tune deter you. No matter the quality, she will love the sound. My favorite song is "Rock-a-bye Baby" complete with rocking and falling motions. But I often just make up my own lyrics to go along with whatever we are doing.

WHAT YOU NEED: *special song*

Echo: Position yourself so that your grandchild can easily see your face. When she coos, squeals, or babbles, respond by imitating the sound she has made. This encourages turn-taking "conversations." As she gets older, you can make a sound for her to imitate. Begin by using the sounds already in her repertoire. Include clicks, hisses, popping sounds, bubble-blowing, and squeals along with more typical vocalizations. Try whispering or speak with drawn-out exaggeration. The purpose of all these variations is to hold her interest.

WHAT YOU NEED: *no props required*

Words and Actions: Recite your favorite nursery rhymes. Add physical actions to capture and hold your grandchild's interest. For *Hickory, Dickory Dock*, run your fingers from her toes to her head, and back down. I could always count on a big smile from 7-month-old Alex when I clapped his hands together as I recited "Pat-a-Cake, Pat-a-Cake, Baker Man." There are many excellent books of Mother Goose rhymes. One recent version is Rosemary Wells's *My Very First Mother Goose*. It has large, colorful, and humorous illustrations.

WHAT YOU NEED: *nursery rhymes*

New Twists

Sing My Song: Make up a song that includes your grandchild's name. This will help her tune into the sound of her own name. It could be your own original lyrics. I made up this song for my first grandson:

> *Jacob, Jacob,*
> *Time to wake up.*
> *Jacob, Jacob*
> *I love you.*
> *Yes I do.*

Or you can simply insert your grandchild's name in a familiar song, for example, "Rock-a bye Jacob in the tree tops. . . . Down will come Jacob, cradle and all."

WHAT YOU NEED: *original song*

Capture the Coos: Use a tape recorder or camcorder to record your grandchild's language milestones. In those early months, capture her coos, cries, gurgles, and laughs. Later, add her babbling and her expanding repertoire of vocalizations. Record a verbal interaction between the two of you, her first words, and a sample of her jargon. Maintain this language history and give it to your grandchild when he or she is older.

WHAT YOU NEED: *tape recorder or camcorder*

One- and Two-Year-Olds

Developmental Insights

Along with that first toddling step, your grandchild typically takes the giant step of saying her first word around her first birthday. At some magical moment those babbling *ma-mas* and *da-das* turn into true words. Slowly at first and then accelerating rapidly, she adds new words. In the first 6 months after saying her first word she will learn another 50, followed by a vocabulary spurt, sometimes labeled the "naming explosion," in which she adds three or more words a day. Many are names of familiar people and objects, but they also include action words and frequently heard expressions. My grandson's early words included *go-gos* (car), *mo'milk, Jako, bye-bye, up, stop, hi,* and *no.* These first words are holophases, one word expressing an entire sentence. Depending on the tone and cadence, *nana* can mean "I want nana" "I see nana," or "Where did nana go?"

Since receptive language develops earlier than spoken language, she understands much more than she can say. When I asked my 1-year-old grandson, "Where is the ball?" he would bring it to me, but it was several months later before he said *ball.* Likewise, he would point to body parts when requested, but still was not be able to say *nose, eye,* or *tummy.*

The next language milestone is the two-word sentence. She takes words learned separately and combines them in new ways. Typically she attaches other words onto pivot words, such as "want cookie," "want Mama," or "want uppy." In a few months, she combines three or more words and can do so in a grammatically correct sequence, for example, "Mama go bye-bye." You may find yourself repeating and extending what she has said. When she says "ball," you respond with "Yes, bring me the ball" or "It's a big, red ball." Using extensions is a naturally beneficial way to "teach" language.

Overloading your grandchild with questions may not elicit the conversation you are seeking. Instead, talk about what she is doing and seeing right now and let her respond when she is ready. For example, you might say, "You are rolling the red ball. Oh dear, it is stuck under the couch and we can't get it out."

As she begins to talk more, you may struggle to make sense of what she is saying. As you spend more time together, you will gradually tune into her unique speech patterns and find her speech more understandable. Don't hesitant to ask her to repeat what she is saying. This shows her you are sincerely interested in what she has to say.

When long-distance grandparents try to have a conversation over the phone, they face an even greater challenge. Your grandchild may listen intently to your voice but say little or nothing in response to your questions. It may help to use a speakerphone and to have a parent prompt her. She usually talks more freely about what she is doing or seeing right now, not some past or future event. Not yet able to take the perspective of another person, she assumes you can see what she sees. A videophone is a good way to overcome this communication hurtle.

Old Faithfuls

Know Your Nose?: This game teaches the names for parts of the body. Ask your grandchild, "Where is your nose?" At first you will need to help her touch her nose. When she has mastered *nose*, add *eyes*, *ears*, *tummy*, and other body parts. For variation you could ask her, "Where is Grandma's nose?"

WHAT YOU NEED: *no props required*

Say and Do Rhymes: Engage your grandchild in songs and rhymes that encourage active participation. Typically, toddlers listen intently and imitate just a few motions, with full participation in both the words and actions coming much later. Begin with easy-to-do movements, ones in which you do what the words say. Here are two examples that toddlers enjoy:

Teddy bear, teddy bear turn around.	*(Stand up and spin around once or twice.)*
Teddy bear, teddy bear, touch the ground	*(Touch the floor.)*
Teddy bear, teddy bear, go up stairs.	*(Walk in place lifting your thighs high.)*
Teddy bear, teddy bear, say your prayers.	*(Put hands together in praying position.)*
Teddy bear, teddy bear, turn out the light.	*(Pretend to click off the light switch.)*
Teddy bear, teddy bear, say good night.	*(Tip head to one side and close eyes.)*
Open, shut them.	*(Extend fingers on both hands in front of you, and then make them into fists.)*
Open, shut them.	*(Repeat above motions.)*
Give your hands a clap, clap, clap.	*(Clap three times.)*
Open, shut them.	*(Repeat extending fingers and making fists)*
Open, shut them.	*(Repeat above motions.)*
Lay them in your lap, lap, lap.	*(Pat lap three times.)*
Up they flutter.	*(Raise hands overhead slowly.)*

Then down they drop.	*(Quickly drop them.)*
Pick them up.	*(Lift them in front of you.)*
And roll them till they stop.	*(Roll hands and forearms quickly around each other.)*

The Eentsy, Weensty Spider: Fingerplays and Action Rhymes is a good source for additional ideas. My granddaughter enjoyed looking at the pictures as we recited the words and performed the depicted motions.

WHAT YOU NEED: *words and motions to fingerplay*

Cows Go Moooo: Teach your grandchild to imitate animal sounds. Look at a picture book of animals. Point to a cow, horse, dog, cat, or duck and make the appropriate moo, neigh, bark, meow, or quack. Then point to an animal and ask, "What does it say?" Eventually, you can omit the pictures and just ask what sound each animal makes. My grandson especially liked to make a fish sound by opening and closing his lips without any vocalizing.

WHAT YOU NEED: *book with pictures of animals*

The Name Game: To encourage learning new words, play this name game. At first, focus on a few highly meaningful words, such as *ma-ma, nana, doggy,* and *car.* Point to it and name it. Then use the word several times again while you talk about its distinctive characteristics: "See the doggy." "The doggy is barking." "The doggy likes to lick your face!" "Do you want to pet the doggy?" "See how soft the doggy feels." Point out other examples of this word, such as pictures of dogs, toy dogs, and neighborhood dogs. Later, test whether she has learned the word by asking, "Where's the doggy?" Or point to a dog and ask her what it is.

WHAT YOU NEED: *familiar objects and pictures of them*

Mary, May I?: This game encourages your grandchild to respond to meaningful questions. Ask her if you may give her a kiss. Wait for her to answer "yes" or "no" and then do as she requests. Make a series of similar requests: May I give you a hug? Tickle you? Touch your nose? Pick you up? Then reverse the directions and ask her to give you a kiss or hug.

WHAT YOU NEED: *no props required*

Simple Stories: Introduce your grandchild to storytelling with your own original story. Include words that she knows and add actions to accompany the words. It can be as short and simple as this example: "The kitty is crying. She wants her mama. Where is Mama? The kitty looks under the chair. No Mama. The kitty looks in the toy box. No Mama. The kitty looks on the bed. Here's Mama! The kitty is so happy!"

When she is 2, add familiar, simple stories with repetitive actions and phrases, such as *The Gingerbread Man* and *The Three Billy Goats Gruff.* Speak with exaggerated expression, use different voices for each character, and improvise sound effects. Encourage her to take an active role in the storytelling by asking her to add the appropriate animal sound or repetitive phase (e.g., the gingerbread man's refrain, *Run, run as fast as you can . . .* or *trip-trap* went the bridge as the goats walked across). This storytelling is a great way to entertain your toddler in the car.

WHAT YOU NEED: *simple traditional stories*

New Twists

Telephone Talk: Pretend phone conversations help your grandchild learn how to talk on the telephone. Use two play phones, one for your grandchild and one for you. Make the phone ring, pick up the receiver, and give an emphatic "hello." Tell your grandchild to respond with her own "hello." Ask a few simple questions: "What is your name?" or "Do you have a teddy bear?" Conclude by saying "good-bye" and asking her to respond with a "good-bye." As she gets older, add a few open-ended questions that require her to talk more: "What are you doing?" or "Tell me about your kitty." You may need to prompt an answer at first, suggesting, for instance, "You could say, I'm playing with my dolly."

WHAT YOU NEED: *two play telephones*

Words to Remember: Continue to record your grandchild's remarkable language growth on a tape recorder or camcorder every few months. At first, you may have to be very creative just to elicit a few words. As her speaking abilities develop, she may be willing to recite a nursery rhyme or carry on a spontaneous conversation. If your toddler has her own original word inventions, be sure to record these as well.

WHAT YOU NEED: *tape recorder or camcorder*

Puppet Play: Hand puppets are a natural for encouraging dialogue, especially if your grandchild is on the shy side. To introduce puppet play, put a puppet on your hand and talk to it and have the puppet answer your questions. Then, have the puppet talk to your grandchild, asking easy-to-answer questions, such as "What is your name?" or "What do you like to play?" You can have your puppet act out everyday routines (eating or going to bed) or more emotion-packed episodes (bumping his head and being afraid to go to the hospital to get stitches). Constructive Playthings (*www.constplay.com*) offers easy-to-use hand puppets at reasonable prices. Lakeshore Learning

Company (*www.lakeshorelearning.com*) has an extensive line of storytelling glove puppets with characters for story classics. My grandchildren especially like the ones with mouths that can "talk" and then snap shut on a finger. However, it was a huggable monkey puppet made by Falkmanis, Inc. that became Jenna's constant companion.

<u>WHAT YOU NEED:</u>   *a hand puppet*

Let Your Fingers Do the Talking: Teaching sign language to toddlers enriches communication options. A child can often learn to sign before she can say the words. This can reduce her frustration at being unable to communicate her wishes. Pick out a few basic signs to teach your grandchild, such as *milk, potty,* and *cookie.* Say the word along with showing her how to sign it. Each day repeat the signs taught previously and add a new one.

<u>WHAT YOU NEED:</u>   *book or DVD with illustrations for basic sign language*

Three- and Four-Year Olds

Developmental Insights

A preschooler's vocabulary grows rapidly, averaging nine new words each day. To accomplish this feat, she uses a process called *fast mapping,* in which new words are associated with their meaning after only a brief encounter. Her sentences become longer and increase in complexity. Most linguists agree that she has an intuitive, working knowledge of the complex rules of language and is able to use most of these by the time she is 5 or 6. She often overgeneralizes the rules, saying "I hurted myself" or "the goodest thing."

Don't be concerned if you overhear your grandchild talking to herself. She is just thinking out loud. She uses this private speech to plan and guide her actions. Four-year-olds may have a hard time getting out what they want to say. This lack of fluency is not surprising, given the phenomenal language growth that is occurring. It usually disappears naturally in a few years. Most speech therapists recommend giving the child plenty of time to get out what she wants to say without calling attention to her "stuttering."

What your grandchild needs most is for you to listen with undivided attention to whatever she has to say. You can extend the conversation with your comments and questions, but let her do most of the talking. When she mispronounces words or makes grammatical errors, model the correct usage or pronunciation by using it in your response. This is more effective than constantly correcting her grammar. Your response to "I runned down the hill" could be "Yes, you ran down a long way." She will talk more freely with you if you focus on the content of what she is saying rather than the correctness of her grammar or pronunciation.

Old Faithfuls

Finger Frolics: Act out rhymes with hand motions. Your grandchild will enjoy imitating the motions and reciting the words. These are great for modeling expressive language and teaching new vocabulary. Here are two of my favorites:

Way up in the apple tree,	*(Point and look up toward the ceiling.)*
Two little apples looked at me.	*(Make two fists.)*
I shook the tree as hard as I could.	*(Shake arms vigorously.)*
Down came the apples.	*(Drop hands from over your head into your lap.)*
Mmmm, they were good!	*(Pretend to eat apple and then rub tummy.)*
Here's a beehive	*(Make a fist with all fingers tucked inside.)*
Where are the bees?	*(Look all around.)*
Hiding inside where nobody sees.	
Now they come creeping out of the hive.	
One, two, three, four, five.	*(Hold up pointer finger, then additional fingers with each new number.)*
Bzzzz!	*(Make fingers fly all around.)*

To add to your repertoire of fingerplays, Liz Cromwell's *Finger Frolics* and *Finger Frolics 2* and Marc Brown's *Finger Rhymes* and *Hand Rhymes* contain both traditional and more recent fingerplays for every occasion and topic.

WHAT YOU NEED: *words and motions for fingerplays*

High and Low/Fast and Slow: This game uses antonyms to increase vocabulary. State a word that has a commonly used antonym: up/down, over/under, in/out, stop/go, tall/ short, happy/sad, hot/cold. Ask your grandchild to tell you a word with the opposite meaning and give her a point for every correct answer. When you are finished, count to see how many points she has earned.

WHAT YOU NEED: *list of antonyms, paper and pencil*

Tell Me a Story: Grandparents have a long history as family storytellers. Keep up this tradition with your grandchild by telling traditional tales or true stories about the family. I often retell a story we recently read together. Any omissions and my grandchildren are quick to set the story straight.

Even better, make up your own original story. Ask what kind of story she would like; should it be sad, funny, or scary? It's easy to make up one based on a recent event. I guarantee a smile of pleasure when your grandchild finds herself the main character in the story. Jake loved to hear about how courageous he was as he rode the inner tube down steep, snowy slopes. Spice up your story with humor or fanciful elaboration.

Children relish the familiar, and so you might want to create a series of stories with the same main characters. For instance, after we acquired a puppy who liked to run out of the yard, I told stories that described her adventures and feelings as she wandered far from home. You can involve your grandchild by asking her to select what the adventure will be in this episode: A car crash? Getting lost? An angry monster?

WHAT YOU NEED: *traditional tales, family stories, made-up stories*

New Twists

Language Stories: Your grandchild's language often shows freshness, humor, and a unique play on words. Jot these down in a journal to share with her when she is older. Here are samples of original expressions and humorous utterances with my grandchildren:

- When he suspected his orange juice had been diluted with water, Jake complained, "It rained in my juice."
- Jake, perplexed upon hearing his great-grandmother's voice on the phone, protested, "But you are dead!" She quickly reassured him that she was very much alive and that it was his other great-grandmother who had died.
- Jenna said emphatically, "I'm not a slowpoke. I'm a fastpoke."
- Jenna said, "I'm up and down sick" to describe her motion sickness.
- When I asked Emerson if he was a girl or a boy, he pondered for awhile and then said, "I'm a truck."

WHAT YOU NEED: *notebook and pen*

The Big Red Circle: This homemade game teaches color, shape, and size. Cut out red, blue, and yellow circles, squares, and triangles from heavy construction paper for a total of nine shapes. Make a second set of smaller ones. Then outline each shape with the appropriate color on a large piece of cardboard.

Your grandchild can match the pieces to the shapes on the board. Hold up a shape and ask, "Where should we put this big red circle?" Follow this same procedure for each of the shapes. You can also use the shapes to sort by color, size, or shape. For example, "Let's put all the circles in this pile and all the triangles in this pile."

WHAT YOU NEED: *red, yellow, and blue construction paper; markers, scissors, ruler, cardboard*

Five- to Eight-Year-Olds

Developmental Insights

Your grandchild now has an extensive vocabulary, including many abstract and difficult words. Her rate of vocabulary growth is even greater than during the preschool years, as she often acquires as many as 20 new words a day.

Her conversational skills improve markedly. She can carry on extended conversations on diverse topics. Her comments and questions are more directly relevant to what you have said, because she is better able to take in what you are saying and modify her responses accordingly. At 5 or 6 she often develops the ability to tell a good narrative about what has happened to her. She includes a series of events leading up to the central event, talks at some length about it, and then tells how things were resolved.

She appreciates having a grown-up who is interested in all her daily activities and who takes the time to listen attentively and understand her feelings and concerns. It may take some warming up before long, intimate conversations can develop between you and your grandchild. Often the best approach is to quietly observe what she is doing. You can make occasional comments and ask a few questions to show your interest. Then follow her lead and be an uncritical listener when she begins to share her deeper thoughts and feelings. Grammy Sonya found that driving a grandchild to the dentist or soccer practice was a good opportunity for conversations.

A good time to informally share your perspectives and values is when you are involved in an activity together that centers on your special interests. Grandma Susan regularly includes her grandchildren in feeding the birds and squirrels and tending her garden. As they do these tasks, she talks about the need to take care of our environment and care for all creatures.

Long-distance grandparents often find that longer, more meaningful phone conversations are possible. To ensure a time compatible with their grandchild's busy schedule, many grandparents set up a regular time to call each week. Keep up-to-date on your grandchild's current interests and activities, so that you can talk about things that especially interest her.

Old Faithfuls

Conversation Starters: To initiate a sustained conversation with your grandchild, wait until she is not heavily involved in an activity. Here are a few suggestions for those occasions when your conversation needs a jumpstart:

- Ask your grandchild to tell you about her best friend.
- Ask about the best thing and then the worst thing that happened today.
- Share photos of special times together and reminisce about the funny things that happened.
- Ask for specifics about a favorite activity, such as what happened at the soccer game or where she rode her bike today.
- Share a newspaper or magazine article that is about children or your grandchild's special interests.
- Watch her favorite TV show or DVD together and then talk about the characters and action.
- Tell stories about her parents when they were young.
- Talk about your childhood—your favorite activities, the place where you lived, or funny incidents. Make this as realistic as possible by showing her a photo of you beside a giant snowman, your report card from first grade, or a manual typewriter.

Creative Collaborations: Encourage your grandchild to make up her own stories. These stories develop her creativity and language skills and also allow her to express her concerns and emotions without fear of criticism. Since she is not the one talking or acting, it's okay to express negative feelings and unacceptable behaviors, such as locking the new baby in the closet or being afraid of all the scary things hiding in the dark.

An effective transitional strategy is to create a story together. Let your grandchild select the main characters and setting. Then start with the traditional "Once upon a time." Take turns adding a sentence or two to the storyline. Let the plot meander all over the place and conclude with a summary sentence: "And that's the story of her many adventures."

WHAT YOU NEED: *no props required*

Word of the Day: To enrich your grandchild's vocabulary, give a new word a whirl for a day. Select a new word, ideally one that has come up spontaneously in conversation or reading. You each try to see how many times you can use it in your conversation. Jake enjoyed learning the distinction between *opaque, transparent,* and *translucent.* He would go around the house pointing out the *opaque* table, the *transparent* window, and the *translucent* plastic container. When I called something a *family tradition,* Jenna delighted in finding other ways to use this new phrase.

WHAT YOU NEED: *new words*

New Twists

Recite a Poem: Help your grandchild select a favorite poem to memorize. It could be a silly poem from *Where the Sidewalk Ends* or a classic from *When We Were Young* or *A Child's Treasury of Poems.* Read the whole poem together several times and talk about its special features, such as the rhyming words, the words that start with the same sounds, and the vivid images. Then read the first line and ask her to repeat it exactly as it is written. Gradually, have her add one more line at a time until she can say the whole poem.

WHAT YOU NEED: *words to a poem*

Phone the Family: Create a family phone book for your grandchild so that she can easily call you and other family members. Use 5 × 8-inch index cards. Punch two holes in the top of each card and attach with ring binders. The cover can be another index card with "My Family Phone Book" as its title. Put a small photo on each page along with "Uncle Joe" or "Grandpa" and his or her phone number. Using her phone book, she can independently keep in touch with you and other family members.

WHAT YOU NEED: *index cards, hole punch, ring binders, family photos, glue, marker*

Hola or Bonjour: Teach your grandchild a few words and phrases in another language. Select those that you can easily use in conversations with your grandchild. Good candidates are: *Hello; Good-bye; How are you?; Thank you; My name is . . .* Learn to count to 10 and the names of colors. Teach your grandchild a simple song or rhyme in that language. If she is already familiar with the English version, it will be easier to learn.

WHAT YOU NEED: *information about common words and phrases in a language that is not your grandchild's native language; song in second language*

Do a Duplicate: This game encourages your grandchild to give clear, complete verbal descriptions of objects. Have her build a LEGOs structure without showing it to you. Then it is your task to build a duplicate structure solely by following her verbal directions. No peeking at her structure! It may help to put a visual shield, such as poster board or a file folder, between her structure and yours. Then reverse roles and see if she can build the structure you have made by relying on your description.

WHAT YOU NEED: *LEGOs, poster board or file folder*

4

Let's Read and Write

Climbing the Literacy Ladder

Jake and Jenna greeted me at the door with their "Did you bring any new books?" refrain. Pouncing on the stack of books I had just checked out of the library, they insisted that I "read them all, right now." We had barely nes-

---

Let's Grandparent: Activity Guide for Young Grandchildren, pages 51–70

tled down on the couch for a long, cozy read when their 1-year-old brother protested about being left out. I soon found myself engulfed by grandchildren, piles of books, and an overwhelming feeling of pride and pleasure. We read our way through the enormous stack down to *There's a Nightmare in My Closet* "just one more time"— a bedtime story guaranteed to generate an extensive flashlight search of every possible place that monsters could hide. After I retold my version of the story with my grandchildren as stars, Jake curled up with a book and flashlight to read it again, and Jenna smiled contentedly as she snuggled under her comforter saying, "I'm going to tell myself a story now."

Why Try It?

By repeating this experience many times over, I hope to pass on my passion for books to my grandchildren. I already see it in their total engrossment in the unfolding story, once even letting a call for ice cream go unheard. I see it in the deep identification with characters, prompting Jake to say, "When I read a book, I want to be that person." I hear it in their questions when we read about elephants, oceans, or volcanoes and in their experimentation with new words and phrases encountered in books.

But the benefits do not stop here. Reading daily to young children significantly increases their vocabulary and strengthens oral language abilities. It lays the foundation for becoming a competent reader. The goal is not how early he learns to read but that he becomes an avid reader for the pure pleasure of it. He will continue to increase in competency as he devours one book after another. Books can also contribute toward healthy emotional development. They are a vehicle for understanding emotions and finding constructive ways to cope with difficulties.

Snapshot of Development

Literacy begins long before formal efforts to teach reading and writing. It can be a natural process, similar to learning to talk. Early pleasurable experiences with books lay a foundation for wanting to learn to read and provide an understanding of how print works.

Tips for Literacy Experiences

Read the Best-of-the-Bunch

In selecting books for your grandchild, a good place to start is with those books you and your children liked. These classics, with their deep, universal appeal, have stood the test of time. My daughter says they bring back pleasant childhood memories of when I read to her.

In addition to storybooks, do include nonfiction books in your selections. Such books teach basic concepts and provide new information. Be sure the information is accurate and up-to-date.

Looking for specific suggestions for books? Pick up a booklist at your public library that makes recommendations about age-appropriateness. The American Library Association website (*www.ala.org*) has reviews of children's books. It also lists award-winning books, including the annual Newbery Medal, given to the author who has made the most distinguished contribution to American literature for children, and the Caldecott Award, given to the artist who has created the most distinguished picture book. The Children's Book Council (*www.cbcbooks.org*) has a guide for choosing the perfect book for a child. I also recommend *The New York Times Parent's Guide to the Best Books for Children* for its detailed information about the quality and content of specific books.

Customize Selections

Select books on subjects of special interest or relevance to your grandchild. For your 2-year-old grandson who plays constantly with cars and trucks, look for books with pictures of vehicles. Since Cassie was fascinated with natural disasters, Grandma Laura shared nonfiction books about tornados, volcanoes, and thunderstorms. When our dog died, 2-year-old Emerson wanted to hear *The Accident*, a story of a dog hit and killed by a car, over and over. Since the theme and pictures were right but the text too complex for him, I just told the story in my own words.

To find a book on a specific topic, use the handy index in *The New York Times Parent's Guide to the Best Books for Children*. A children's librarian also can help you find books that fit your grandchild's age and interests.

Elicit Participation

Keep your grandchild actively involved in the reading process. Be quick to respond to his questions or comments, even though this interrupts the story.

Start by having your infant grandchild handle the book. Encourage the 2-year-old to name objects as you point to them. The preschooler can join in when you come to repetitive and predictable phrases. The kindergartner can point out words or letters he recognizes and take a turn reading to you.

Support your grandchild's efforts when he chooses to read to himself. Pleased with Alex's excellent memory and expressive retelling of *We're Going on a Bear Hunt,* Grandma Laura told her, "You really read that well." To this, Alex replied very seriously, "Grandma Laura, you are a good reader, too!"

Be a Drama Queen

Energetic, expressive reading will command the attention of even your most book-adverse grandchild. Make it a theatrical performance with different voices for each character. Whisper or shout, pause or speed up, growl or cry to make the story come alive.

Read for Fun

Although reading is packed with educational value, keep your focus on having an enjoyable experience. The by-product may be an early and competent reader, but leave the academic emphasis to others. Consider it a child-directed activity. Suggest it as an option, but follow your grandchild's lead about when and what to read.

Write Regularly

Writing is the flip side of reading. To create an interest in writing, find frequent opportunities to do so with your grandchild. Write his name on his artwork, have him dictate a thank-you note, or have him suggest items for a grocery list. When your grandchild tries his hand at writing, the combination of fine motor and cognitive challenges can generate frustration, but also a great sense of achievement. Applaud his efforts to write and keep them spontaneous and authentic. There should be a real purpose for what he writes. View it as *using* writing, not just *practicing* writing. Displaying examples of his writing shows you value his efforts.

Activities

This chapter continues with the same organization of activities as in earlier chapters, with reading activities divided into *Old Faithfuls* and *New Twists*. **Old Faithfuls** are basic everyday activities that are easy to do with minimal preparation and important to do on a regular basis. **New Twists** take more planning and materials. They include ways to document your grandchild's reading development and suggestions about creating original books for your grandchild.

The First Year

Developmental Insights

How soon should you begin to read to your grandchild? Take your cues from his responses. Even in his early months he enjoys listening to your voice. As his vision improves, he focuses on the pictures as well. At first, it is the outline of the object that draws his attention rather than the details, so choose illustrations with one object on a plain background.

By 6 months he may want a more active role in the reading process. Let him explore the physical properties of books, letting him touch, hold, and taste them as well. (Is this the first step in developing a lifelong taste for books?) He may want to start at the back, quit in the middle, or turn the book upside down. The important thing is to surround him with books, whether he is sitting on your lap, playing in the highchair, or crawling on the floor. Let books be as familiar and loved as those ubiquitous stuffed animals.

Your grandchild figures out quickly that the two-dimensional pictures in books represent real objects. Look for books that have brightly colored, simple pictures of familiar objects. You will not be reading so much as using a point-and-say strategy. Your eager page-turner may not be interested in hearing that "The cow jumped over the moon," but you can point to the picture and say, "See the cow" and "That's the moon."

Old Faithfuls

Sturdy as He Grows: Are you alarmed at the prospect of your grandchild, with his penchant for search-and-destroy missions, manhandling the expensive and fragile books you have purchased? One solution is board books. Made of heavy cardboard, these stand up well to all his touching, poking, and tossing about. They are great for teething too. He will find it easier to hold the book and turn the sturdy pages. Likewise, cloth or vinyl books are made to withstand his demolition efforts.

WHAT YOU NEED: *board, cloth, or vinyl books*

Handle and Hear: To heighten interest in books, make it a multisensory experience. Touch-and-feel books let your grandchild explore many tactile textures—the soft bunny tail, the rough sand, or the lacy curtains. *Pat the Bunny* has remained an all-time favorite. Dorling Kindersley Publishing (*http://us.dk.com*) has an extensive touch-and-feel series. Books with buttons to push for playing songs or nursery rhymes let your grandchild explore cause-and-effect as he plays them over and over again.

WHAT YOU NEED: *touch-and-feel books, books with sound buttons*

New Twists

Grand Books: Make your own unique board books. Cut poster board into 6-inch squares. Add photos, pictures, and a word or two on each page and cover each page with clear contact paper. Assemble into a book by punching two holes on the side of each page and fastening together with ring binders or pipe cleaners. Here are some suggestions for themes:

- *My Family:* Attach a photo of a family member on each page. Be sure to include one of your grandchild, the family pet, and yourself.
- *Things That Go:* Cut out pictures of tricycles, trains, planes, cars, and trucks from magazines or download computer images and put one on each page.
- *My Favorite Toys:* Take photos of his favorite toys and attach one on each page of the book.
- *My Favorite Foods:* Use pictures from magazines and labels from food products. Include as many healthy foods as possible. What are his favorite fruits? What about yogurt, nuts, and cheese?

WHAT YOU NEED: *poster board, clear contact paper, hole punch, ring binders or pipe cleaners; photos or pictures*

One- and Two-Year-Olds

Developmental Insights

Many toddlers engage in reading-like behavior, turning the pages and looking at the pictures. At 16 months, Emerson, with his strong bent for imitation, would get his own book and study it intently whenever I read to his older brother and sister. When Jenna was 2 and in that "I want to do it myself" stage, she would insist on "reading" a new book to herself before asking me to read it.

Reading to a toddler is one of the best ways to increase his vocabulary. Also, it's a great opportunity for cuddling up together and having a sustained conversation, a break from his typical whirlwind of activity. Expect to read the same book over and over and over again. You may be bored by the second or third time, but not your grandchild, who will give you his persistent "Again!"

Look for picture books that have illustrations on every page and minimal text. Books, such as *The Carrot Seed* or *Freight Train*, with their simple storylines about familiar events, are easy for your grandchild to understand. Stories with frequent repetition in the words and actions are predictable and easy to follow, so try such traditional tales as *The Three Bears*. Stories that invite participation, such as *Brown Bear, Brown Bear, What Do You See?* will keep your grandchild actively engaged. Pause and let him fill in the appropriate word or phrase. Include concept books that teach colors, shapes, or counting. I like Tana Hoban's series of concept books, with such titles as *Push-Pull, Empty-Full: A Book of Opposites* and *Is It Rough? Is it Smooth? Is It Shiny?*

Books that deal with typical toddler concerns, such as getting in trouble or being left alone, often have a strong appeal. *The Owl Babies*, with its theme of separation from mother, was one of my grandchildren's favorites. They beamed with relief when mother owl returned. My great niece, Cassie, wanted to hear the story, *No, David!* over and over, identifying with the boy who in spite of his misbehavior still receives a big hug and unconditional love from his mother. She always asked for her own big hug after each reading.

Toddlers begin making marks on paper with crayons or markers. These scribbles are a precursor to writing. They later diverge into clearly distinguished writing or drawing, but at first he just enjoys seeing his marks on the page.

What about teaching the letters of the alphabet? Since letters are prominently featured on baby toys and alphabet books, it's easy to do. But don't do it in order to give him a head start in learning to read. It will be a long time yet before these symbols become connected to meaningful words and sounds.

Old Faithfuls

Books with Fun Features: Toddlers love lift-the-flap books. Your grandchild's delight in opening the flap to discover what's underneath is great for active involvement and predicting. Eric Hill's *Where's Spot?*, the story of a mother dog searching everywhere to find her hiding puppy, is an especially good example, because the flaps are integrated effectively into the storyline.

Pop-up books, with their three-dimensional expansions, are sure to produce chuckles of surprise. Look for ones with bright colors and a variety of pop-up designs. Any story or text is of secondary interest. A word of caution: Those flaps and pop-ups are very tempting to touch, tug, and tear, so keep your tape handy.

WHAT YOU NEED: *lift-the-flap and pop-up books*

Screen Time Stories: High-quality children's literature is a good choice for computer programs, videos, or DVDs. Beware that some may be too scary or upsetting for toddlers, for they are still trying to distinguish fantasy from reality. I was surprised to see tears streaming down 2-year-old Jenna's face as she watched *Corduroy Lost*, so deep was her empathy for the little teddy bear who was all alone and lost in a dark store. This experience convinced me to watch along with my grandchildren. Then I am there to deal with questions and concerns and can engage in retelling and acting out the story afterward.

Some software programs with interactive story formats are appropriate for older toddlers. My grandchildren especially liked those long-time favorites, Dr. Seuss's *The Cat in the Hat* and *Green Eggs and Ham* by The Learning Company (*www.learningcompany.com*). In these your grandchild can choose between hearing the story read straight through or stopping to "play" along the way.

WHAT YOU NEED: *computer or DVD player, CD or DVD*

My Marks: To foster your grandchild's first attempts at "writing," hand him a brightly colored washable marker and help him make marks on paper. Point to what he has drawn and encourage him to repeat his efforts. Give him frequent exposure to easy-to-use markers, and soon he will be making deliberate scribbles.

WHAT YOU NEED: *paper, washable markers*

New Twists

Grand Books: Create books especially designed for your own grandchild. Here are a few ideas to get you started.

- *My Favorite Things:* Use a three-ring binder to create a picture book of your grandchild's favorite things. On each piece of notebook paper glue pictures from magazines or images downloaded from the Internet, and write a word or sentence under each. You can easily add new pages as his interests grow.

  WHAT YOU NEED: *three-ring binder, notebook paper, glue, pictures, markers*

- *Where's Our Child?:* Make a lift-the-flap book using poster board for both the pages and the flaps. Punch holes on the left side and fasten together with ring binders or yarn. Paste pictures of a mother and father animal on the page and a picture of their baby under the flap. On each page repeat the query, "Where's our child?" On the last page, place a photo of your grandchild's parents and one of him inside the flap.

WHAT YOU NEED: *poster board, hole punch, ring binders or yarn, animal pictures, family photos*

- *My First Words:* A book that includes pictures of your grandchild's budding vocabulary serves as a tool to reinforce his early language efforts and later as a memento of his first words. An easy way to do this is to take photos of people, objects, and actions for which he has a word. People and objects are straightforward and easy to depict. Action words are more challenging. For *bye-bye* show him waving; for *uppy* show him in the act of being picked up; for *all gone* show an empty bowl. Attach each photo to heavy paper, punch holes in the margins of each page, and fasten together with ring binders or yarn.

WHAT YOU NEED: *camera, photos, heavy paper, hole punch, ring binders or yarn*

- *Our Time Together:* Use photos to illustrate a recent time spent with your grandchild. It could be a special event like the fireworks on the Fourth of July or a chronicle of all the activities you did together on an extended visit. When I came to stay for a week with my 1-year-old grandson, I took photos of all our activities and assembled these into a book about my visit. The book begins with "Once when I was one, my grandma came to visit." I put a photo of myself here to help him remember me until my next visit. Simple rhymes ("Rub-a-dub-dub, one boy in a tub") accompanied each photo.

WHAT YOU NEED: *camera, photos, heavy paper, hole punch; ring binders or yarn*

Baggie Books: For a more interactive experience, make a book with plastic zipper baggies. Use a report cover with quick-clip binding to clip the baggies together on the side opposite the zipper. Here are some suggestions:

- For a *How Does It Feel?* book, draw or copy downloaded clipart pictures on pieces of 8 × 6 heavy paper. Glue items with different textures on your pictures. For example, cotton for a bunny's tail, feathers on a bird, sandpaper in a sandbox, velvet on a party dress, wax paper over a window, and foil on a snowman. Put each picture in a zip-lock baggie and assemble in a binder. Let your grandchild unzip the baggies and handle the items inside. Talk about how soft, rough, smooth, or slippery each item feels.

WHAT YOU NEED: *plastic baggies with zippers; quick-clip binder; cotton, feathers, sandpaper, wax paper, foil, velvet, and other items with interesting textures, heavy paper, glue*

▪ For a shape theme, cut out circles, squares, rectangles, triangles, and stars in several sizes and colors. Put all the circles in one baggie, all the squares in another baggie, and so on. As he pulls them out, talk about the round circle, the three points on the triangle, and the big and little star.

WHAT YOU NEED: *plastic baggies with zippers; stapler and tape or quick-clip binder; scissors, heavy construction paper*

Three and Four-Year-Olds

Developmental Insights

Your grandchild's expanded attention span and cognitive advances allow for longer and more focused reading sessions. He may no longer be content with reading the same books over and over again, but instead be interested in books he hasn't read before. Offer a variety of books, knowing some will be laid aside after a quick read, while others will merit a big smile and an immediate request to "read it again."

Your grandchild is ready for stories with significantly more print and complex storylines, such as *Mike Mulligan and His Steam Shovel* or *Sylvester and the Magic Pebble*. Since illustrations still facilitate his understanding of the text, look for ones that are aesthetically pleasing and that add interesting details to the story. Occasionally, include a book of poetry, such as the humorous *Jamberry*. I like to read poems from the classic work by Robert Louis Stevenson, *A Child's Garden of Verses*, for I have fond memories of my mother reading them to me more than 60 years ago.

Curiosity about a wide range of subjects is a sign of his rapidly expanding ability to understand ever more of his world. So, in addition to stories, include informational books about nature, the human body, machines, or whatever subjects especially interest him.

Make reading times occasions for extended conversations. Discussing a new book before beginning to read it arouses interest and focus. It can be as simple as looking at the illustrations on the cover and wondering together what the story could be about. When reading informational books, it helps to ask questions to see what your grandchild already knows and where you can provide clarification. Books with themes touching on your grandchild's current concerns (e.g., fear of the dark, making friends, or adjusting to a new baby sister or brother) often inspire meaningful follow-up discussions.

You can help your grandchild lay a firm foundation for future reading success. Utilize strategies similar to those for language development; first and foremost, provide a responsive, literacy-rich environment. Skip the flash cards, drills, and formal lessons. Instead, as you are playing and reading together, reinforce what he already knows about reading and assist him in taking the next step on the literacy ladder. This includes learning to recognize both upper- and lowercase letters, getting the print–language connection, learning the sound–symbol relationships of letters, and acquiring sight words. Teach these incidentally in the context of fun, meaningful activities. You could point at each word in the title of the book or read the labels on cereal boxes.

Be supportive and interested in his early efforts to read or write, recognizing that these are complex and challenging tasks. Look for evidence of what he understands and is able to do, keeping your suggestions and corrections to a minimum. When my grandson pointed to "now" and said excitedly "no," I praised him for noticing the print and recognizing the word *no* and then showed him how the addition of "w" made it into another word. Scribbled lines across the page or markings that look like letters of his own original alphabet show that your grandchild knows what writing looks like. He may use invented spelling, writing down his best phonetic rendering of words. When your grandchild writes "LAFT" for "elephant," it shows an understanding of the sound–symbol relationship.

Reading and writing letters and words becomes much more meaningful to your grandchild when he sees how much grown-ups use them in their everyday activities. Call attention to environmental print (words appearing in settings other than books) every chance you can. Study the cereal boxes for letters to identify. When you go for a walk, read the signs. Read the commands in computer games, for example, *play, quit, yes, no.* Write a label or sentence to go with a picture he has drawn. Encourage him to write a note to his parents or best friend. It may start as pretend writing but soon includes his name and "I lov U." The emphasis is upon writing authentic messages rather than practicing how to write letters or words. This keeps it fun and meaningful.

Old Faithfuls

Time to Rhyme: Rhyming develops sensitivity to sounds and makes it easier to read words in the same "word family" (rhyming words with similar spellings). Help your grandchild tune in to rhyming words with this game. Ask, "Can you think of a word that rhymes with. . . . cat [pig, dog, see, go]?" Take turns coming up with as many words as possible. Write the words down as you say them. Then go back and read them with your grandchild.

WHAT YOU NEED: *paper and pencil*

Onscreen Stories: If your grandchild would rather watch TV or DVDs than read a book, lure him into the enchantment of books with onscreen children's classics. To encourage the transition to reading, provide the book version of what he has been watching. Here are my tried-and-true options:

- The Jumbo Box of Storybook Classics on DVD (Scholastic Video Collection) includes 35 old-time favorites, such as *Where the Wild Things Are, Harold and the Purple Crayon,* and *Pete's a Pizza.*
- Interactive books are available on CDs. *Arthur's Computer Adventure* (Learning Company) and *Stellaluna* (Living Books) are two my grandchildren especially enjoyed.
- Supplement your personal collection of videos and DVDs with those available at your local library. It is sure to have an extensive selection of classics and currently popular items.

WHAT YOU NEED: *videos, DVDs, or CDs with stories*

Letter of the Day: Pick a letter and write it on an index card. The goal for the day is to see how many times you can find this letter. It could be hidden in storybooks, food labels, road signs, or computer games. Put a gold star on the index card each time your grandchild finds this letter. Count the stars at the end of the day. Compare tallies for different letters on subsequent days. The initial letter in his name is a good choice for the first time.

WHAT YOU NEED: *marker, index cards, gold stars*

It's in the Mail: If you are a long-distance grandparent, inundate your grandchild with letters and cards. It could be a picture in a magazine or a photo of something that would be of special interest to him. One way to up the odds of getting return mail is to include a self-addressed envelope and a specific question to answer related to the picture that you sent.

When on vacation, send him postcards with special kid appeal, such as one picturing animals, vehicles, or children. Just print a simple sentence or two about the picture. Then after his parents' initial reading, he can "read" it himself. It could be a simple as, "Dear Jake, We rode this train. It is very fast. Love, Grandma." He will be thrilled to find his name on a piece of mail. It lets him know you are thinking of him and provides a reason to read what you have written.

WHAT YOU NEED: *paper, envelopes, postcards, stamps, pen*

My Name: The first word your grandchild writes will probably be his name. Write his name in large print at the top of a piece of paper. Tell him that this spells his or her name and then point to each letter as you say it. Encourage him to write a few of the letters below yours. Write his name on an index card and have it available for him to copy on his artwork.

WHAT YOU NEED: *paper, markers, index card*

New Twists

Record-a-Story: Long-distance grandparents can record their grandchild's favorite books on audiocassettes. At the end of each page, ring a bell to indicate that it's time to turn the page. Send the book along with the cassette. Grandma Sonja regularly sent her grandchildren stories she had recorded. Each time, Jenna would beam with delight, "It's Grammy reading to me!"

WHAT YOU NEED: *tape recorder, child's book, call bell*

Story Board: Dramatize familiar stories using a story board. Select a favorite story with lots of action and repetition, such as *The Gingerbread Man* or *The Three Bears*. Make cutout figures of the main characters. Perhaps you can photocopy these from the storybook or buy an inexpensive second copy of the book from which you cut out characters and props. Another alternative is to download images from websites. To find templates for traditional stories, google "preschool templates." Then, attach a piece of magnetic tape to the back of each cutout figure.

Use a magnetic board, cookie sheet, or your refrigerator as your story board. As you tell the story, add or remove pieces to illustrate the action. For example, make the Gingerbread Man run across the board as each of the other characters chases him. Then it is your grandchild's turn to use the board and characters to retell stories in his own words or to make up new stories.

WHAT YOU NEED: *magnetic board, cookie sheet, or refrigerator; magnetic tape, scissors, pictures of characters and props*

turns them face down again. The goal is to remember where the cards are and find the pairs. The winner is the player who finds the most pairs.

WHAT YOU NEED: *index cards, marker*

Letter Lotto: To give preschoolers practice in letter recognition, play Lotto using letters instead of pictures. The object of the game is to get matches for all the letters on your card. One player turns over the first card in the deck and asks, "Who has the . . . ?" The person with this letter then puts it on his matching letter. Continue to play until one person has matches for all his letters or until everyone fills his board.

Making a Letter Lotto game is easy. Use heavy construction paper to make three boards. Draw a grid with nine squares on each, and write a different letter in each square. (Since this leaves one board with only eight letters, fill in the last square with a question mark or exclamation point.) Then make a small card for each letter. Use this deck of cards to match and cover the letters on the boards, or make it even more quickly on the computer. To make it more colorful, draw each extra-large letter in a different color. Then duplicate the letters of each "board" and cut them out, storing them in a zip-lock bag.

WHAT YOU NEED: *heavy construction paper, scissors, marker; computer, paper*

File of Favorites: Write your grandchild's favorite words on 3 × 5-inch index cards—*Mom, love, ice cream, stop, train,* or even a few potty talk words. Keep these in a file box and add new ones upon request. As his collection grows, he will enjoy reading and writing these words. He can use them to write labels on his drawings or write notes to friends and family. With your assistance, he may be able to make sentences with his word collection.

WHAT YOU NEED: *index cards, markers, file box*

Playing Post Office: Add an element of pretend play to writing activities by providing props for creating and delivering mail. Set out paper, envelopes, stickers for stamps, and pencils and markers for writing and addressing letters. Your grandchild may write letters or words that he knows or simply use pretend writing, making letter-like markings or scribbled lines across the page. Props for delivering the mail could include a canvas bag, a large carton with a slot in the top for a drop box, and several boxes set around the house as delivery destinations.

WHAT YOU NEED: *paper, envelopes, stickers, pencils, markers, canvas bag, large carton, smaller boxes*

Five- to Eight-Year-Olds

Developmental Insights

Learning to read and write is the major emphasis in first grade and often in kindergarten as well. It is crucial that your grandchild becomes a competent reader during his early school years. If he falls behind, he may become too discouraged and embarrassed to persist later. You can support his efforts through informal, authentic literacy experiences. Continue to read together, introduce new books, and praise his efforts at mastering the reading and writing process.

For your grandchild's early reading efforts, introduce him to books designed especially for emergent readers. *Bob Books First* by Scholastic (*www. scholastic.com*), a set of 12 little books, teaches a few new sounds in each book and uses words that are phonically regular, adding humorous illustrations to keep the reader entertained. The *Wright Group Story Box* uses repetition, picture cues, minimal print, and interesting stories to make reading successful and fun. Introduce these books to him and soon he will be reading a bedtime story to you!

The next step on the literacy ladder is the many easy-to-read books designed especially for the early stages of reading. They have illustrations that provide content clues, simple vocabulary, slightly enlarged type, and simple plots. Stories with suspense and humor may help your grandchild stick with this difficult task. Most libraries and bookstores have sections with easy-to-read books. I recommend Arnold Lobel's *Frog and Toad* series and Dr. Seuss's beginning reader books (e.g., *The Cat in the Hat* and *Go, Dog, Go*). Although written with limited vocabulary and simple sentences, they are still entertaining stories with vivid illustrations. Have your grandchild show off his new skills by reading to you, but provide assistance as needed to move the story along. One strategy is to take turns reading pages.

Simple chapter books with a combination of pictures and text are the next big step in reading. Many children gravitate toward book series such as *Encyclopedia Brown*, *The Magic School Bus*, and *Arthur*. These books have the advantage of familiar names and characters, making them easier for the beginning reader to follow.

Don't let the fact that he is becoming an independent reader deter you from continuing those special reading sessions that promote intimacy and sharing. Since his comprehension and interests are far ahead of his reading competencies, you may want to read him informational books that introduce new concepts and vocabulary and longer chapter books, such as those in the *Harry Potter* series.

The development of writing skills typically goes hand-in-hand with learning to read. It can be a daunting task to combine the fine motor challenge of forming letters accurately along with the struggle to decode sounds. Praise your grandchild's efforts and leave the fine-tuning for later. Many schools encourage the use of phonetic, but unconventional, spellings in the early stage of writing. Too much stress on spelling may simply frustrate the beginning writer and get in the way of progress. The important thing is to support his efforts and find meaningful writing tasks to do together.

Old Faithfuls

Return to Sender: Long-distance grandparents can keep in touch with frequent two-way mail correspondence. Send your grandchild a letter via regular mail with a photo, drawing, joke, or riddle enclosed. An easy insert is a page from an activity book, such as a maze or page to color. Ask him to return the completed activity in the enclosed self-addressed envelope.

WHAT YOU NEED: *paper, envelopes, photo or page from activity book*

Easy E-Mail: For quicker turnaround time, keep in touch with your grandchild via e-mail. Write a brief message and attach a photo that has kid-appeal: you, dressed up in your clown costume or blowing out all those candles on your birthday cake. Add a question as a hook to encourage a reply. "What would you like for your birthday?" is sure to get a quick response. You will probably need to elicit the help of a parent to read and write the messages.

WHAT YOU NEED: *computer with Internet access, willing parent*

Same Sound: Reinforce phonics learning with this game that focuses on isolating initial sounds. Take turns sayings words that begin with the same sound, for example, *sun, sand, see,* and *sit.* Write them down, read them to your grandchild, and encourage him to read them too. See how many of the words you can put in a sentence, such as, "Silly Susan sat on the sunny, sandy seashore sipping soda."

WHAT YOU NEED: *paper and pencil*

Search the Signs: This is a great game to play in the car. First look for the letter *A* in signs, license plates, or bumper stickers. Then look for a *B* and continue doing this for each letter of the alphabet. It can be a joint effort or a race to see who finishes first.

WHAT YOU NEED: *car trip, signs*

New Twists

Leaps in Literacy: Keep a record of your grandchild's emerging reading and writing abilities. Include a list of his favorite books, samples of early writing, and the names of the first books he reads all by himself. Keeping these in a loose-leaf notebook makes it easy to add new pieces.

WHAT YOU NEED: *loose-leaf notebook, hole punch, pen*

Book-of-the-Month Club: Long-distance grandparents may like to have a grandparent–grandchild book club. Each month send your grandchild a book and set up a special time to talk with him by phone about it. Plan some open-ended discussion questions. You could read a paragraph and ask why this character felt or acted the way he or she did. You could ask him to read you his favorite page in the book and then discuss why he liked this part.

WHAT YOU NEED: *duplicate books, phone*

Cartoon Scramble: This game capitalizes on the appeal of brightly colored comic strips. First read a cartoon from the newspaper to your grandchild. Then cut it into individual frames. See if your grandchild can put the frames in the correct sequence and tell the story. Make it more challenging by using comics with six or eight frames.

WHAT YOU NEED: *comic strips, scissors*

What's New?: The comics aren't the only section of the newspaper of interest to your grandchild. Show him how to check the weather forecast or the listing of special community events for children. Point out pictures that might interest him and summarize the accompanying story. My grandson was fascinated with those that showed snowstorms, tornadoes, and floods.

WHAT YOU NEED: *newspaper*

Word Bingo: A fun way to drill basic sight words (such as *the, and, up,* and *in*) is to make a Bingo game that uses words instead of pictures. Include your grandchild's favorite words along with those basic, but boring sight words. Write out a list of 40–50 words and then cut out the words and put them in a bowl. For each playing card, make a 5 × 5 grid. Label the columns in the traditional way (B-I-N-G-O). Write one of the words from the list in each of the squares. Although each card may include words used on other cards, the words should be placed in a different pattern.

Here is a quick review for how to play Bingo. The caller draws a word from the bowl and reads it. Anyone who has this word on his or her playing card puts a marker to cover this place. The winner is the first person to complete a vertical, horizontal, or diagonal row.

WHAT YOU NEED: *heavy paper, pen, scissors, bowl, pennies or poker chips for markers*

Grand Books: Create a family history book with a separate chapter for each person. Write a story about a significant or interesting event in his or her life. Especially appealing are the adventures and misadventures of your grown-up children—the more action-packed and mischievous the better. "How Uncle Steve Won the Demolition Derby" or "The Car That Rolled Away" are favorites of my grandchildren. Use large print, limit the amount of text per page, and include photos or illustrations. For a finished look, add a cover and spiral binding.

WHAT YOU NEED: *construction paper, typing paper, marker, photos or illustrations, spiral binding*

Kid Books: Encourage your grandchild to create his own storybook. Have him tell you a story. It could be an account of a real event, his version of an old favorite, or an original story. Then have him dictate a sentence for you to write on each page. Your older grandchild may be able to write the sentences himself. He can illustrate the story on the top half of the page. When he has completed all the pages, add a title page on the front and staple them together.

To the query "What should my story be about?" you could suggest:

▪ Tell me about your best friend.
▪ What happened on your trip to see the snow?
▪ Make up a story about a beautiful princess (or Spiderman or a Tyrannosaurus Rex).
▪ "Once there was a little mouse who was very, very hungry . . ." (or some such one-sentence story starter)

WHAT YOU NEED: *typing paper, markers, construction paper, stapler*

Photo Journal: Provide your grandchild with photos of memorable events in his life: vacation trips, birthday celebrations, pets, friends, and favorite games. He can select his favorites and glue each on a separate page. Then he can write an explanatory sentence or two below each photo. Arrange in chronological order in a loose-leaf notebook.

WHAT YOU NEED: *photos, paper, glue, marker, loose-leaf notebook*

5

Let's Go

Exploring the Community

Busy with purchasing tickets for the zoo, I told my two young grand-children, "Wait right here." *Wait* not being in their vocabulary, they were nowhere to be seen when I turned around. Duly alarmed, I took off at a fast pace. The ticket taker reported seeing two small children zip by at a high rate of speed. When the path divided, my alarm turned to panic. Would I ever find them in the labyrinth of paths winding through the zoo, or, worse yet, find them splashing in the polar bear moat or climbing into the gorilla's cage? Fortunately, Jenna slowed down her more adventuresome brother enough that I finally found them "waiting" for me.

Why Try It?

In spite of such potential frustrations, these trips away from home are guaranteed to be among the most memorable times spent with your grandchild. When I ask grandparents what they like to do with their grandchildren, they often describe a favorite place that they take them. Both grandparents and grandchildren find trips exciting, and they provide many opportunities to get to know one another. The trip can be as simple as taking a one-year-old to see a neighbor's friendly dog or as extensive, and expensive, as a trip to Disneyland when she is 6.

Snapshot of Development

Whatever is just around the corner is a new and exciting experience for a toddler. In a few years, her interests will expand to include many places in the local community and, eventually, to outings that teach her about diverse cultures, religions, and places far from home. The length of time feasible for trips likewise expands: at first, brief, 30-minute outings, and later, those lasting several days.

Tips for Outings

Take only one grandchild. Often, I have found that one is fun, but two is too much. Taking one child at a time lets you select an outing that matches his or her age, personality, and interests. You can focus exclusively on one without having to settle a dispute about whether to see the lions or ride the train around the zoo. Having two little ones running in opposite directions can be disconcerting, to say the least. So take just one or take a second grandparent.

Let her do it. Young children soon get impatient with the observer role. They need hands-on experiences. Wherever you go, ask yourself how your grandchild can become actively involved. At the farm, she can climb on the tractor, pick an ear of corn, and feed the chickens. At the farmer's market, she can weigh the fruit, put it in a plastic bag, and hand the money to the cashier.

Plan ahead. An ounce of prevention is the best antidote for children's pound of impatience and inflexibility. Get as much advance information as possible before visiting a new place. Drive by an unfamiliar playground to check out its equipment or call the museum to make sure it is open and has convenient parking. Be prepared for the unexpected, such as delays in traffic, motion sickness, or a sudden downpour. Bring plenty of snacks, drinks, a change of clothing, and favorite toys and blankets. And don't forget the camera to document your outings. A cell phone with a camera is lightweight, convenient, and readily available.

Be road wise. Do give some forethought to the travel portion of your outing. If your grandchild quickly becomes restless when riding in the car, keep travel time to a minimum. I like to plan in-car activities, such as singing, telling stories, playing a game, or listening to children's songs. If the activities provide previews of the place to which you are going, so much the better. Visiting a farm? Sing "Old McDonald Had a Farm," or see how many different types of farm animals you can name. On the return trip, make up stories about what you saw. Doing things together is the best way to head off the bickering and teasing between grandchildren that is all too common on car trips.

List the options. Of course, nothing has a bigger impact on the success of your trip than selecting the right destination. Time and thought invested in making an informed choice is well worth the effort. A good first step is to list places to visit and events to attend in your community. Then add to your list as new possibilities occur to you. When I find myself wishing my grandchild was with me so that I could share an experience—seeing the underside of my car as the mechanic changes the oil or getting our puppy to "sit" at obedience school—that is my cue to add this place to my list. For special community events, check your local newspaper, online community calendars, or local parenting magazines. Libraries often have story times, puppet shows, and other events for children, and museums may have special family days or programs for young children. I also like to ask other grandparents and parents for their recommendations.

Make it match. With your list of potential trips in hand, the next step is to choose one that is a good fit for your grandchild, one that takes into account her developmental level as well as her special interests and personality. Ask yourself: Is it appropriate for her age? Does it mesh with her temperament and interests? Is my 2-year-old grandchild up to dealing with the full day of excitement, crowds, and long waits typical of a theme park visit? Is my very active 4-year-old going to sit quietly through a long movie without disturbing others? If not, put these trips on hold for now. Does your grandchild have any special fears? Since my grandniece Cassie had a fear of tunnels, her grandmother wisely let her watch the zoo train go through the tunnel but let her decide whether to ride the train. A good way to include your grandchild in the decision about where to go is to let her choose between two alternatives.

Pick your passions. Don't skip this step in the decision-making process. Consider what you like best and for which you have the time and energy. You want to have a good time, too. If you are an animal lover, you could visit the zoo, attend a pet show, or take a pony ride. Are you an exercise enthusiast? A bike ride, dip in the pool, or hike in the woods would be a good fit. If reading a good book is more your speed, consider instead a library story time, a children's theater production, or a visit to a bookstore.

Play It Safe: Be sure that you have the right child car seat and have it installed correctly, especially since the models change as your grandchild grows. Consumers Union, a nonprofit group that tests products, strongly recommends that you always use car seats for young children. It points out that all states require them for children under 4 years of age, and many also require booster seats for older children. It suggests that you keep the car seat in the rear-facing position as long as possible and, if there is only one child, that you put it in the center of the back seat, as this is the safest place in the car. You can learn more by subscribing to its articles on its website, *www.ConsumerReports.org.* These car seats can present a challenge, but don't let your grandchild be among the 80 percent that the U.S. Department of Transportation estimates are improperly restrained.

Activities

I have divided ideas for outings into *Old Faithfuls* and *New Twists*. **Old Faithfuls** are basic everyday activities that merit frequent repetitions. Since they require little advance preparation, they can be spur-of-the moment events. When you want to do something extra special, try an outing in the **New Twists** section. These add the excitement of novelty, but take more time and planning.

The First Year

Developmental Insights

In those first few months your grandchild is mostly tuned into her own physical needs and has only brief times of alert wakefulness. Her visual world is in best focus just 10 inches from her face, while the rest of the world is a blur of colors and shapes. Therefore, you and her parents are the primary benefactors of trips. For you, it can be a time alone with this new person in your life or an opportunity to show her off to friends; while for the exhausted, sleep-deprived parents, it can provide a quiet interlude.

As she develops an increasingly predictable pattern of sleeping, eating, alertness, and, yes, fussiness, you can anticipate the best times to take her out. But don't trust this predictability too far. Those few short blocks suddenly felt like miles when my 3-month-old grandson decided he had enough of being in the stroller and, scheduled or not, wanted to be fed immediately, if not sooner. It is well worth the few extra minutes it takes to pack an emergency kit of food, drink, pacifier, and diapers.

As vision and hearing acuity develop, your grandchild begins to appreciate more of the sights and sounds that she experiences on outings. Those things so familiar to you are new to her. Find opportunities that maximize all her senses. Let her hold a rock or leaf, smell a fragrant flower, listen to a barking dog, feel the bark of a tree, and watch an airplane zooming across the sky.

As she develops her motor skills, she may want to get out of the stroller and crawl nonstop and taste everything along the way. It is well worth the effort to find a grassy hill or sandy beach for her to explore. You will need to be alert in case she decides to put something in her mouth, but fortunately, she is still easy to distract when you offer a substitute. After a good crawl, she may welcome a relaxing stroller ride home.

The second half of the first year is also the peak time for stranger wariness (a fear of unfamiliar people) and separation anxiety (fear of being separated from her mother or father). Children vary considerably in how strongly they exhibit these fears, but if your grandchild does cry and cling to her parents, just keep in mind that these are signs of cognitive and social growth; she knows who is familiar and trusted and has formed strong emotional attachments. If you have not been around your grandchild recently, she may protest vehemently about going on that fun trip to the park without her mother. Much as you want time alone with her, allow her to warm up and feel comfortable with you before whisking her away.

Old Faithfuls

Out and About: Since most babies enjoy riding in the car, it often works well to take your grandchild along with you on short trips around town. I enjoyed taking ten-month-old Emerson with me when I ran errands. He liked all the new sights and sounds, as well as the relaxing car ride. Safely strapped in the child seat in the shopping cart, he was content to hold small items and appreciative of the obligating adults who so cheerfully retrieved them when he did his gravity tests. I liked all the "What a cute baby!" comments and someone to entertain me along the way.

WHAT YOU NEED: *car, infant car seat*

Walk and Talk: There is nothing like a walk in a stroller or baby carrier to sooth a fussy baby. The cool air, new sights and sounds, and, most of all, the gentle motion can distract her and lull her to sleep. I took many a stroll around the neighborhood with each infant grandchild. On your walks, you can support her emerging language. Talk about what you are doing and repeat the names of all those familiar objects that you are seeing. She will understand more than she can say and will probably add her own vocalizations to your monologue. Even young infants learn to take turns in vocal interactions, so it's fun to engage in a "conversation" as you stroll.

WHAT YOU NEED: *stroller or baby carrier*

Show-and-Tell Time: Grandparents love to share photos and stories about their grandchildren. Even better is showing off the real thing. During your grandchild's first 6 months, it is relatively easy to take her to the homes of family and friends. She will enjoy all the smiling faces and charm them with her own beguiling smile.

All that changes when she becomes mobile and wary of strangers. Instead of smiling, she may wail in protest when a stranger comes near. Suggest to friends that they let her warm up to them from a distance and let her be the one to initiate interactions. As if this is not enough trouble, now, instead of sleeping comfortably in her car seat, she wants to explore forbidden corners and prized antiques. It may help to bring your own supply of toys and to monitor her every move.

WHAT YOU NEED: *car, infant car seat, toys*

Swings and Things: Visiting a local playground provides a chance to be outside with new people and things to observe. Look for parks that have baby swings and soft surfaces for crawling. Be aware that she will have no qualms about tasting leaves, rocks, or dirt.

WHAT YOU NEED: *playground, stroller or car and infant car seat*

New Twists

Music and Movement: Take your grandchild to a series of music classes specifically designed for infants. These encourage grown-ups to actively participate in the songs and actions. Music Together and Kindermusik are examples of such national programs. Or attend a music/movement session at a fitness center for infants. National chains that offer such programs include Gymboree, My Gym, and The Little Gym. Check out what's available in your area by visiting websites. Some offer a free pass for the first visit. Look for special classes for infants under 6 months and for crawlers in which the accompanying adult participates along with the child. At a class for nonmobile children, my sister found that her granddaughter Alex was especially delighted with the musical games, the giant parachute, and the colorful bubbles to pop.

WHAT YOU NEED: *car and infant car seat, infant fitness center or infant music session*

Pet the Pet: Find someone with a friendly pet to visit, perhaps a dog, cat, bird, guinea pig, turtle, or rabbit. Encourage your grandchild to approach the pet slowly and only touch and handle as the owner directs. She may want to stay on your lap and observe from a distance, especially if the animal is large or active. Respect her need to take time before interacting with this strange new creature. Let her feel how soft the bunny or kitty is or what a hard shell the turtle has. Listen carefully to any sounds the animal makes and do your best imitation. Perhaps your grandchild will try to do the same.

WHAT YOU NEED: *friend with docile pet*

One- and Two-Year-Olds

Developmental Insights

You don't have to plan something elaborate to entertain your toddler grandchild. There is much that is new just around the corner. Short and sweet is my motto, an hour or less is best. Look for destinations close to home, ideally those within walking distance. You may discover, as did my sister Carolyn on a trip to the zoo, that what most interested her 1-year-old granddaughter was not the tigers and bears, but running across a grassy field to catch a butterfly. I like to keep in-car time short, especially when I am the sole grown-up, to minimize those quick exits from the freeway to retrieve a dropped pacifier or teddy bear that has fallen on the floor.

Allow your grandchild plenty of time to explore and repeat experiences. She may want to climb up and down the neighbor's steps over and over or drop a huge pile of pebbles into the storm sewer. My grandchild wanted to explore every driveway and sidewalk several times. Observing and talking are secondary to touching, manipulating, and using her whole body to explore what she is experiencing. Toddlers definitely do not like to be hurried, so allow extra time for everything. They are living in the moment, enjoying what they are doing right now. Perhaps there is a lesson here for us hurried, overly time-conscious adults.

Your 2-year-old grandchild becomes increasingly aware that she is a separate, autonomous person. Enter here the ubiquitous *no* and *mine*. No matter how fun the event, doing what she wants in her own way and at her own pace is going to win out over all else. Avoid getting into a power struggle. Instead, provide choices and be flexible. Although you have planned a trip to a garden to see the spring flowers, she may only be interested in running up and down the paths, always in the opposite direction from you. It may be best to join in her game and save smelling the roses for later. If the outing takes a direction you had not planned, enjoy the detour. Foster her growing sense of independence by letting her do those little tasks like putting money in the parking meter or unlocking the car door with the remote.

Plan outings around her regular schedule. When she is hungry, thirsty, or tired, she wants her needs met *right now*. If you delay too long, your fun outing could end in a major meltdown. Come provisioned with snacks, drinks, comfort items, and a stroller for when she suddenly cannot take another step.

Toddlers typically play alongside each other; they notice what other children are doing but focus more on the toys than each other. This parallel play marks the start of future peer relationships. Playing with a child a few years older often results in more positive and sustained interaction, since the older child can utilize his more advanced social skills to adapt to the toddler's abilities. Take into account this increasing interest in other children by planning a trip to a place where your grandchild can engage in parallel play with other children, such as at a playground or in a discovery museum.

Many of the destinations described in the section for preschoolers are fun for 2-year-olds as well, provided you make appropriate modifications. A toddler may be more fearful of new experiences, have a shorter attention span, and be less tolerant of changes in routines and delays. A visit to the train station could include watching trains arrive, walking across the tracks, and seeing how the crossing guards come down to stop traffic. You may want to omit taking a ride on the train until she is older, since this could mean some long, unexpected waits. I found this out the hard way. As we were waiting for the return ride on the commuter train, I noticed a puddle forming on the ground beneath 2-year-old Jenna, and unfortunately, I had not brought along a change of clothes.

Old Faithfuls

Push and Pull: If your grandchild is no longer content to tour the neighborhood in her stroller, suggest that she take a baby doll for a ride. When she gets tired of all the pushing, she can ride in the stroller on the return trip. Or exchange the stroller for a wagon—they're great for hauling treasures found on the way and providing a different, bumpy kind of ride.

WHAT YOU NEED: *baby doll, stroller or wagon*

Windy Weather Walk: Capitalize on windy weather when you take a walk. Take along something to flutter in the breeze—a silk scarf, crepe paper streamers, balloon, or pinwheel. Notice leaves scurrying across the road, flags flapping, and the sound of the wind in the tree branches. Talk about how the wind feels blowing on your face and hair. Run into the wind, then turn around and let the wind hurry you along. When you get back home, blow bubbles and watch as they drift away.

WHAT YOU NEED: *windy day and a scarf, crepe paper streamers, balloon, or pinwheel; bubble solution with wand*

Story Time for Tots: Attend a story time at your neighborhood library. Most have weekly story times designed specifically for toddlers. They intersperse books with songs, fingerplays, and musical games. Afterward, let your grandchild choose a book to take home. The first time I took Jenna to the library, she clutched her chosen book tightly, not wanting to relinquish it even long enough to check it out. Only after seeing another child use the self-checkout machine did she jump up on the stool and check it out "all by myself."

WHAT YOU NEED: *library story time, library card*

Splish-Splash: So what if it's raining outside? Just don boots and raincoats and put up the umbrella. You are sure to find some puddles perfect for splashing. Perhaps you can float leaves or twigs in the water as well. You may find a few earthworms or a downed tree branch to explore. Do take along some wipes and a towel in case your toddler gets too wet and muddy.

WHAT YOU NEED: *rainy day, rain gear, wipes, towel*

Picnic in the Park: Playgrounds specifically designed for toddlers have low, enclosed climbing structures and slides with wide steps rather than ladders. Take along a few shovels and pails for playing in the sandbox. Sprinklers or a wading pool during hot weather are sure to be favorites, as are the randomly squirting jets of water now common in many playgrounds. Pack some finger foods, cold drinks, and a blanket, so you can have a little picnic in the park before heading home.

WHAT YOU NEED: *toddler playground, shovels and pails, change of clothes, finger foods, drinks, blanket*

Wet and Wonderful: For a leisurely afternoon in the sun, find a community center with a kiddy pool. Take along a variety of water toys for filling, pouring, and floating and swim diapers. A full-sized pool requires that you assume a more active role. Encourage your grandchild to jump to you, bob up and down in the water, or take an exciting inner-tube ride.

WHAT YOU NEED: *wading or swimming pool, water toys, swim diaper*

Play It Safe: Swimming pools, lakes, and beaches can provide the best in summer fun, but each year that fun turns into tragedy for some families. Children slip through inner tubes or hit their head when diving. At the family gathering where "everyone is watching," sometimes, in fact, no one is watching a specific child. Children of all ages, especially the young and nonswimmers, need constant, personal supervision around water.

New Twists

Play Date: If you have friends with young grandchildren, you could plan brief visits to their homes. Although the most frequent interactions may be disputes over toys, toddlers also watch and imitate each other. This is the first step toward learning how to play with peers. It helps to have two balls, two trucks, or two dolls, so that both can play simultaneously with these toys.

WHAT YOU NEED: *friend with young grandchild, duplicates of toys*

To the Beach: If you are fortunate enough to live near the ocean or a lake with a sandy shore, your grandchild can enjoy many hours of sensory play there. Take a supply of pails and shovels for filling and dumping sand, water, or shells over and over again. Of course, wading in the water and playing tag with the waves may be the biggest thrill of all. Since she is especially vulnerable to sunburn, do take all necessary precautions.

WHAT YOU NEED: *sandy beach, pails, shovels, sunscreen*

Does It Neigh, Moo, or Quack?: Although toddlers see many pictures of farm animals, it may take a special effort for them to experience real ones up close. If you know someone with a gentle horse or pony, ask them to supervise a visit to the stables, where your grandchild can feel its mane, strokes its nose, and feed it an apple. Petting zoos provide opportunities for children to pet and feed sheep, cows, goats, and ducks. My grandchildren enjoyed visiting a large pond, where they fed the ducks bread crumbs and delighted in making them scatter as they ran into their midst.

WHAT YOU NEED: *gentle horse or pony, a petting zoo or a duck pond; appropriate food for the animals*

Play It Safe: Some diseases can be transmitted from animals to humans. As a safety precaution, have your grandchildren wash their hands or use disinfectant wipes after touching farm animals.

Three- and Four-Year-Olds

Developmental Insights

Your preschool grandchild is ready for longer, more diverse trips, so open the door and help her explore the community. On your way to the car wash, supermarket, or hardware store? Take your grandchild along. She is sure to find something new and interesting to learn. The trick is to allow extra time and look at the world from her point of view.

How you make use of the places you visit is every bit as important as where you go. Be creative about ways to include as many hands-on activities as possible. Think of the trip as going somewhere to do a specific activity—to buy a hammer and nails, pick strawberries, or paddle a boat. You may see many interesting things along the way, but center the event on a specific activity.

Before leaving home, talk about what you will do and see. In addition to increasing her excitement, it can help you figure out her current level of knowledge and how best to build on it. Before visiting an apple orchard, ask her where the apples come from and how they get from the tree to the store. On the way to the circus, talk about clowns, trapeze artists, and trained animals. And do talk about your behavioral expectations, such as staying close to you and not running or yelling.

During your trips, talk about what you are seeing and doing. Include questions that encourage careful observation and problem solving: "What do you think that bulldozer is trying to do?" "Why are the animals in cages?" "How did the watermelons get here?" "What would happen if someone filled up the creek with big rocks?"

Follow up your trips with activities that reinforce and expand on what was experienced during the outing. A book, video, or DVD on a related topic encourages reminiscing and adds new knowledge. You might browse through *Eating the Alphabet* to find pictures of fruits and vegetables that you saw at the supermarket. Or watch a DVD that shows a lion stalking a deer or caring for her cubs, instead of, like the one at the zoo, only sleeping. After seeing the circus, pretend to be clowns or tight-rope walkers. If you take photos on your trips, you can share them with your grandchild on your next visit; this should spark an animated conversation about what you did together.

Since the possibilities for activities increase so greatly for preschoolers, consider the following examples merely as representative of the range of options. They may stimulate your thinking about others readily available to you and of special interest to your grandchild.

Old Faithfuls

Fun Focus: Sometimes you can enliven a walk around the neighborhood with a special focus. In the fall collect multicolored leaves or pine cones to use in a collage; in the spring search for flowers and learn their names. Another time, look for words and numbers on mailboxes and road signs. Since one of the first words that Jake learned to read was "no," it was fun to find and read the "No Parking" and "No Entry" signs. Or look for interesting trees and pick your favorites.

WHAT YOU NEED: *a safe, walkable neighborhood*

Playground Repertoire: Playgrounds continue to be a top option, great for impromptu outings with minimal planning and easy supervision. For variety, try playgrounds new to you and your grandchild. Each may have a special attraction: a water sprinkler, a long slide built into the hillside, or a fountain in the sand box. For new ideas, check the playgrounds shown on a local map. For more complete information, visit a community website. These often have listings of neighborhood parks as well as locator maps, available facilities, and photos. I like to drive by any new park to see if it looks like a place my grandchildren would enjoy.

After developing a playground repertoire, you can let your grandchild choose the one for that day. Will it be "the crayon park," or "the one with the super slide"? Since playgrounds lend themselves to social play, ask a friend with a grandchild to join you. Even when we go by ourselves, my grandchildren typically manage to make a friend or two at the park. It helps when we bring along a few toy trucks and pails that we are willing to share.

WHAT YOU NEED: *knowledge of local playgrounds, sand or water toys*

Pool Play: Your preschooler may want to upgrade from a kiddy pool to the challenge of a regular swimming pool. Perhaps you or your grandchild's parents belong to a recreational center with a pool, or there may be a community pool nearby.

To get your grandchild to put her face in the water—a first step toward becoming a swimmer—blow bubbles, retrieve objects from the bottom of the pool, and play ring-around-the-rosy, ending by going under water. To add variety to the water play, bring along beach balls, kick boards, toys that float, or weighted rings. An inflatable shark sparked the imagination of my grandchildren, with a surprise reversal when they pretended to rescue the shark from drowning.

WHAT YOU NEED: *swimming pool, beach ball, kick boards, floating toys, or weighted rings*

Surf and Sand: A trip to a lake or seashore has the additional appeal of sand, waves, and waterfowl. This does require close supervision; I suggest one adult for each child. Build castles in the sand and decorate them with shells and rocks, splash in the shallow water, and take a walk along the shore to explore rock formations, vegetation, and wild life. Dig a deep hole in the sand big enough to crawl inside.

WHAT YOU NEED: *sandy beach, shovels, pails*

To Market, To Market: To make trips to the supermarket interesting and educational, select a focus on each visit. On one trip, check out the fruits and vegetables. On another, buy the ingredients for a favorite recipe that you will prepare together. Take your grandchild to order a special birthday cake and investigate all the other bakery items as well. Maybe you'll be lucky enough to see someone decorating a cake.

WHAT YOU NEED: *supermarket*

Books and More: I like to take my grandchildren to the library each week to pick out new books. In addition to regular story times, most community libraries offer special programs for children, such as magic, puppet, or animal shows.

WHAT YOU NEED: *library, library card, schedule of events*

Dining Out: When you take your grandchild out to eat, be sure to go to a child-friendly restaurant. The easiest option is one with fast food service and kid meals. Those with climbing structures or other activities for young children give your grandchild safe and appropriate opportunities for play while you linger over your coffee.

When your grandchild is ready, take her to other restaurants that have relatively quick service and offer informal settings. Some have special menus for children, which include smaller portions and children's favorites, like macaroni-and-cheese or hot dogs. You may want to take along some of your grandchild's favorite foods, such as fruit, yogurt, or granola bars, just in case the wait is too long or the selection not to her liking. Come armed with a few books, crayons, and table activities to pull out as needed. I recommend going early and finding a corner booth.

WHAT YOU NEED: *child-friendly restaurant, a few table activities and snacks*

Clean That Car: Next time you head for the car wash, take along your grandchild. She will enjoy all the suds, brushes, and action as your car goes through the automatic car wash. Or get into the action at a do-it-yourself one. It is worth the few extra quarters, wet clothes, and not perfectly clean car. You may want to take along a change of clothes or a raincoat for your grandchild. When I let my grandson put in the quarters and spray, soap, and rinse the car, he was impressed with "how fast the water comes out."

WHAT YOU NEED: *car, car wash, quarters, extra clothes or raincoat*

Tasty Tidbits or Squeaky Toy: Take your grandchild to a pet store to pick out a toy for a pet. While there, explore all the interesting items for cats, dogs, birds, and other pets. Some have pets for sale that are fun to observe, but I hope you won't be tempted to take one home!

WHAT YOU NEED: *pet store*

New Twists

All Aboard: If your grandchild loves playing with trains, take her on a train ride, whether it be a kiddy train at the zoo or a shuttle train at the airport. Most exciting of all is a train with open cars and a steam engine, such as the Thomas the Tank Engine excursions that are available at multiple venues. If you live near a commuter train, ride it for several stops, then get off and ride another train back to your original station. Take time to watch the crossing guards as they go up and down, inspecting the tracks up close and then climbing up to the top level of the train. After taking my grandson on such a trip, I heard him perform a surprisingly accurate vocal rendition of crossing guards coming down as he played with his train set.

WHAT YOU NEED: *train*

Up, Up, and Away: Consider visiting a small, private airport. Observe the planes take off and land. Then get up close to the planes and inspect their wings, tail, and propellers. Maybe someone will let your grandchild climb inside, see all the buttons and dials, and put on a headset. My grandchildren also enjoyed visiting a major airport. The fascination was not so much the planes as the shuttle train, the moving walkways, escalators, baggage screening machines, and long hallways for running and getting lost.

WHAT YOU NEED: *airport*

Bears, Bats, or Baboons: A trip to a large city zoo is sure to provide new and fascinating experiences. Children are curious to see the wild animals they are learning about in books. The penguins swimming by or the monkeys swinging on the trapeze are more likely to keep their interest than the tiger that just lies there. But even the bears and big cats wake up when it is feeding time. Seek out hands-on options; feed the birds, pet the farm animals, and play with the insect puppets in the Bug House. With my grandchildren, I found it worked best to strike a balance between zoo animals and the merry-go-round. Take a stroller for carrying supplies and a tired child at the end of the day.

But don't limit your wild animal experiences to full-scale zoos. Look for venues that have some small, often native, animals. My grandchildren especially like to watch otters darting through the water at the Coyote Point Regional Park near San Francisco or the giant bats hanging quietly upside down at the Palo Alto Children's Museum.

WHAT YOU NEED: *zoo*

Underwater World: Experience the special magic of the underwater world at an aquarium, with its diverse fish, eels, jellyfish, and sea lions. Perhaps best of all, it is a world in constant motion. Be sure to plan your visit to take in special animal shows of seals and dolphins, and look for exhibits where a child can touch a starfish, ray, or mollusk.

WHAT YOU NEED: *aquarium*

Ships Ahoy: Take a ride on a paddleboat, rowboat, or sailboat. Model wearing a life jacket and be sure your grandchild has one on and securely fastened. Maybe your grandchild can help to steer or paddle the boat. While in the harbor, stroll along the pier and point out special features of different kinds of boats. Perhaps you can see the underside of a boat before it is launched and observe the process of getting it from the trailer to the water. Or there may be fishing boats and a fish market that you can investigate.

WHAT YOU NEED: *boat, life jackets, harbor*

Plants Galore: A visit to a nursery is especially fun in the spring when an abundance of flowers and plants are on sale. Select a few plants to bring home and start your own garden. While there, see how many different types of plants you can find. What about a cactus, a lemon tree, or a rose bush?

WHAT YOU NEED: *nursery*

Pet a Pig/Pick a Pumpkin: A visit to a small family farm with both crops and animals is the ideal choice for learning about a farm. Your grandchild can climb up on the tractor, pick apples or tomatoes, walk among the corn stalks, climb up in the barn loft, collect eggs from the chicken nests, or do any of those activities so often shown in children's storybooks.

If a traditional family farm isn't an option, find a farm or orchard that allows active participation and up-close exploration. Even though your grandchild may only pick a quart of strawberries, the experience of doing it herself will make these berries the most delicious ever. Or visit a pumpkin patch that has activities and displays specifically for young children. Your grandchild can pick out a pumpkin or two to take home for making jack-o-lanterns and perhaps take a bumpy wagon ride through the fields. If you visit a dairy farm, you can see where the cows live and what they eat, how they are milked with complicated machines, and the large holding tanks for the milk.

WHAT YOU NEED: *kid-friendly farm*

Fresh and Friendly: A farmer's market with its small individual stalls is a good place to browse with your grandchild. Vendors will usually have an abundance of fresh produce, flowers, and homemade goods. To get your grandchild actively involved, suggest she pick out and weigh several items and then pay the cashier for her selections. For example, she could choose a tomato, cucumber, and lettuce for a salad that you prepare together when you get home.

WHAT YOU NEED: *farmer's market*

Hard Hat Zone: Is your grandchild fascinated by powerful construction equipment? There is usually some roadwork or other construction project going on not too far from home. From a safe distance, watch the backhoes, bulldozers, and steamrollers as they dig holes or flatten surfaces. Then return after work to see the machines up close. On a repeat visit, note the changes and speculate about what will come next. If a new house is being built nearby, it's a great opportunity to observe each step in the construction process. Watch the cement trucks pour the foundation, the carpenters put up the framing, the plumbers install pipes and drains, the electricians do the wiring, and the roofers attach the shingles. You might want to read a book about building before or after a visit. My sister Laura found that her 4-year-old granddaughter was just as fascinated by Richard Scarry's *What Do People Do All Day?* as her father was at the same age.

WHAT YOU NEED: *construction site, book on construction equipment*

Pulleys, Bubbles, and Waterspouts: Most large cities have discovery museums that emphasize hands-on science activities. Some include art and pretend play as well. For instance, the award-winning San Jose Discovery Museum lets children blow giant bubbles, lift bowling balls with pulleys, drive an ambulance with the siren blaring, and roll tennis balls through mazes. My grandchildren's favorite activity is the Water Works, with its combination of balls, wheels, vacuum tubes, whirlpools, and spouts. Grandma Laura found that her granddaughter especially liked the imaginative play at the Magic House in St. Louis. In the miniature supermarket, Cassie became first a shopper filling her cart with milk and bananas and then a cashier ringing up the sales. On the construction site, she put on her hardhat and lifted the foam bricks with a pulley.

WHAT YOU NEED: *discovery museum*

Five- to Eight-Year-Olds

Developmental Insights

As your grandchild matures, you can take more involved outings. She will find it easier to tolerate delays and comply with adult expectations, such as sitting quietly during a show. An all-day trip becomes more feasible. You may be the one that is irritable and fussy before the day is over, while she is still going strong. She may even be ready for an overnight or weekend trip with you.

Take into account her developmental advances as you plan your outings. She is now able to understand more abstract concepts and knows a great deal about the world. Moreover, she can concentrate on one thing for an extended period of time and learn through observation without always needing physical involvement. As a result, you can spend more time looking at and talking about what you are seeing, but balance this with opportunities for active participation.

She is now ready to learn about people and places beyond her own family and immediate community. You can expand her knowledge of the wider world and her appreciation of diverse cultures through positive firsthand experiences with different religious and cultural groups. Teach her to read maps. Show her how to use the map of a zoo or theme park. Print out a map from MapQuest and show her your route to local venues. Soon she will be telling you where you made a wrong turn!

Your grandchild may be developing special skills and interests through music lessons, sports teams, or gymnastics or dance classes. Plan outings that capitalize on these, such as attending a concert or professional sports event or exploring a specialty store together.

Jazz up your previous outings through more complex exploration and involvement. Instead of a trip to the neighborhood pool, go to a water park. Your boat trip could include some fishing or instruction in how to sail. When you go to the library, take a tour through the stacks, note how books are organized, and use the computer to search for a specific book. On a trip to the zoo, you can focus on one group of animals, such as bears or reptiles, and learn about their special characteristics.

Old Faithfuls

The Big Screen: Your grandchild will doubtless know the movie that "everyone is seeing" and be thrilled if you take her. Even though it's a children's film, it may have content that is too scary or violent for your grandchild, so talk to someone who has seen it or read a review before deciding to go. You can get information on current movies at *www.parentpreviews.com*. Minimize the temptation of all that junk food by bringing along a few healthy snacks.

WHAT YOU NEED: *movie theater, review of film, healthy snacks*

Hiking/Biking: Your grandchild is doubtless full of energy, so join her in some vigorous aerobic fun. If you like to hike, explore nature trails where you can experience different habitats—wetlands, woods, or meadows. Walk across a high bridge over a river or explore a cave. Hike up to a mountain overlook or waterfall. Stroll beside a river, lake, or stream. A picnic lunch at a scenic spot can be a relaxing break along the way.

Or take a challenging bike ride up a mountain or down a meandering country road. Carrying on a family tradition of intergenerational cycling, Jake and his grandpa often take bike rides together. Recently when Jake rode on the tandem behind his father, he whooped with pleasure as he stood up to get maximal power and left his grandpa in the dust.

WHAT YOU NEED: *trail for hiking or biking, bikes, picnic lunch*

A Table for Two: Take your grandchild out for a meal at a special restaurant. If she is adventuresome enough to sample new foods, try an ethnic restaurant, such as Chinese, Mexican, or Greek. The decor may prompt discussion of a particular culture. Although she is better at waiting than she was a few years ago, you still may want to bring along a deck of cards or paper-and-pencil games to play while you wait.

WHAT YOU NEED: *restaurant, deck of cards or paper-and-pencil games*

Take Me Out to the Ball Game: Share your enthusiasm for your favorite spectator sport with your grandchild. I recommend that you first take her to a local and inexpensive game, perhaps at a high school, where you can sit close to the field and won't mind leaving early if she gets restless. As her interest grows, a professional game may be in order.

WHAT YOU NEED: *tickets to ball game*

Explore the Store: Take your grandchild on a shopping trip to buy a particular item in a specialty store, such as one selling camping equipment or electronics. Take a little extra time to investigate the wide range of equipment while you are there. Look inside tents that are set up; try to identify the purpose for all the electronic equipment. When you go to a hardware store to buy nails, wood, and sandpaper for your grandchild's own construction project, look at all the tools and try to guess their functions. Since your grandchild is beginning to understand the value of money, use this opportunity to provide a real-life illustration of how much items cost and how to make a purchase.

WHAT YOU NEED: *specialty store and money for purchases*

A Special Night: Spending the night alone at a grandparent's home is a special treat. Do some careful planning the first time, making sure you have all those familiar blankets, toothbrushes, and toys for her bedtime rituals. Following her regular bedtime routine will make it go more smoothly. It helps to plan some special things to do together, such as watching a new DVD, reading a book, or playing a card game. Granddad Tom always has whatever grandchild is sleeping over help him fix waffles for breakfast.

WHAT YOU NEED: *favorite blanket and stuffed animals, new DVD, book, or game, pajamas and toothbrush*

New Twists

Dinosaurs and Dioramas: Many natural history and science museums have interactive exhibits that stimulate learning. Abstract science concepts make more sense when you can manipulate equipment and see the results. Your grandchild can push buttons on many display cases or computer screens. Perhaps she can make robots stack cubes or go on a virtual roller-coaster ride. She may be able to walk through a replica of a human heart, experiment with pendulums, see a real dinosaur skeleton, or view dioramas of early indigenous peoples.

WHAT YOU NEED: *science or natural history museum*

Space Exploration: If your grandchild is fascinated with space travel, plan a trip that capitalizes on this interest. Take her to a planetarium for an exciting and educational viewing of the night sky or visit an observatory to look through a telescope at the moon and planets. Also, check to see whether your science museum has a display on spaceships or the solar system.

WHAT YOU NEED: *planetarium, observatory, or science museum*

Strike This Pose: The key to a successful visit to an art museum is to get your grandchild actively engaged. It is better to discuss a few pieces in depth than to look superficially at a great many. Ask open-ended questions: "What is happening here?" "How does it make you feel?" "What do you find most engaging or puzzling?" You could focus on pieces with themes of special interest to your grandchild, such as animals, children, or boats. See if you can find ways to incorporate some doing along with the viewing. "Can you assume the pose of the statue?" "Can you draw a clown like the one in the painting?" Let your grandchild buy postcards of pieces that she likes. Follow up your visit with an art activity that relates to what you just saw—some modeling clay to create your own sculptures or watercolors to paint a vase of flowers like the one by a famous painter.

WHAT YOU NEED: *art museum; pencil and paper, modeling clay, or watercolors*

Chinese Dragons and Mexican Piñatas: To show your grandchild the richness that other cultures bring to our country, attend festivals put on by different ethnic groups. Events associated with special holidays, such as the Chinese New Year, Cinco de Mayo, and St. Patrick's Day, are great occasions to participate in the joyful celebration of another culture. These typically provide opportunities to try out new food, hear traditional music, and view special performances, all in a lively setting with activities that encourage children to participate. Often there is a special section with activities planned for children.

WHAT YOU NEED: *ethnic festival*

Sacred Places: Visit a church, synagogue, or mosque to learn about and appreciate other religions. If you have a friend who attends one, ask him or her to serve as your guide. Your friend's knowledge and appreciation of a particular religion will make it especially meaningful. He can point out the significance of the paintings, statues, altars, and books. Pay special attention to the architectural features, like the domed ceiling or raised altar.

WHAT YOU NEED: *church, synagogue, or mosque*

Off Broadway: Live musical or theatrical performances provide an exhilarating mix of music, costumes, scenery, and lighting effects. That opening curtain may open up new possibilities for your grandchild. Seeing real people acting, dancing, singing, or playing instruments may inspire her to become a performer.

Check your local paper for children's music and theater performances. Your grandchild may be ready for some that are not just for kids, such as *The Nutcracker* around Christmas time. If professional shows are not available, community and school productions can be every bit as exciting to your grandchild, especially if she knows one of the performers.

Because Jenna was so excited about her ballet lessons, I took her to a performance of *The Sleeping Beauty*. We read the story many times before going. During the performance, I was surprised how many of her comments included observations of the music, scenery, and dancing. Afterward, as she sashayed to the car, she declared that someday she would play the part of the good fairy.

WHAT YOU NEED: *tickets to live performance*

Camping Adventure: Introduce your grandchild to camping by setting up a tent in the backyard and spending the night there. Flashlights, sleeping bags, and bedtime stories in the dark can be a real adventure. If it's not working, you can always retreat to the house. The next step is to find a campground near by where you can swim, hike, or paddle a boat. Take along balls, bikes, or Frisbees to use in the campgrounds. Your grandchild can help with such camping chores as getting water, collecting firewood, and setting up the tent. Try some easy campfire cooking, such as roasting hot dogs or marshmallows.

WHAT YOU NEED: *tent, sleeping bags; balls, bikes, or Frisbees; roasting forks, hot dogs or marshmallows*

6

Let's Explore

Discovering with Sand and Silly Stuff

J enna giggled with delight as the ball of dough oozed between her fingers, dripping slowly to the ground. She ran her fingers through the silky texture and squeezed it in her hands. Wide-eyed with surprise when it changed from a solid to a liquid, then back again, she became an observant little scientist

Let's Grandparent: Activity Guide for Young Grandchildren, pages 93–107

experimenting with this odd substance. What was this marvelous substance that so held the attention of a 2-year-old for the better part of an hour? Just cornstarch and water mixed together on a tray. I hope Jenna's rapture will entice you to try similar exploratory materials with your grandchild.

Why Try It?

Your grandchild can have many hours of fun with water, sand, and other materials that invite open-ended exploration. Most are inexpensive and readily available. These materials, with an emphasis on soothing touch, provide relaxing, unstructured play. They're great for releasing tensions, especially important for that more intense grandchild.

All this carefree messing around strengthens your grandchild's motor development and eye–hand coordination. Less evident, but perhaps even more important, it also promotes cognitive development by strengthening sensory integration, observational skills, concept development, and analytical thinking.

Snapshot of Development

Through sensory-motor experiences, a baby learns to integrate perceptions from seeing, hearing, and touching into a comprehensive view of his world. Soon he begins experimenting with materials and repeating actions over and over to confirm his findings. As he gets older, he can more consciously experiment with variations and verbalize what he is discovering.

Most exploratory experiences do not require precise fine motor skills. This makes them especially well suited for young children, whose finger and hand muscles take many years to develop fully.

Tips for Exploratory Activities

Maximize amounts. To make the most of exploratory experiences, don't skimp on the materials. Fortunately, most are readily available and inexpensive. Water is there at the turn of the tap, and sand and dirt are just a few steps away in the backyard. Other materials, such as flour, cornstarch, baking soda, food coloring, and dish detergent, are standard items in most kitchens.

Supersize supervision and preparation. Even though materials may be close at hand, do these exploratory experiences only when you can prepare carefully and give constant supervision. The best solution to the dilemma of allowing your grandchild to explore freely without creating a gigantic mess is to do these messy projects outside where Mother Nature, not grand-mother, can do the cleanup. When doing them inside, rely on many layers of newspaper on the table for soaking up spills. Cleaning up spills with soapy sponges and absorbent bath towels can be part of the fun. For many of these experiences I use a large, shallow plastic container, the bigger the better, especially if more than one child is playing. Even better is a sensory table, a large tub on legs with a drain in the bottom.

Set reasonable limits. Although you want your grandchild to feel free to explore the materials in many ways, be realistic about how much messiness you can tolerate. It helps to set clear rules before beginning. And, yes, be ready quickly to terminate the activity if it gets out of hand.

Talk it up. Talk to your grandchild as he explores materials. Describe what he is doing and seeing. Provide new vocabulary and ask questions that call his attention to what is happening. Suggest other things to try. It is of-ten better simply to play with the materials yourself and model possibilities rather than give too many directions about what to do.

Activities

Exploratory experiences include *Old Faithfuls* and *New Twists*. **Old Faithfuls** are basic everyday experiences that merit frequent repetitions. These are quick and easy to set up with readily available materials. When you want to experiment with something new, try one in the **New Twists** section. These typically take a bit more time, equipment, and planning.

The First Year

Developmental Insights

Exploring by touch is a major way your grandchild learns about his world. At birth he can grasp your finger or a rattle. Soon he reaches out to touch and explore objects. He learns eye–hand coordination as he reaches for the toy you dangle in front of him. But his exploration isn't going to stop with touching. Most objects end up in his mouth, so restrict objects to those that are safe if ingested and that have no small detachable parts that pose a choking hazard.

Sensory experiences encourage him to integrate perceptions from all the senses. As he splashes water, he hears the sound it makes and sees the ripples and spray. When he squishes the banana and licks his fingers, smell-ing, tasting, and touching all come into play.

During the first year you can nest many sensory experiences within such caregiving routines as feeding and bathing. Encourage your grandchild to squeeze the soapy sponge or crumble the cracker. For play time, select toys and materials that provide a variety of sensory experiences. Touch-and-feel books are a good choice for early book experiences. That all-time favorite, a cuddly teddy bear, provides a clear contrast to the hard rattle, while a cold ice cube feels and behaves so differently from warm water.

Old Faithfuls

Icy Cold: An easy trick for distracting a fussy baby is to put an ice cube on the play table or highchair tray. He will push it around the tray, struggle to pick it up for a lick, and be surprised by the cold, slippery sensation.

WHAT YOU NEED: *ice cubes, play table or highchair*

Splash and Splatter: On a hot summer day, a grassy, shaded spot is great for setting up a kiddy pool filled with warm water. Add a pail to fill and dump, a sponge to squeeze, a duck to float, and your grandchild. But never leave him alone in the water even for a minute. Unattended children have drowned in kiddy pools.

WHAT YOU NEED: *kiddy pool, warm water, pail, sponge, toy duck*

Sandy Sensations: By the time your grandchild is big enough to sit alone, he will enjoy playing in a sandbox. Initially he may just pat, stroke, and dig in the sand with his hands. As he gets older, you can extend the possibilities by adding sand toys—spoons, scoops, pails, funnels, and sieves. If you wet down a patch of sand, he can feel the contrast in texture and temperature.

WHAT YOU NEED: *sandbox, sand toys*

New Twists

Jiggle That Jello: Gelatin blocks are loaded with sensory potential. They are brightly colored, have a yummy taste, and, best of all, have a cool, slippery texture. To make blocks, add 1 cup boiling water to a small package of flavored gelatin. Do not add the usual cold water. Pour into an 8-inch square pan. Chill for several hours until firmly set. Dip the bottom of the pan in warm water just long enough to melt it slightly. Cut into blocks and put on the highchair tray for your grandchild to jiggle, poke, pick up, and taste.

WHAT YOU NEED: *box of flavored gelatin, water, 8-inch square pan, knife*

Squish-Squash: If playing with food is not too repugnant to you, try a glob of pudding, yogurt, or whipping cream on your grandchild's highchair tray.

You may want to capture on video his delightful exploration, beginning with a tentative poke, progressing to whole-hand swirls, and ending up a delicious mess.

WHAT YOU NEED: *highchair; pudding, yogurt, or whipping cream*

Shake-a-Sound: Make shakers from plastic pill bottles with childproof lids. Put a different item in each (rice, dried beans, marbles, pebbles, or a few pennies). Your grandchild can easily grasp and shake them to hear the contrasting sounds. Since Emerson always headed straight to one particular kitchen drawer, I stored these shakers on the front row.

WHAT YOU NEED: *plastic pill bottles; rice, beans, marbles, pebbles, or pennies*

One- and Two-Year-Olds

Developmental Insights

It is through creative experimentation that your toddler grandchild discovers how the world works. He needs to repeat his actions many times and in various ways in order to make basic concepts his own. The best way to support this cognitive growth is through open-ended, hands-on experiences. Actions do *teach* better than words.

Freely exploring is a good fit for your toddler's fine motor and emotional needs. He can use his whole hand and arm without the need for precise hand and finger manipulation. The "I want to do it myself" 2-year-old can do most of these activities with only a little help. You may be surprised to discover that his typically short attention span grows much longer when exploring new materials.

Old Faithfuls

Wonderful Water: Children can never get enough of water play. On a hot summer day set up a sprinkler in the yard and let your toddler run in and out of the spray. When it is too cold or rainy to play outside, set up a large plastic container on a low table and cover the table and floor with towels and your grandchild with a waterproof smock. Then supervise diligently to avoid flooding the floor with a whole container of water.

Here are ways to add variety:

- Put a few drops of food coloring in the water.
- Add cups, funnels, sieves, plastic squeeze bottles or sponges.
- Make bubbles by adding dish detergent to warm water.

- Float ice cubes on the water and provide a spoon for stirring and scooping.

WHAT YOU NEED: *sprinkler; large plastic container, low table, towels, child's waterproof smock; food coloring, dish detergent, cups, funnels, sieves, plastic squeeze bottles, or sponges*

Dig and Dump: Your 1-year-old grandchild mostly likes to scoop, pour, and dig in the sand. Just provide a shovel and pail and companionship. By age 2, he may be ready for pretend play. Model driving a truck down a super-highway or adding sticks as candles to a sand cake. Make it very clear you are only pretending to eat the cake or your grandchild may end up with a mouthful of sand! A few props can inspire new pretend play: bulldozers and cranes, cardboard tubes for tunnels, small plastic animals, or even pebbles and twigs. Wetting down the sand adds a whole new dimension to the play. Add water and stir until the sand holds its shape. Show your grandchild how to pack the wet sand into a container. When he turns it upside down, he will delight in finding that it all comes out in one piece. Decorate with rocks and twigs.

WHAT YOU NEED: *sandbox, shovel, pail; props such as a dump truck, a bulldozer, cardboard tubes, plastic animals, pebbles, or twigs*

Bowl of Bubbles: Put a generous amount of dish detergent in a large mixing bowl with several cups of warm water. Have your grandchild whip up a foaming bowl of bubbles with an eggbeater or wire whisk. Use plastic straws to blow bubbles of different sizes. First practice blowing out, not sucking in, so he doesn't end up with a mouthful of soapy water.

WHAT YOU NEED: *dish detergent, large mixing bowl, water, eggbeater or wire whisk, plastic straws*

Rice Is Nice: Water or sand too messy? Try uncooked rice, beans, or pasta in a large plastic container. Add funnels, cups, and spoons for scooping and pouring. Provide several strainers and sieves with different-sized holes. Let your grandchild sift and separate materials by size. Or add play dishes to encourage pretend play.

WHAT YOU NEED: *plastic container, uncooked rice, beans, or paste; funnels, cups, spoons, strainer, sieve, play dishes*

Beautiful Bubbles: Ready-made bubble solutions are a quick and easy way to provide bubble-blowing experiences. Your grandchild will watch with wide-eyed fascination as rainbow-colored bubbles drift gently down and suddenly pop. The bubble solution works best outside on a calm, cool day.

Most toddlers have trouble blowing bubbles. Blowing not too little, not too much, but just right can be frustrating. You can demonstrate how to get just the right amount of air by saying "whoosh" close to the loop of the wand. Your grandchild may be more successful by gently waving the wand or be satisfied with just watching and chasing the ones you blow.

WHAT YOU NEED: *ready-made bubble solution with wand*

New Twists

Cornstarch Concoction: Here is the recipe that so delighted Jenna: Mix one part cold water to two parts cornstarch on a large tray. Observe how it thickens into a solid and then drips from your hands like a liquid. Even grandparents may find the contrasting textures and properties fascinating. Yes, it's messy, but it does have the virtue of being easy to sweep up and to wash out of clothes.

WHAT YOU NEED: *cornstarch, water, large tray*

Foamy Fun: Put mounds of foamy shaving cream on a child-sized table outside and let your grandchild spread it around and squish with his hands. Or put a half cup of the shaving cream in a zip-lock bag, cut a small hole in one corner and let him squirt it out. For easy clean-up use on the shower wall during bath time.

WHAT YOU NEED: *foamy shaving cream, child-sized table, zip-lock bag*

Touch-and-Taste Play Dough: This recipe for edible play dough eliminates any concern if it ends up in your grandchild's mouth. Mix 1 cup creamy peanut butter, 1 cup corn syrup, 1 teaspoon cinnamon, 1 cup powdered sugar, and 1 cup powdered milk in a large bowl. Knead together with your hands until well blended. Add more powdered milk until it is pliable but not sticky. Show your grandchild how to pat, poke, and pound the dough. It has a slippery texture, cinnamon and peanut aromas, and a pleasing taste.

WHAT YOU NEED: *peanut butter, corn syrup, cinnamon, powdered sugar, powdered milk, mixing bowl*

Three- and Four-Year-Olds

Developmental Insights

Your grandchild now enjoys exploring new materials with unusual properties. Along with his sensory and motor exploration, he becomes more observant of physical characteristics and changes. This leads to experimenting with intentional variations. What if I make bigger holes in my sieve? What if I add flour instead of baking soda to the vinegar?

His great leap forward in language ability means he can talk about what he is seeing and doing. Learning new words to describe his experiences deepens his understanding of concepts and physical properties. You can encourage him to observe carefully and tell you what he is doing and seeing. Extend his vocabulary by adding your own descriptive commentary. For example:

Grandparent: "What is happening to the ice?"

Grandchild: "It's slippery and wet and going away."

Grandparent: "Yes, it's melting. The ice cube is turning into water. It's not solid anymore, it's a liquid."

Old Faithfuls

Bigger and Better Bubbles: For a more elaborate bubble-making experience, make your own bubble solution with this simple recipe. Mix 4 cups water, 1 cup corn syrup, and 1 cup liquid dish detergent. For best results, use Joy or Dawn. Let the solution sit for a few hours before using. Then pour into a dish pan and use a large, ready-made bubble wand or one improvised from pipe cleaners. Your grandchild can dip the bubble-maker into the solution and wave it around to produce his own beautiful bubbles. You can also use a funnel as a bubble-blower. Dip the wide end in solution and blow on the other end. Blowing on a straw that has been dipped in the solution makes tiny bubbles. Try plastic six-pack holders to make six bubbles at a time.

WHAT YOU NEED: *Joy or Dawn liquid dish detergent, water, corn syrup; ready-made bubble wand or pipe cleaners, funnel, plastic six-pack holder*

Icebergs: Freeze water in several plastic margarine tubs. Remove from containers and float in a large bowl of water, along with some ice cubes. Encourage your grandchild to push them around on top of the water, submerge them, explore how they feel, and observe their melting. Inspire pretend play by adding small plastic animals or figurines and a boat. Four-year-old Jenna reenacted the sinking of the Titanic with her iceberg.

WHAT YOU NEED: *several margarine tubs, water, ice cubes, large bowl; small plastic animals or figurines and a boat*

Car Wash: On a warm day get out the tricycles and wagons and have a car wash. Supply a bucket of water, sponges, a squirt bottle, and small towels. Then have fun getting your vehicles sparklingly clean.

WHAT YOU NEED: *tricycle, wagon, bucket, water, sponges, squirt bottle, towels*

Float or Sink?: Fill a plastic container half full of water. Collect both heavy and light objects, such as a plastic ball, cup, wooden block, marble, rock, and feather. Before your grandchild drops each in the water, ask him to guess whether it will float or sink. He may verbalize that some sink because they are big or heavy. Even if you show him contradictory evidence, like the big boat that floats, he will probably persist in his original explanation, because the concept of displacement is far too difficult for him to grasp. Instead, just focus on predicting and observing, without trying to explain why.

WHAT YOU NEED: *large plastic container, water; plastic ball, cup, wooden block, marble, rock, or feather*

New Twists

Rainbow Goop: Combine a delightful tactile and visual experience with the discovery of creating new colors. First prepare the goop. Mix together ⅓ cup sugar, 1 cup cornstarch, and 4 cups water. Cook over a low heat until it boils and thickens. Your grandchild can witness the transformation of a cloudy white liquid into a translucent gel and the blending of vibrant colors into the still-warm mixture. Separate into three containers and color each one with red, yellow, or blue paint. When the mixture cools slightly, put heaping tablespoons of red and yellow goop in a zip-lock bag and tape shut. Do the same with red and blue and with yellow and blue. Your grandchild can poke, pat, and squeeze the soft and slippery bags. He will delight in the brilliant new colors he creates.

WHAT YOU NEED: *mixing bowl, sugar, cornstarch, three bowls, spoon, red, blue, and yellow tempera paint, zip-lock bags, tape*

Fun Fountains: Explore how water flows through homemade sieves. The quickest way to make sieves is to punch holes in Styrofoam cups with a pencil. For a sturdier product use a metal can or plastic container. Turn the container upside down on a workbench and punch holes on the sides and bottom with a hammer and nail.

Fill the bathtub or a large plastic tub with water. Scoop up water in the sieves and observe the different patterns as the water flows out. Compare the amount of flow through big and small holes. Raise and lower the sieves and observe how this changes the splashing and bubbles created in the water. My favorite sieve has a vertical row of holes up the side. The force and location of the spray dramatically change as the water level gets lower.

To extend the play:

- Help your grandchild make his own sieves. As he is making them, call attention to the size and placement of holes.
- Use the sieves in the sandbox. With a tub of water close by, you can compare the flow of sand and water through the sieves.

WHAT YOU NEED: *large plastic tub, water, Styrofoam cups, and pencil; metal cans or plastic containers, nails, hammer; sandbox, water, sand*

Silly Slime: This transforming substance is as much fun to make as it is to play with. Mix 2 cups water with ⅛ cup Borax (available in the laundry detergent section of supermarkets). In another container mix ½ cup water, ½ cup glue, and a few drops of food coloring. Let your grandchild stir the two solutions together and observe the surprising results. After you pour off the excess water, give your grandchild a large piece to manipulate. It has an interesting texture and intriguing properties—slippery, slimy, stretchy, oozy, and brittle. You can stretch it out by pulling it slowly or break it by giving a quick jerk. Since it sticks to paper, use it on a plastic, wooden, or metal surface. My grandchildren especially enjoyed letting a large piece ooze slowly off the table onto the floor.

WHAT YOU NEED: *glue, Borax, food coloring, water, two mixing bowls, spoon*

Feel to Find Out: Insert a small item, such as a spoon or block, inside a large, heavy sock. Have your grandchild put his hand inside the sock and guess what the item is. No peeking allowed! Ask him to describe what he is feeling, for example, "It's hard. It's round. It's heavy. It's a marble!" Try with increasingly harder items, such as a funnel, paperclip, or pipe cleaner.

WHAT YOU NEED: *large, heavy sock; spoon, wooden block, toy car, funnel, paperclip, or pipe cleaner*

Seeds and Soil: Designate a spot in your garden as a digging hole. Mix in a bag of garden soil or mulch into the dirt to make it easier to dig. Give your grandchild a small shovel and plastic containers to fill. With a watering can he can make delightfully messy mud. When the season is right, help him plant some seeds. Large ones, such as sunflower seeds or beans, are easier for his little hands to hold. Rye grass seeds are tiny but have the advantage of quick germination. Put them in a salt shaker and let your grandchild shake seeds out onto the dirt. He can water his garden each day and check on the progress, as the seeds sprout and grow into flowers or vegetables.

WHAT YOU NEED: *garden soil or mulch, small shovel, plastic containers; seeds, watering can*

Five- to Eight-Year-Olds

Developmental Insights

Your grandchild now explores the properties of materials through more controlled experimenting. He compares results and tries to predict what will happen. You can encourage this scientific investigation by asking questions that arouse his curiosity. "What would happen if you make the ramp steeper?" "What if you add more marbles to your boat?" These hands-on experiences bring new meaning to basic science concepts. Your grandchild understands the transformation from solid to liquid to gas as he heats ice cubes. He intuitively uses the scientific method when he carefully observes, makes variations, and compares results. Encourage him to verbalize what he is observing. For example, "I can get the water to go up the tube when I raise the other end."

According to Piagetian theory, children between 5 and 7 begin to understand and apply abstract concepts in concrete situations—those with real objects and observable actions. This milestone in cognitive development, called the stage of concrete operational thought, is evident as your grandchild experiments with materials. He takes both the width and the height of a container into account in determining how much water it can hold. He understands that the shape of a container affects whether it can float. He may move beyond a description of what is happening to an understanding of why it is happening. Ask your grandchild, "Why does this container hold more water?" You may need to help him verbalize what he intuitively grasps: "This container holds more water because it is wider."

Old Faithfuls

Castles, Tunnels, and Waterfalls: Combining generous amounts of sand and water opens up possibilities for elaborate construction projects. The beach is the ideal site, but many playgrounds also offer combination water and sand facilities. Or run a garden hose over to your sandbox and attach a nozzle that lets your grandchild easily turn the water on and off. He may start with the traditional sand castle and then add a water-filled moat around it. Encourage him to extend his repertoire to include a meandering stream with islands or a lake created by a dam. Suggest that he construct a tunnel or create a waterfall. Ask him what will happen if his stream runs down a much steeper hill. Change the direction of the water flow by placing rocks in the path of the stream.

WHAT YOU NEED: *large space, sand, and water*

Magic Magnets: Use a strong horseshoe magnet to demonstrate how magnets attract metal objects. Collect a number of metal objects, such as paper clips, aluminum foil, nails, coins, and small toy cars, as well as objects made of wood, paper, or plastic. Let your grandchild discover which objects the magnet will pick up.

Try these variations. See how many paper clips the magnet can pick up at one time. See if the magnet will attract metal objects through paper, fabric, plastic, or glass. Put paperclips inside the lid of a cardboard box. Then move a magnet under it to make the paperclips move. Experiment with several bar magnets to see whether they attract or repel each other.

WHAT YOU NEED: *horseshoe and bar magnets, small metal objects, wooden, paper, and plastic objects; paper, fabric, sheet of plastic, paperclips, lid of cardboard box*

What Do You Hear, Feel, Smell?: To encourage awareness of all of the senses, take your grandchild to a secluded spot in the backyard and sit quietly with your eyes closed for a few minutes. Then ask, "What do you hear? What do you smell? What do you feel?" If the last question stumps your grandchild, suggest the warmth of the sun, the breeze on your skin, or the roughness of a rock.

WHAT YOU NEED: *quiet outdoor location*

New Twists

Up and Over: Can water really flow uphill? Learn how with this siphoning task. Buy a long piece of plastic tubing at a hardware store and insert funnels on the ends. Add a few drops of blue food coloring to a gallon of water. Hold up both ends of the tubing at the same height and add water until the tubing is full of water. Let your grandchild experiment with raising and lowering the ends to get the water to flow from one place to another. It is especially exciting when you get the water to flow up the tubing. To start this process the tube must be filled with water. The best place to try this is outside, either in a kiddy pool or with several large plastic tubs.

WHAT YOU NEED: *plastic tubing, funnels, water, blue food coloring, large plastic tubs*

Erupting Volcano: Children love the dramatic chemical reaction that occurs when baking soda and vinegar combine. The addition of dish detergent produces thick, foamy bubbles. Measure ⅓ cup vinegar into a tall plastic cup, add a squirt of dish detergent, stir in 1 tablespoon baking soda, and watch as it fizzes and foams. Then put a pitcher of vinegar, bowl of baking soda, bottle of dish detergent, teaspoons, and clear plastic cups on a tray, and let your grandchild experiment with mixing in whatever proportions he likes. To make a volcano, mix red food coloring, vinegar, and detergent in a tall glass jar. Insert the jar in a mound of sand with just the top visible. Then add the baking soda to make the volcano erupt with foamy, hot lava.

WHID YOU NEED: *baking soda, vinegar, liquid dish detergent, plastic cups, spoon, tray; for volcano: red food coloring, tall glass jar, sand*

What Dissolves?: Prepare a tray with a pitcher of water, teaspoons, clear plastic cups, and separate bowls of rice, salt, flour, vegetable oil, and sugar. Have your grandchild put a spoonful of salt in a glass of water, stir briskly, and observe what happens. Ask "Where did the salt go?" Do the same with the sugar and ask, "Can you tell which contains salt or sugar just by looking?" Try tasting each to decide what each solution contains. Then mix a little flour in water and compare to the salt and sugar solutions. Do the same with rice and then vegetable oil. Provide verbal descriptions for what you are observing: "It dissolved and disappeared. It became cloudy. It was so heavy it sank to the bottom. It separated and is floating on top of the water." After trying each ingredient separately, my granddaughter liked to make different combinations and have me guess what ingredients the mixtures contained.

WHAT YOU NEED: *tray, pitcher of water, teaspoons, clear plastic cups, bowls, rice, salt, flour, vegetable oil, sugar*

Rising Raisins: This simple observational experience takes only a tall glass, raisins, and a clear carbonated drink, such as 7-Up. Pour the soda in the glass and add half a dozen raisins. Watch as they sink to the bottom, rest awhile, and then float to the surface. They may linger there and then settle to the bottom, repeating this cycle over and over. Observe the tiny bubbles that form on the raisins and speculate about why some rise while others don't. For comparison, put raisins in a glass of water and see what happens. Raisins will rise more quickly if first soaked in hot water.

The first time I tried this with my grandchildren they enjoyed it much more than I had anticipated. They tried to catch the raisins that rose to the surface before they sank again. We also used dried cranberries and discovered that they would rise and fall with even greater regularity than raisins.

When I asked Jenna why the raisins and cranberries rose, she first said that maybe there was no gravity in the water, but then she changed her mind and speculated that the bubbles made them lighter. What I hadn't expected was that my grandchildren talked excitedly about the raisins as if they were alive. (Was this perhaps because they moved so erratically?) Jenna explained that the dried cranberries bobbed up and down so much because they were "more adventuresome."

WHAT YOU NEED: *raisins, clear carbonated drink, tall clear glasses, water*

Short and Fat or Tall and Thin?: Put out a tall, narrow container and a short, wide container (such as a water bottle and a mixing bowl). Ask your grandchild, "Do you think this tall, thin bottle will hold more water than this short, fat bowl?" To test his prediction, he can completely fill one container with water and pour it into the other one. Does it overflow or does it still need more water to fill it? Take turns predicting volume with other pairs of containers. Encourage him to verbalize how both height and width affect the amount of water.

To take this experience a step further, have your grandchild compare the volume of all the containers. Start by asking, "Which one will hold the most water? Which one will hold the least water" Then have him line up all the other containers between these two. To test his predictions, he can count how many cups of water it takes to fill each container.

WHAT YOU NEED: *plastic containers of various heights and widths, water, measuring cup*

Ships Ahoy: Help your grandchild make a barge and an ocean liner out of 6-inch squares of aluminum foil. To make a barge, turn up the edges of the foil slightly, leaving the rest of the foil flat. To make an ocean liner, crunch up the sides so that the bottom of the boat gets very small. Try floating them in the water and modify the shape as needed to make them float. Then have him gently add marbles to the boats until they sink. Ask him to predict which one will hold the most marbles before it sinks. He may see that the shape of the boat is the important factor. Introduce the concepts of *displacement* by talking about how the shape changes the amount of water pushed aside by the boat. To test further the relationship between shape and *buoyancy*, put 10 paper clips in the foil barge and 10 inside a foil square of the same size that has been crumpled into a ball. The former should float while the latter sinks to the bottom—same weight but different shape.

WHAT YOU NEED: *aluminum foil, tub of water, marbles, paper clips*

Faster and Farther: Build two ramps that are the same length but are different heights. Use heavy cardboard for the runway and blocks to support the ramps. Put a car at the top of each ramp and, without pushing them, let them roll down the ramp. Compare which car goes farther. Vary the height of the ramp and predict which car will be the winner. Instead of cars, you could use marbles or tennis balls. Talk about how the height of the ramp affects speed and distance.

WHAT YOU NEED: *heavy cardboard, blocks, toy cars, marbles or tennis balls*

$\underline{\qquad\qquad}$

7

Let's Play Games

Playing with Cards and Computers

"**L**et's play *War!*" exclaimed 5-year-old Jake, as he dealt out seven cards to each player, surreptitiously selecting some high cards for himself. When his younger sister Jenna had the high card, she swept them all in, exultantly crying, "I'm winning! I'm winning!" When she ran out of cards, she just scooped up the undealt cards. Although Jake at first objected that she can't take them all, he allowed the game to proceed, especially since he had his own way of assuring success. A king of spades kept reappearing all too frequently to capture all the jacks and queens, but he denied peeking at his cards.

Was I concerned that he was on the road to becoming a confirmed cheat and liar bent on winning at whatever cost? Not at all! We were playing a delightfully exciting game of *War*, each at our own developmental level. Jake was going through the arduous transition to playing competitive games with rules. Three-year-old Jenna still focused exclusively on the excitement of each play. I was the only holdout for playing by the "official" rules.

Why Try It?

Games are a fun and versatile way to interact with your grandchild. Are you looking for a quiet activity? One that requires no preparation or equipment? A game that both children and grown-ups can enjoy? A way to reconnect with your grandchild after a long separation? No problem! You are sure to find a game to match your specific needs. Games are easy to initiate, and everyone quickly gets caught up in the excitement of the action.

Just in case this isn't enough, games are packed with potential educational value. You can use them to reinforce academic skills, replacing boring reading and math drills with the fun of playing a game that requires identifying words or counting accurately. Many games also strengthen cognitive skills. From the simple game of *Concentration* to the complex one of chess, they encourage your grandchild to pay close attention and remember information. She sharpens her logical thinking abilities as she plans effective strategies and anticipates what other players will do. Active games provide physical exercise, promoting large motor development, aerobic endurance, weight control, and an outlet for releasing an overabundance of energy. Games can teach important social skills as well. In competitive games your grandchild learns how to strive to do her best, to compete fairly, and to win or lose graciously. They can also emphasize teamwork and cooperation. She learns how to coordinate efforts with a partner or teammates.

Snapshot of Development

There is a strong link between cognitive development and game-playing ability. Younger children enjoy rituals that feature a sequence of actions building toward a pleasurable conclusion. Older children are ready for games with rules; these have a clear goal and usually involve competition.

Expect the transition to games with rules when your grandchild is about 5 years old. Games that primarily rely on chance, such as the draw of the cards or the roll of the dice, work best at first. When she becomes more proficient with following rules, add the additional challenge of games that include skill, such as remembering where cards are or planning effective strategies.

Tips for Playing Games

Make a mental match. Take into account your grandchild's stage of cognitive development when selecting and playing games. Choose games that reinforce developing skills. If she is learning to count, play a board game that requires accurate counting. If she is learning to kick a ball, take turns kicking one back and forth. Modify games to match her current stage of cognitive development. For example, instead of playing a competitive game of *Chutes and Ladders* with your 4-year-old, simply serve as her coach as she moves her pieces along the board to the finish line.

Promote prosocial behaviors. Unfortunately, competitive games can bring out a host of negative behaviors. Your grandchild may become very clever at cheating, brag about how well she is doing, erupt with angry frustration, or dissolve into tears of disappointment. Modeling appropriate behavior and maintaining an attitude that having fun together is more important than winning can go a long way toward overcoming these difficulties. If games become too intense, look for ways to make them less competitive and anxiety-producing. You could pair up a younger child with a grown-up or older child on a team. Sometimes giving younger children a handicap, like allowing two hits instead of one in playing croquet, can keep them in the game. If sibling rivalry is high, you could put them on the same team or play with each separately.

To foster prosocial values, balance competitive games with those that emphasize teamwork and cooperation. Cooperative games emphasize working toward a common goal. It can be as simple as keeping all the balloons in the air or as complex as a board game in which you work together to save the whales or solve a mystery.

Be game savvy. Develop a spontaneous repertoire of games to play any time, anywhere. Have a few board games and a deck of cards on hand to use at a moment's notice. When a long-distance grandparent comes for a visit, playing a new game with his or her grandchild is a great way to renew their friendship. For an extensive list of games, along with clear explanation of the rules, check this website: *www.gameskidsplay.net.*

Strike a balance on the video game controversy. What should be your position on all those popular, but controversial video games for your grandchild? Are they too addictive? Do they promote a message of violence? Do they take too much time away from the social interactions, hands-on learning, and physical play that she needs? Or are they a fun way to learn academic skills, foster computer literacy, and develop eye–hand coordination? Which games you choose and how you use them with your grandchild are crucial in determining whether the positives outweigh the negatives.

Activities

Games include *Old Faithfuls* and *New Twists*. **Old Faithfuls** are traditional games that merit frequent repetitions. Most take minimal preparation or supplies. After a quick review of the rules, you will probably remember playing them yourself when you were young. When you are looking for something different, try a game in the **New Twists** section. These often take advance preparation or time to study unfamiliar rules.

Most of the games described below require only two players. For those that take a third player, elicit a sibling, playmate, or spouse to join in the fun. I emphasize games that have a long history of popularity. I hope they will spark pleasant memories of when you played them as a child.

The First Year

Developmental Insights

Melt-your-heart smiles and squeals of delight are guaranteed when playing games with your new grandchild. They capitalize on her enjoyment of rhythmic motion, high-pitched sounds, and gentle touches. You provide the language and assist her in performing the actions. She provides eye contact, smiles, and coos. These frequent playful interactions lay the foundation for a lifelong positive relationship. I recommend developing your own simple games to initiate frequently with your grandchild. The following ideas can serve as stimuli to make up your own special games. When you find something that gets a positive response from your grandchild, elaborate on it and develop a set sequence of words and actions. Here are some *Old Faithfuls* to use with your newest grandchild. I have not included any *New Twists* because simple and familiar are what works best for infants.

Old Faithfuls

Monkey See, Monkey Do: This game capitalizes on your grandchild's innate fascination with the human face. Hold your grandchild on your lap facing you and make eye contact. Make funny faces and sounds. Stick out your tongue, open your mouth very wide, and make high-pitched squeaks. It is surprising how much even a newborn can imitate.

WHAT YOU NEED: *no props required*

Buzzing Bee: Encourage your grandchild visually to track a moving object with this game. Make a buzzing sound; wiggle your finger in a circuitous path in large circles, spiraling in until you poke her gently in the tummy. She will watch with rapt attention and then laugh with glee when "stung" by the bee.

WHAT YOU NEED: *no props required*

Watch the Rattle: This game also encourages visual tracking. Hold a rattle or squeaky toy about 10 inches from her face. Shake or squeak it as you move it slowly side to side in her line of vision.

WHAT YOU NEED: *rattle or squeaky toy*

Touch and Talk: Even though she can't understand the words, your grand-child enjoys the rhythm and rhyme as you recite nursery rhymes. Add the extra pleasure of movement and touch as you move her arms to "pat-a-cake" or wiggle each "little piggy."

This little piggy went to market,	*(Wiggle each toe, beginning with the big toe.)*
This little piggy stayed home,	
This little piggy had roast beef,	
This little piggy had none.	
And this little piggy cried, wee, wee,	
All the way home.	
Pat-a-cake, pat-a-cake, baker's man.	*(Clap her hands together.)*
Bake me a cake as fast as you can.	
Pat it and prick it and mark it with "B"	*(Massage her tummy, ending with a gentle poke.)*
And put it in the oven for baby and me.	*(Spread her arms wide open.)*

WHAT YOU NEED: *no props required*

Bouncy Baby: Turn your grandchild's love of bouncing into a game. Sit her on your knee facing you, and bounce her up and down while chanting one of these nursery rhymes:

To market, to market, to buy a fat pig.
Home again, home again, jiggity jig.
To market, to market to buy a fat hog.
Home again, home again, jiggity jog.
To market, to market, to buy a new gown.
Home again, home again, all fall down! *(On this line straighten your legs and let her slide down to your feet.)*

The grand old duke of York— *(Lift your grandchild up high and down*
He had ten thousand men. *low to correspond to words of the song.)*
He marched them up the hill
Then marched them down again.
And when you're up, you're up.
And when you're down, you're down.
And when you're only halfway up,
You're neither up nor down.

WHAT YOU NEED: *no props required*

Peek-a-Boo: At about 8 months your grandchild begins to acquire the concept of object permanence. She understands that objects and people continue to exist even when out of sight. This game reinforces this emerging understanding. Hide behind the crib, and then pop up, saying "Peek-a-boo, I see you," repeating many times in a row. Another variation is to hold her on your lap facing you. Cover your face with a baby blanket, slowly take it off, and conclude with a big "peek-a-boo." Then reverse the procedure by putting the blanket over her face, saying, "Where's Susie?" Take it off and proclaim, "Here she is."

WHAT YOU NEED: *crib or baby blanket*

Hide and Hunt: Another game that fosters object permanence is looking for hidden objects. Show your grandchild a ball, and then, while she is watching, hide it under a baby blanket. Ask, "Where's the ball?" If she doesn't look under the blanket, swish it off announcing, "Here it is." Repeat with other toys and hiding places.

WHAT YOU NEED: *baby blanket, ball, small toys*

Knock the Blocks: Build a tower of small, soft blocks. Then show your grandchild how to knock them all down with a swipe of your hand. Build another tower and help her knock them down. Each time they fall down give an emphatic "They all fall down!" After a few times, she will spontaneously delight in toppling the tower.

WHAT YOU NEED: *soft blocks*

Crawl and Catch: When your grandchild starts crawling, crawl around on the floor or lawn with her and announce, "I'm gong to catch you!" Crawl after her and give her a big hug.

WHAT YOU NEED: *soft surface for crawling*

One- and Two-Year-Olds

Developmental Insights

Your grandchild rapidly progresses from those first hesitant steps to running at high speed everywhere, especially away from you. Since fine motor skills lag way behind large motor development, active games that utilize large muscles are most successful. Also take into account that games in which you both do the same thing are easier for your grandchild. Since she is much better at imitating than following verbal directions, keep the explanations super simple and show by your actions what to do.

I recommend at most an occasional computer game with a toddler. She is much better off playing with real objects. To make the experience more interactive for your grandchild, who probably can't yet manipulate the mouse, have her touch items on the monitor to make selections, which you then carry out. Software programs with interactive stories, rather than games, are a better choice for toddlers.

Old Faithfuls

Play Ball: Sitting on the floor opposite each other, roll a large, soft ball back and forth. As your grandchild becomes more adept, increase the space between you. By the time she is age 2, you can stand facing each other and kick or bounce the ball back and forth. Your grandchild can also roll the ball into a large cardboard box tipped on its side or try to knock down a tower of several boxes. My grandson liked to use a giant exercise ball. It was easier to kick and catch.

WHAT YOU NEED: *large, soft ball*

Follow the Leader: Since toddlers like to imitate actions, play a simple game of *Follow the Leader.* Ask, "Can you reach up high?" as you stretch both hands high overhead. Praise her when she does her own version. Then quickly follow with a series of actions, accompanied by a verbal description. For example: Turn around; touch the floor; clap your hands; jump up and down; lie down on the floor. End with: Give me a big hug. An older toddler may be able to take a turn as leader.

WHAT YOU NEED: *no props required*

Making Matches: If your grandchild sees others playing cards, she may want to play with them too. A better alternative than 52 Pick-Up is to use the cards for matching and sorting. A deck of picture cards, such as those in an *Old Maid* game, works better than regular playing cards. Suggest that she find ones that are alike and continue until all have matches. For the first few times limit the number of cards. When you use a regular deck of cards, sort them by color, number, or suit.

WHAT YOU NEED: *deck of cards*

But Here She Is!: Toddlers do not understand the need for secrecy in playing hide-and-seek. They don't yet take into account what is going on in the other person's head, but your grandchild can still enjoy a modified version of the traditional game. She likes finding a cozy place to hide and the anticipation of "being found." Even though you know exactly where she is hiding, since it was where she hid the last three times, look for her in other places first, saying, "She is not under the bed" and "not behind the chair" and "not in the closet." When you come to her hiding place, loudly announce "But here she is!" At this point my granddaughter would always pop out, squealing with delight.

WHAT YOU NEED: *living room or bedroom*

Songs with Actions: Here are a few longtime favorite games played to the lyrics of a song. They have simple tunes with easy, large motor actions.

You can play *Ring-Around-the-Rosy* with just you and your grandchild, but it is more fun with two or three children. Jenna always found falling down in Ring-Around-the-Rosy exhilarating and asked to play it again and again, giving my aging knees quite a workout.

Ring-around-the-rosy.   *(Join hands and walk around in a circle.)*
A pocket full of posies.
Ashes, ashes,
We all fall down!   *(Sit down quickly still holding hands.)*

A Hunting We Will Go provides the satisfaction of getting a big hug at the end.

A hunting we will go.   *(Walk around quickly.)*
A hunting we will go.
We'll catch a fox,   *(Catch your grandchild and give her a big hug.)*
And put him in a box.
And never let him go.

When your grandchild does the inevitable jumping on the bed, chant this *Monkeys Jumping on the Bed* rhyme. If she wants to act out falling off, suggest she flop down on the bed instead. A further enactment would be to have five stuffed animals jump and fall off the bed.

Five little monkeys jumping on the bed.
One fell off and bumped his head.
Mama called the doctor and the doctor said,
"No more monkeys jumping on the bed."
(Repeat for four, three, two, and one monkeys.)

WHAT YOU NEED: *bed, five stuffed animals*

Whirl and Twirl: Toddlers often dance spontaneously whenever they hear music. Add to your grandchild's repertoire by dancing to music of varying tempos. Play fast, rhythmic music and demonstrate making crisp, defined movements. Next, play music with a slow tempo and model making flowing movements with your arms. Cheer your grandchild on, encouraging her to improvise her own movements.

WHAT YOU NEED: *CD player, music CDs*

Stop and Plop: Your older toddler may enjoy the added challenge of this game. It requires that she listen carefully to the music. Encourage her to dance to the music and then sit down quickly when it stops. The first few times cue her that you are going to stop the music in the middle of the song and model plopping down on the floor immediately upon turning the music off.

WHAT YOU NEED: *CD player, music CDs*

Balloons in the Air: Blow up a balloon and tie securely. Toss it into the air and show your grandchild how to tap it to keep it from falling down. Encourage her to help you keep it up. Add to the challenge by using two or even three balloons.

WHAT YOU NEED: *balloons*

New Twists

Beat the Drum: Show your grandchild how to make sounds by hitting a metal pie pan with a wooden spoon. Let her experiment with making lots of noise. Then suggest, "Let's hit it fast. Now let's do a slow beat. Can you make it very, very soft? Now hit it very hard and loud." Next compare the sounds made with the metal pie pan to those on plastic or cardboard containers. End by parading around the room, banging away as you go, to the music of an energetic march.

WHAT YOU NEED: *metal pie pans, wooden spoon, plastic or cardboard containers, marching music*

Fill and Spill: Cut a slit in the plastic lid of a coffee can. Give your grandchild a big pile of poker chips. Show her how to put them in the slot and fill up the can. Then she can dump it out and do it all over again. My grandson modified the game, choosing to put first the blue chips, then the red chips, and finally the white chips in the can.

WHAT YOU NEED: *coffee can, poker chips*

Beanbag Toss: Show your grandchild how to toss a beanbag into a large plastic container. At first, suggest she stand close, so she will be successful most of the time. Then encourage her to stand farther back to make it more challenging. To add color recognition to the task, spread out four colors of construction paper in the center of the floor, and suggest that she toss a beanbag onto a specific color.

WHAT YOU NEED: *beanbag, plastic container, colored construction paper*

Three- and Four-Year-Olds

Developmental Insights

Your preschool grandchild relishes active play that utilizes her developing motor skills. If she wants to test them out in unsafe, risk-taking adventures, like standing on the railing at the top of the jungle gym, redirect them into active, challenging games. When Jake wanted to ride his new scooter full speed ahead down our steep, winding road, I took him to the neighborhood track, away from steep hills, cars, or rocks, where he raced at break-neck speed around and around the track and then found a ramp to zip down with a soft, grassy landing.

Preschoolers are seldom ready for competitive games with rules. Their focus is on what they are doing independent of other players. Try playing

Tic-Tac-Toe with a preschooler. She will blithely concentrate on getting her three X's or O's in a row with no attempt to block your efforts. My 3-year-old granddaughter made it clear at the outset where her X's would go and pointed out I could use another row for my O's.

Adapt competitive games to make them more suitable for your preschool grandchild. Instead of racing to see who is fastest, enjoy the exhilaration of running as fast as you can together. For board games, getting to the finish line, not getting there first, is the objective. Play along with your grandchild, and let her determine the rules. There are many excellent board games for young children. Those in which you move pieces around a path to a finish line by using spinners, dice, or cards are good for beginners. Luck, not skill, determines the winner. Some classics are *Candyland*, *Chutes and Ladders*, and *Hi Ho Cherry-O*. You can find similar games that capitalize on currently popular toys and television shows. My grandchildren enjoyed a *Thomas the Tank* board game, to which they added an element of pretend play.

There are many preschool computer games available either for purchase or on the Internet. Some focus on quick response and eye–hand coordination, while others have an educational emphasis.

When your grandchild learns to play independently, a major concern may be that she spends too much time playing these games. Discuss with her parents what is a reasonable amount of computer time and enforce this time limit, perhaps by setting a timer. Although most of these computer games are designed for solitary play, you can make them a joint activity by taking turns or cheering her along as she plays.

Old Faithfuls

Sam Says: In the traditional game of *Simon Says* everyone imitates the leader when he says "Simon says..." but not when he omits the "Simon says" before giving a command. This is harder than you might think for preschoolers, because they pay more attention to the physical cues than the words. This modification provides an added cue to make it easier. When the leader says "Sam says..." then you are not supposed to imitate the action. Explain that she is to do what Simon says but not what Sam says. At first, hesitate after giving a command and ask, "Now who is telling us to do this?"

WHAT YOU NEED: *no props required*

Sing and Do: You can do these action songs with just you and your grandchild but a third or fourth player adds to the fun.

> Here we go round the mulberry bush,   *(Join hands and walk around in a circle.)*
> The mulberry bush, the mulberry bush.
> Here we go round the mulberry bush,
> So early in the morning.
> This is the way we get out of bed,   *(Pretend stretch and get out of bed.)*
> Get out of bed, get out of bed.
> This is the way we get out of bed,
> So early in the morning.

(Repeat the first verse and then add other words and actions in the second verse. For example, Take a bath; put on our clothes; eat our breakfast; brush our teeth; wave good-bye.)

> You put your arm in,   *(Put arm in front of you.)*
> You put your arm out,   *(Put arm behind you.)*
> You put your arm in,   *(Put arm in front of you again.)*
> And shake it all about.   *(Shake your arm vigorously.)*
> You do the Hokey Pokey   *(Raise arms over your head.)*
> And you turn yourself around.   *(Turn around.)*
> That's what it's all about.   *(Clap hands.)*

(Repeat for foot, elbow, shoulder, head, and whole self.)

WHAT YOU NEED: *no props required*

Card Count: Here are some simple ways to teach math concepts with a deck of cards. Give your grandchild a small pile of cards and ask her to count them. Divide the cards into two piles and figure out which has more cards. Next, see if she can make two stacks that have the same number of cards. Another task is to sort the cards into suits, remove the face cards, and then arrange each suit in numerical order.

WHAT YOU NEED: *deck of cards*

Treasure Hunt: Hide a little box with a special treat inside (such as a balloon, cookie, or sticker). Take your grandchild on a treasure hunt in her room to find it. Give a hint, such as, "It's under something soft and white." You can take turns hiding the treasure box. When I played this game with my 3-year-old granddaughter, she knew enough to tell me, "In a treasure hunt you are not supposed to tell where it is," but she found it difficult to give hints that were not complete giveaways.

WHAT YOU NEED: *small box, special treat*

Until We Meet Again: My grandchildren invented this game and played it each day on a path near their preschool. They would run in opposite directions around the circular path, gleefully hug each other when they met, and then start off promptly in opposite directions. You can play this game with your grandchild. Tell her to run one direction around your house, while you run the other way. The first time she may be a bit startled to see you coming around the corner.

WHAT YOU NEED: *circular path or house with free access all around it*

Search and Find: Identify three easy-to-find items (e.g., a dog, a yellow house, and a trailer truck) to look for while riding in the car or going on a walk. Both you and your grandchild search for the same items. After you have found all three items, start over with a new list.

WHAT YOU NEED: *Car ride or walk*

A Clue for You: This is a great game to play on the ride home after an outing. Give clues about something you just saw, and see if your grandchild can guess what it is. For example, after seeing flamingos at the zoo, ask "I saw something pink that stands on one foot. What was it?" After a trip to the farmer's market, the question could be, "I saw a big, orange vegetable. What was it?"

WHAT YOU NEED: *outing*

New Twists

Lots of Lotto: Lotto games typically have a set of boards with six or nine pictures on each and a deck of cards containing the pictures on all the boards. The object of the game is to get matches for all the pictures on your board. One player turns over the first card in the deck and asks, "Who has the (duck)?" The person with this picture puts it on the matching picture. It is a simple game that teaches vocabulary and matching skills. You can continue to play until one person has matches for all her pictures or until everyone fills their boards.

It is easy to make your own lotto games that target concepts especially appropriate for your grandchild. A game for 3-year-olds could involve matching colors and shapes, while one for older preschoolers could provide practice in number and letter recognition. Use heavy construction paper to make three boards. Draw a grid with nine squares on each. For color and shape recognition fill the squares with circles, squares, rectangles, diamonds, triangles, and stars in different colors. Then players must find matches for both color and shape (e.g., a yellow circle or a green triangle). Then make duplicates on small cards. Use this deck of cards to match and cover the letters on the boards. To make a numbers game with only single digits, use several colors along with the numbers, and match for both color and number.

WHAT YOU NEED: *lotto game; construction paper, scissors, marker*

Amazing Maze: Build an obstacle course for your grandchild to navigate. Use chairs, pillows, blankets, tables, and large blocks to construct a bridge to walk over, a tunnel to crawl through, stairs to climb up and down, and low barricades to step over. My grandchildren love to construct intricate bridges to climb over and insist I traverse them too, sometimes to my peril, being considerably heavier and less agile than they are.

WHAT YOU NEED: *chairs, pillows, blankets, tables, large blocks*

Strikes and Spares: Set up a bowling alley on your patio or sidewalk. Use 5–10 plastic bottles (such as disposable water bottles) as the pins and a large, soft ball. Put sand or pebbles in the bottles to make them more stable. Show your grandchild how to roll the ball toward the bottles in order to knock them down. Have her stand close to the bottles at first, and then increase the distance as she becomes more proficient. Throwing or kicking the ball at the target is another way to make it more challenging.

WHAT YOU NEED: *plastic bottles and large, soft ball; sand or pebbles*

Five- to Eight-Year-Olds

Developmental Insights

When children are 5–6 years old their cognitive abilities take a giant step forward, allowing them to better understand the thinking and intentions of others. This increased ability to take into account the perspective of another person opens up the option of playing competitive games with rules. During this transitional period, start with games that are based more on chance than skill (*Candyland, Bingo*) and ones in which all players perform the same actions (such as running a race and *Slap Jack*). These simpler games mean your grandchild can concentrate on learning how to play by the rules. As she becomes more proficient, add the challenge of games where it helps to anticipate your opponent's actions and to plan strategies based on these expectations (such as *Tic-Tac-Toe* and *Go Fish*). You can also add games with complementary rather than parallel roles. For example, in *Tag* one person chases while the others try to avoid being caught. This requires understanding two different roles and coordinating them with others.

On a more practical note, your grandchild may find it difficult to hold more than a few cards spread out in her hand. Since secrecy is important for many card games, one solution is to have her put the cards inside a shoe box tipped on its side. Decks with small cards are easier to hold, as well as handy to transport in purse or pocket. Or you can purchase cardholder fans.

Old Faithfuls

Ready, Set, Go: All that energetic running around can be turned into competitive races. This means everyone must start at the same time and from the same place. Decide on definite starting and finishing lines and use the typical, "Get ready. Get set. Go!" To add variety and practice other gross motor skills, have a race in which you must skip, hop, or jump all the way.

WHAT YOU NEED: *large, open space*

Two for Tag: Already done your share of chasing after your grandchild? In a game of *Tag* she now has to take a turn chasing you. The person who is "it" chases and tries to touch someone. Then this person becomes "it." You can play with just you and your grandchild, but it's more fun if you can add a few more players. One variation is to have a designated spot where you are safe from being tagged.

WHAT YOU NEED: *large, open space*

Ready or Not: The traditional game of hide-and-seek is a favorite for many children. The "seeker" hides her eyes and counts to 20, while everyone else scurries away to find a hiding place. After counting to a designated number, the seeker states, "Ready or not, here I come" and begins hunting. When she finds someone, they both see who can make it back to the home base first. You will know your grandchild understands the complementary roles of hider and seeker when she starts using a variety of hiding places, hides very quietly, makes sure she is well concealed, and knows the seeker is not supposed to peek while counting.

WHAT YOU NEED: *yard or large house*

Remember and Match: The card game of *Concentration* fosters memory skills. Put cards face down. Players alternate turning up two cards at a time. If they match (e.g., two red sixes), you keep them. If not, you turn them face down again. The goal is to remember where the cards are and find the pairs. Simplify this at first by using only six or eight pairs. The winner is the player who ends up with the most cards. When I first played this game with my 5-year-old grandson, he was more interested in our together finding matches than in getting the most cards. Many grandparents, myself included, find that their grandchildren consistently beat them at this game.

WHAT YOU NEED: *deck of cards*

This Is War: Determining which numeral is higher adds an element of skill to *War*, a simple game of chance. After removing the face cards, deal out the rest of the cards. Two or more people can play. Each player keeps her pile face down and turns up the top card. The person with the higher number takes all the cards. If two players turn up the same number, then both turn up another card and the higher number takes all the cards. The winner is the one who ends up with the most cards.

WHAT YOU NEED: *deck of cards*

Lonely Lady: To be politically correct, I have changed the name from *Old Maid* to *Lonely Lady*. Playing with the traditional Old Maid picture cards adds the fun of interesting characters, but you can also use a regular deck of cards. Play with only two suits and one queen, who becomes the "Lonely Lady." You need at least three players. Deal out all the cards face down. The object is to avoid ending up with the Lonely Lady. Each person looks at her cards and removes any pairs from her hand. The first player lets the player to the left pick a card from her hand. If it matches a card in her hand, she can discard the pair. If not, she keeps it in her hand. Then she lets the next player draw a card from her hand. This continues until all cards except the Lonely Lady have been played. The person holding this card loses that hand.

WHAT YOU NEED: *deck of cards*

Slap That Jack: *Slap Jack* is a super simple, super silly game; perhaps that's why it's unexpectedly so much fun. Deal everyone a stack of cards face down. Everyone turns over their top card at the same time without looking at it and tosses it into the center. You continue until someone turns up a jack. The first person to slap the jack wins the whole pile. Continue playing until you run out of cards. The winner is the one who gets the most cards. Solve any disagreement about who slapped the jack first by seeing whose hand is on the bottom.

WHAT YOU NEED: *deck of cards*

Xs and Os: We have all played the simple but intriguing game of *Tic-Tac-Toe* as children. Draw two vertical lines and cross them with two horizontal lines. Take turns putting an X or O in one of the nine spaces, trying to get three marks in a line, vertically, horizontally, or diagonally. When my 5-year-old grandson tired of playing the traditional way, he devised ever more complex diagrams and rules to follow.

WHAT YOU NEED: *paper and pencils*

Go Fish: You can buy picture cards for playing *Go Fish* or use a regular deck of cards. Although two can play this game, it's more interesting with three or more. Give each player seven cards and spread the rest face down in the middle of the table. Players remove and save any pairs they have. One player begins by asking any other player if she has a particular card. If she does, she gives it to the requestor; if not, she says "Go fish," and the requestor takes a card from those that are face down on the table. Then the next player takes a turn asking. This continues until all cards have been put down as pairs. The winner is the player who makes the most pairs.

WHAT YOU NEED: *deck of cards*

Ten Again: *Make Ten* is a great game for reinforcing addition facts. After removing the face cards, deal out the remaining cards face down to two or three players. Players take turns placing one of their cards face up in the center. When your card and any other card or combination of cards in the center equals 10, you get to take these cards. Continue until you have gone through your original stacks. The winner is the one who has taken the most cards. Jake's variation is to have everyone turn up a card at the same time and see who is first to come up with a winning combination. The need for speedy recognition adds to the excitement.

WHAT YOU NEED: *deck of cards*

New Twists

Tunnels: Make your own miniature golf game. Create tunnels from cereal and shoe boxes by opening up both ends. Place them around the room and put a number on each. Tape to the floor for greater stability. Use rackets or spatulas to hit tennis balls through each of the boxes in the proper sequence. To make it a competitive game, take turns hitting your balls.

WHAT YOU NEED: *cereal and shoe boxes, tape, marker, rackets or spatulas, tennis balls*

Math in a Can: Use this homemade game to reinforce math skills. Cut a slot in the lid of a coffee can. Give each player the same number of poker chips. Then take turns rolling one die and putting that number of chips in the can. The winner is the player that gets all her chips in the can first. Increase the math challenge by using two dice. To practice addition, add the numbers on both dice. To practice subtraction, subtract the lower number from the higher one.

WHAT YOU NEED: *coffee can with plastic lid, poker chips, dice*

Fishing Fun: Making this game is half the fun. To make a fishing pole, attach a 2-foot piece of heavy string to the end of a 2-foot long stick. Then tie a magnet to the end of the string. Help your grandchild draw and cut out fish and other marine animals from construction paper. Attach a paper clip to each animal and place in the ocean—a large piece of blue paper on the floor. Now it's time to see how many fish, octopi, or turtles you can hook with your fishing pole!

WHAT YOU NEED: *heavy string, stick, magnet, construction paper, markers, scissors, paper clips*

Family Faces: Make a game of *Concentration* with family photos. Make duplicate photos of 10 or more family members and glue these on 2 × 3-inch index cards. Use to play the game of *Concentration,* as described above. I sent this game to my grandson who lived across the country as a way for him to remember us. I also printed each person's name under his or her photo, so that he could learn to spell our names.

WHAT YOU NEED: *family photos, index cards, glue, marker*

8

Let's Pretend

Becoming Pirates and Princesses

I stomped around the house shouting, "I'm going to throw you off the cliff, then drag her away to my kingdom." A high-powdered laser beam thwarted my plans, toppling me to the ground. While I lay there gasping my last breath, I looked up to see the visiting workman standing at the door with a look of amusement (or was it concern?) on his face. Jeharta quickly revived. Aladdin put down his laser, and Jasmine came out from her hiding place under the bed. I covered my embarrassment with a feeble, "It's our favorite pretend game."

Why Try It?

Do you have pleasant memories of your favorite game of "Let's pretend"? Do you remember the many hours when you lined up your dolls to play school or the fierce fights you staged with your dinosaurs? Then you will appreciate the intense pleasure that your grandchild experiences as he immerses himself in the world of pretend play, and for that reason alone you will want to encourage it. During these early years pretend play is packed with value for your grandchild. When he pretends, he controls whatever happens, whether it is slaying monsters or overpowering bullies. He learns to understand different perspectives, as he becomes the parent, the baby, or the new puppy. It is a way to work through his fears, anger, and sadness, helping him cope with these troubling and intense feelings. Children often reenact unpleasant events, but modify them to emphasize the positive parts. After a major cut on her forehead, Jenna repeatedly acted out having her doll fall on her head and go to the hospital to get stitches, while she took the role of the comforting parent.

Although pretend play may seem effortless, in reality it is an intellectually demanding activity. Not convinced? Try coming up with your own pretend script and getting others to help you act it out properly. Perhaps this intellectual component is why children who engage in extensive pretend play tend to score high on cognitive and creative abilities.

It is often in pretend play that children begin to interact and play cooperatively with others. At first they take parallel roles; both take care of their baby dolls or drive their cars all around the living room. Later, they assume complementary roles, declaring, "You be the Mommy and I'll be the baby." or race and crash their cars. Whether playing alone or with others, pretend play is rich in language. When alone, a child often engages in extensive monologues about what is happening. When playing with others, he moves back and forth between talk and action, first discussing who they are and what they will do and then dramatizing it. In these play episodes conversations are often complex and highly improvisational, as children bounce ideas off each other. Pretend play hones social skills as your grandchild learns to cooperate, resolve conflicts without disrupting the play, and be assertive about his ideas.

Snapshot of Development

Pretend play is more than one of the simple delights of childhood; it is serious business linked to the child's increasingly sophisticated use of symbols as a way to make sense of the world. He isn't born with this ability; he has to learn how. The infant can only experience the world directly, through what he sees and hears and his own bodily movements. He slowly grasps that he is a separate entity and that objects have a permanent existence apart from his own experience of them. Only then, when he is well into his second year, is he ready to make the great leap forward to using symbols. We see the beginnings of using symbols in his first words, and we also see it in his first pretend play, when he uses a simple object to represent something else. A pebble becomes a cookie; a doll becomes a baby.

Gradually his pretend play becomes more complex. He takes his toy cars to fill up at the gas station or puts his teddy bear in timeout for being bad. From this simple, realistic role-playing evolves elaborate thematic play. He often has a few favorite themes that he plays repeatedly, but with variation in the plot and dialogue. Common themes are family life, princesses, or the latest superheroes. You may find your grandson engaged in fast-paced, action-packed adventures, while your granddaughter spends more time in the planning stage and chooses less violent themes.

Sometimes your grandchild pretends through his toys. He acts out a pirate scenario with his miniature pirate ship and crew. Toy sets for many pretend themes are readily available and make great gifts. Other times he himself becomes a pretend character and acts out that role. With his pirate hat and sword he fights to defend his ship and plunders for gold. A few props and dress-up items encourage this type of pretending. Either way, he is using his imagination to visualize and act out the drama.

Like daffodils in spring, pretend play sprouts during the toddler years, then bursts into full bloom during the preschool years, a vivid display of imagination and emotion. All too often it wilts and fades away as the child grows older.

Why this decline? One explanation is that it shrinks as critical thinking abilities grow. Or perhaps social constraints simply push public pretend play underground into interior monologues and daydreams. It may resurface in imaginative art and stories. Another factor that may contribute to its decline is that the more structured and realistic activities of school, sports teams, and music or dance lessons leave little time for leisurely pretend play.

Tips for Pretend Play

Choose your role. As adults we rarely, if ever, play pretend games. We mostly focus on real events, and whatever fantasy life we have is channeled into books, films, and computer games or is hidden away in the interior monologue of our private daydreams. So, we may feel uncomfortable with the pretend play of our grandchild and uncertain about how to proceed. Consider these options for ways to participate:

- As an **accepting observer**, you support your grandchild's play with a few acknowledging words and no hint of judgment or efforts to intervene. You just sit back and enjoy his forays into the world of make-believe and gain insights into his thoughts and feelings.
- As **stage manager**, you may set the stage for a specific theme by defining a space and setting out props. If the play lags, you ask open-ended questions to move the action along: "What else does a doctor do?" or "Where is your rocket ship going?"
- As **co-player**, you get to be an actor, too. To jump-start pretend play, you could model simple, realistic pretending. When 4-year-old Cassie said she didn't know how to play school, Grandma Laura modeled reading stories and giving snacks to the dolls. Your grandchild may ask you to assume a role in his pretend play episode. Let him be the director, while you dutifully carry out your assigned role.

Prepare a prop box. To encourage dressing up and acting out pretend roles, assemble an assortment of items that can tweak your grandchild's imagination. Search your drawers and closets for unused shoes, hats, costume jewelry, fabrics of various textures, scarves, eyeglasses, ribbons, purses, and robes. Add inexpensive items from garage sales or thrift stores—a white jacket, cape, cane, Halloween costume, medical scrubs, a clown nose, wigs, hard hat, ballet outfit, shiny dresses with sequins, lace curtains, and a frilly blouse. Seeing his reflection in a full-length mirror is sure to bring giggles, posing, and funny faces, followed by acting out the part of clown, knight, doctor, or magician.

Link to special event. A good time to set up a new pretend play center is after a special outing. Your grandchild can draw on his firsthand experience to add new roles, details, and conversations to his play. This enhances his understanding of what he experienced. Create a special space with some interesting props and dress-up clothes. You can assume the role of waiter, clerk, or doctor to get the play started.

Have fun with fiction. To promote storybook themes, pretend to be a character from a story you have just read. Act out the story as you retell it. *The Three Billy Goats Gruff* works well to initiate this process. You can make a bridge from cushions; stuffed animals can go *trip-trap* across it while you roar out the troll's warning.

My grandchildren often used stories to extend their repertoire of pretend play. When Jake was 2 he liked to act out Winnie the Pooh episodes, especially Pooh getting stuck in Rabbit's hole when he ate too much honey. My role was to be the hole. The Nightmare hiding in the closet (*There's a Nightmare in My Closet*), Miss Clavel coming fast and faster (*Madeline*), and the mean Jafaro (*Aladdin*) are among my other starring roles.

Activities

Pretend activities include *Old Faithfuls* and *New Twists*. **Old Faithfuls** are basic everyday ones that merit frequent repetitions. They use materials that are readily available. When you want to do something different, try an activity in the **New Twists** section. These add the enticement of novelty, but take a bit more equipment and preparation. Some are linked to a special event that your grandchild has had.

One- and Two-Year-Olds

Developmental Insights

It is during the second year that simple forms of pretend play emerge. To nurture early pretend play, model the behavior you want your grandchild to imitate. Make a cake out of play dough and pretend to take a bite. Feed the baby doll some cereal. Talk about how the airplane is taking off into the sky and landing at the airport. Your smiles and "I'm pretending to . . ." indicate that this is not for real. Set up props to encourage acting out real-life situations, such as those described below.

Old Faithfuls

My Baby: Pretending that a doll or teddy bear is a baby is an early and universal form of pretend play. Model simple nurturing routines: hugging and singing to a doll, sitting her in a chair and feeding her with a baby spoon, and covering her with a baby blanket when it is time for sleep. For more complex play, set up a tub of warm, bubbly water for bathing the baby doll, along with a small towel and washcloth. A bottle, spoon, bib, and highchair for feeding the baby and a stroller for taking her for a walk extend the play.

WHAT YOU NEED: *doll or teddy bear, chair, baby spoon, baby blanket; washtub, water, towels; bottle, bib, stroller*

What's for Dinner?: A child-size kitchen center with stove, refrigerator, sink, and oven are sure to inspire pretend cooking. However, toy dishes, pans, and spoons on a little table are usually enough to spark such play. Play dough or dried pasta can serve as food. For something different, you could provide a small pitcher of water tinted with food coloring.

WHAT YOU NEED: *toy dishes, pans, spoons; play dough or dried pasta; pitcher, water, food coloring; kitchen center*

Mommy and Daddy: Provide a few simple props that mommies and daddies use: a necktie, hat, briefcase, purse, necklace, or cell phone. Help your grandchild put on the necktie and hand him the briefcase, so he can wave good-bye and drive off to work. Add a small toolbox, broom, or vacuum cleaner for working around the house.

WHAT YOU NEED: *a necktie, hat, briefcase, purse, necklace, or cell phone; child-size toolbox, broom, or vacuum cleaner*

Cozy Corner: Capitalize on your grandchild's delight in little enclosures. Make a hideaway under the table with blankets draped over the side, or build one out of chairs and cushions. Pretend to be bears snuggled up in their warm little den, and then crawl out to look for berries. Or use the hideaway as a safe haven from the fierce dinosaur stomping around the jungle.

WHAT YOU NEED: *several blankets, chairs, table, cushions*

All Aboard: Make a train or bus with the kitchen chairs, and put a doll or teddy bear in each seat. Your grandchild can take the front seat and drive everyone to the park or zoo. You can be the conductor who collects the tickets.

WHAT YOU NEED: *kitchen chairs, dolls, and stuffed animals*

Mean Monster: Pretend to be a giant monster. Stomp around and wave your arms as though trying to catch your prey. Growl, "I'm coming to get you." Then sweep up your grandchild in a big hug. Afterward, he may want to be the monster who tries to get you, as you cower in the corner.

WHAT YOU NEED: *no props required*

New Twists

Kitties and Puppies: Children enjoy pretending to be animals. My grandchildren especially liked to be kitties or puppies. Model making purrs, meows, barks, and whines and extend the play possibilities with a bowl of water, leash, and ball. To make a simple costume, tuck a scarf into the back of your grandchild's pants for a tail. Cut out ears from heavy construction paper, and attach to a headband made from a 1-inch wide strip of construction paper. When we acquired a new puppy, my grandson spontaneously pretended to be a dog, lapping water from a dish and crawling in the cage to sleep. However, I was not able to get him to "sit" or "stay" on command.

WHAT YOU NEED: *scarf, construction paper, tape, headband*

Candles on the Cake: Birthday parties, with their rituals of candles, balloons, presents, and guests, make a great theme for pretend play. Sit dolls in a circle on the floor or around a small table, and give each a cup, plate, and play food. Ask the dolls what they would like to eat and then speak for them, using a different voice. Make a cake from play dough, decorated with toothpick candles. Sing "Happy Birthday" and pretend to blow out the candles. Add some balloons and a few boxes wrapped in tissue paper to open as gifts.

WHAT YOU NEED: *dolls, play dishes, play dough, toothpicks, boxes, tissue paper, balloons*

City Traffic: Use a large sheet of brown wrapping paper (at least 3 × 4 feet) to create a network of roads that wind around all corners of the layout. Pencil them in, and then use a black marker to make them stand out. Add a parking lot, bus stop, and school, plus a variety of stores and houses. You could add some train tracks and a train station. Then get out some toy cars, trucks, and trains and show your grandchild how to drive them over the roads and tracks.

WHAT YOU NEED: *brown wrapping paper, pencil, marker, toy cars, trucks, and trains*

Read It/Do It: Let's Pretend, a board book for toddlers, has colored photos and a short sentence on each page about a pretend play role. For example, one page has a photo of a toddler with a doll and the text "Let's pretend I'm the mom." Reading this book to your grandchild can be an entree into pretending these realistic roles.

WHAT YOU NEED: *Let's Pretend board book*

Three- and Four-Year-Olds

Developmental Insights

During the preschool years pretend play bursts into full bloom with elaborate dramatizations and conversations about what is happening. No longer simply pouring water or floating a toy in the bathtub, the preschooler pretends to save the duck from drowning in the huge waterfall. He instantly transforms a rock into a buried treasure, a tricycle into a speeding race car, or a jungle gym into a spaceship. Now, whether playing with trains, blocks, crayons, or board games, pretend play infiltrates them all.

Plots for pretend play become more complicated, allowing your grandchild to explore new situations and try out many roles. Themes expand to include fantasy characters from stories or from his rich imagination. Dangerous, scary, or violent situations with heroes who overcome all obstacles let him face his fears, be all-powerful, and be in control of everything that happens. Emerson obliterates all the scary monsters lurking in dark corners or becomes the big, bad bully, who ends up protecting the little guys. These games reflect the preschooler's view of the world, one of sharp contrasts—right and wrong, heroes and villains; he is not yet ready for flawed heroes or ambiguous situations. Such subtlety comes much later.

Complex pretend play requires ample unstructured time and freedom from grown-up censoring. Provide encouragement simply by accepting and enjoying your grandchild's play. Occasionally add a prop—a hose for the firefighter, menus for the restaurant, or a backpack for the hiker. When he asks for you to play with him, let him provide the leadership. My grandchildren are quick to tell me what character I get to be and how I am suppose to act.

Old Faithfuls

Go for Groceries: When your grandchild plays store, he can draw on his many supermarket experiences. Set up a cash register on a low table to serve as the checkout counter. Stock the store with plastic food and empty food boxes. Labels provide opportunities to practice reading. Add a shopping cart or basket, grocery bags, a purse or wallet, play money, and credit cards. Then take turns being the customer or clerk.

WHAT YOU NEED: *table, cash register, plastic food, food boxes, shopping cart or basket, grocery bags, purse or wallet, play money and credit cards*

May I Take Your Order?: To create a fast food restaurant, put a cash register on a small table to serve as the counter and post a menu listing items and their prices. Provide play food, dishes, and money. Set up a table and chairs where the customers can eat. If you have a play kitchen center, use it to prepare the food. To create a more formal dining experience, add a waiter, menus, and a pad and pencil for "writing" orders. Dolls and stuffed animals can be your customers.

WHAT YOU NEED: *play cash register, paper, markers, play food, dishes, money; toy kitchen center; writing pad, pencil, heavy paper; dolls or stuffed animals*

A Night in the Forest: Pretend to go on a camping trip. Hike through a forest filled with streams to ford, hills to climb, and bears to avoid. Build a campfire with Lincoln Logs for roasting hot dogs and marshmallows on sticks. Set up a tent by draping a sheet over several chairs. Your grandchild can crawl inside with a flashlight, sleeping bag, and snacks—enough provisions for a dark, scary night in the forest. Enhance the mood with the hoot of an owl or howl of a coyote.

WHAT YOU NEED: *backpack, boots, sheet, chairs, flashlight, sleeping bag, snacks*

Say Ah: Playing doctor can help your grandchild deal with anxieties associated with visiting the doctor. Set out a stethoscope, bandages, cotton balls, syringe, pill bottles, flashlight, tongue depressor, and white coat. A pillowcase on a chair can serve as the examining table and a doll as the patient. You can take turns playing the role of the patient, parent, or doctor. When you are the doctor, give a running commentary about what you are doing and why. When you are the patient, express your fears about getting a shot or having to undress. When you are the parent, give your child reassuring support and comforting hugs.

WHAT YOU NEED: *stethoscope, bandages, cotton balls, syringe, pill bottles, flashlight, tongue depressor, white coat, pillowcase, chair, doll*

Fight That Fire: The drama of a fire truck speeding down the road with its siren blaring and the firefighter dousing the fire with a blast of water and rescuing a child or puppy from the flames makes playing firefighters a popular theme. Supply a rain slicker, boots, hard hat, 3-foot piece of hose, and a wagon or tricycle to serve as the fire truck. Your grandchild will be glad to supply the siren and excitement.

WHAT YOU NEED: *rain slicker, boots, hard hat, 3-foot hose, wagon or tricycle*

New Twists

Spaceship or Playhouse: Sometimes a cardboard box is all it takes to get your grandchild's imagination working. A box just big enough to sit in becomes a boat; several tied together make a great train. Turn one on its side for a dollhouse, and create a second floor by adding another box on top. A large appliance box can be turned into a playhouse. He may want to decorate it with markers or paint while you cut out a door or window. A tall, slender box makes a good spaceship. Paint it silver on the outside and draw dials and a steering wheel on the inside. Cut a window in the front, so he can see where he is headed. This would be a great time to read the book *Not A Box*, which describes the many pretend possibilities that a box can elicit.

WHAT YOU NEED: *large cardboard boxes, markers or tempera paint, scissors, string*

King and Queen: The medieval world of knights, princesses, kings, and queens is a favorite theme for many preschoolers. Heroes and heroines always win out over the bad guys. Perhaps there is a dragon to slay or a princess to rescue. To add to the allure, provide a knight, king, or princess costume.

Here are directions for making a golden crown to complete the outfit: Use a 9 × 12 piece of heavy gold construction paper. Cut off a 2-inch strip of paper along the long edge. Fold the larger piece in half with the short ends together. Draw a zigzag line on the paper with a high point in the middle and cut it out. Help your grandchild add "jewels"to the crown by gluing on glitter and sequins. Tape the 2-inch strip to the crown, fitting it to your grandchild's head size.

WHAT YOU NEED: *princess gown, knight's costume; gold construction paper, scissors, glue, glitter, sequins*

The Big Top: Introduce this pretend theme after a firsthand experience with a circus. Use string to make a large circus ring on the floor. Your grandchild becomes a lion tamer with a child's chair, stick, and stuffed animals. Give the clown a balloon and floppy shoes. The tightrope walker needs an umbrella and a rope stretched out on the floor. The acrobat can do his tricks on a soft mat. Take the role of master of ceremonies and introduce each act with enthusiastic fanfare.

WHAT YOU NEED: *string; child's chair, stick, stuffed animals; balloon, adult shoes; umbrella, rope; soft mat*

Five- to Eight-Year-Olds

Developmental Insights

The increasing demands of school, organized sports, and music or dance lessons can fill much of your grandchild's time. Relaxing, unstructured pretend play provides a needed balance, for it has no rules or pressure to succeed. When given adequate time and support, pretend play typically becomes more elaborate and fantasy-based. Themes often anticipate adolescent roles or action-packed episodes of powerful superheroes.

Include more fantasy themes in your prop box. Your grandchild appreciates complete, authentic-looking outfits and can come up with creative ways to utilize available materials. He probably has explicit ideas about what character he wants to be. Favorites include clowns, knights, princesses, fairies, cowboys and cowgirls, pirates, and action heroes. Help him create costumes from what you have on hand or select additional items at a thrift shop. Looking for ideas? Check out the delightful photos in *Make Believe: A Book of Costume and Fantasy*, featuring costumes made with household items and much imagination.

Old Faithfuls

Bye-Bye Baby, Hello Dolly: As your granddaughter rehearses for her adolescent and grown-up roles, Barbie dolls and her counterparts may usurp baby dolls in her play. There is an extensive collection of clothes and accessories available to equip Barbie for her busy social life and many career options. As your granddaughter acts out these roles, play along with her, modeling appropriate dialogue and actions. Although some criticize Barbie for presenting an unrealistic body image and emphasis upon possessions, others counter that she shows girls the variety of career roles available to them, comes in multiethnic versions, and provides the pleasant and therapeutic fantasy of being an assertive, beautiful young woman.

Another popular doll these days is the American Girl doll. The company has 18-inch dolls that, unlike Barbie, are younger and more rounded. The selection includes dolls from American historical periods and books that go along with the dolls. As with Barbie, many clothes and props are available.

WHAT YOU NEED: *dolls, clothes and accessories*

Superheroes: For enacting adolescent and grown-up macho roles, your grandson can choose from many action and superhero figures. As he dramatizes action-packed, often highly violent themes in which he vanquishes the evil enemy, he feels powerful and able to express his own strong emotions in an acceptable way. If you can tolerate all the gory details and frequent slayings, you may decide to play along with him, perhaps even assuming the role of the bad guy before being annihilated.

WHAT YOU NEED: *action figures and accessories*

School Days: If you play school with your grandchild, you will gain insight into his feelings about this increasingly important part of his life. Create a classroom with a table, chairs, and chalkboard. Add paper, pencils, chalk, and books. He may like to be the teacher, who asks you difficult questions, reads to the class, or gives detailed instructions about how to complete a worksheet. You can throw in a bit of humor by being the naughty kid who won't pay attention and makes too much noise.

WHAT YOU NEED: *table, chairs, chalkboard, paper, pencils, chalk, books*

New Twists

Buried Treasure: A pirate theme is sure to generate action-packed adventures. Cut out swords from heavy cardboard and cover the blades with foil. Create a treasure chest by covering a small box in gold foil and filling it with coins and shiny jewels. Draw a map that shows where buried treasure can be found. Dress the pirate in a bandana, eye patch, and pirate hat. To minimize overly aggressive sword fights, focus on sailing the ship to far distant shores and searching for buried treasure. The couch or picnic table can be the pirate ship. Dig for buried treasure in the sandbox or under a pile of cushions.

WHAT YOU NEED: *cardboard, scissors, silver and gold foil, bandanas, eye patches, small box, coins, bead, shovel*

Act It Out: This guessing game encourages your grandchild to pretend to be a specific animal. Purchase a set of animal cards or make your own by gluing animal pictures from magazines or clipart on index cards. The first player draws a card and acts out the movements and sounds that animal makes. The other players try to guess what animal it is. The person who guesses correctly gets to have the next turn.

WHAT YOU NEED: *set of animal cards or index cards, animal pictures, glue*

Mirror, Mirror, on the Wall: To go along with her glamorous outfits, your granddaughter may like to beautify herself with makeup and new hairstyles. Create a beauty salon with cape, brushes, combs, clips, curlers, squirt bottle filled with water, hair dryer, ribbons, and hand mirror (no scissors please!).

Do manicures with a bowl of water, hand lotion, and children's fingernail polish. For makeup, assemble a supply of discarded blush, lip gloss, face power, rouge, toilet water, and cleansing cream. An easy alternative is to purchase a makeup, hairstyling, or manicure kit designed for young girls.

WHAT YOU NEED: *cape, brushes, combs, clips, curlers, squirt bottle filled with water, hair dryer, ribbons, hand mirror; bowl, water, hand lotion, children's fingernail polish; blush, lip gloss, face power, rouge, toilet water, cleansing cream*

The Puppets Perform: It's fun to put on a puppet show. A stage can be as simple as a card table turned on its side for the puppeteer to hide behind. Or you can cut out a large window in an appliance box, tack on a curtain, and have your grandchild crawl inside to perform. Act out familiar stories or improvise your own. *The Little Pigs Puppet Book* has step-by-step directions for putting on a full-scale puppet show. Although you can purchase many delightful puppets, you may enjoy creating your own, using one of these methods:

- **Paper bag puppets:** Make puppets from lunch bags. Draw a face on the top third of the bag, stuff this part with newspaper, and secure with a rubber band for the head. Cut out two holes on either side of the bag for thumb and index finger to go through. Glue on paper strips or yarn for hair, arms, legs, or a tail. Or make a talking puppet by using the fold in the bag as the mouth. Put fingers around the bottom fold and make the fold open and shut for a mouth. Glue teeth or a tongue inside the mouth, or draw on big red lips, one above and one below the fold.

  WHAT YOU NEED: *lunch bags, newspaper, rubber bands, glue, yarn, construction paper, markers*

- **Stick puppets:** Stick puppets are a good way to act out a classic story. Draw the story characters on lightweight cardboard, such as file folders. Three to 4 inches tall is a good size. Cut out and glue on craft sticks or cardboard strips. If you don't want to draw the characters, you can trace or photocopy figures from storybooks or find templates online to color and cut out. I found many of these when I googled "preschool templates."

  WHAT YOU NEED: *lightweight cardboard, glue, craft sticks*

9

Let's Cook

Making Special Treats and Cute Creations

"Let's make the cake for Granddad's birthday party," exclaimed 3-year-old Emerson and 7-year-old Jenna. Of course I agreed enthusiastically. After all, what could go wrong with this simple project? First, Emerson broke

Let's Grandparent: Activity Guide for Young Grandchildren, pages 141–160
Copyright © 2008 by Information Age Publishing
All rights of reproduction in any form reserved.

the eggs into a bowl. So what if there were traces of shells in the cake! It wouldn't affect the favor. Jenna commandeered the mixer and was doing fine until she too quickly removed the whirring beaters from the batter. So what if batter splattered all over the place! We could clean it up. Then in our haste to remove the cake from the pan, it broke into several pieces. Jenna whispered, "We won't tell anyone!" and quickly plastered the fractured cake back together with gooey chocolate frosting. As we added the 70 candles to the cake, Jenna and Emerson had different ideas about their placement. So what if the cake had multiple holes all over the top from their extensive rearrangements! It still looked delicious. We had our share of laughs as we created this uniquely delicious cake; so really, nothing went wrong, did it?

Why Try It?

Cooking with your grandchild is a fun-filled recipe for memorable good times together. Start with the anticipation of tasting, pour in the pleasure of preparing, sprinkle on the surprise of discovery, and top with the pride of accomplishment. Stir it all together with a pinch of good humor and a pint of patience. The result is a deliciously successful experience that you will want to repeat again and again.

Along with all the pleasures of cooking, your grandchild is developing a skill that has lifelong usefulness. She experiences pride in learning such a useful, grown-up task. A great sense of accomplishment comes from completing seemingly simple tasks. When my grandson was 4, he worked diligently for a good 20 minutes slicing a huge chunk of cheese and beamed with pleasure at his newfound skill.

Cooking together is a backdoor way to encourage healthy eating habits. Nutrition advice to eat a variety of foods and limit sweets runs counter to children's natural tendencies. They typically prefer candy to carrots and seem programmed to be cautious about new foods. Cooking can encourage your grandchild to become more adventuresome and, at least, give the new food a taste. She may be more enthusiastic about tasting the papaya she sliced or the broccoli with the creamy cheese sauce she prepared.

Cooking is a fun way to strengthen science, math, and reading skills. Abstract science concepts become concrete as your grandchild observes physical changes that result from combining, heating, and cooling food. Counting, measuring, sequencing, and using time concepts are an integral part of the cooking process. Reading may be as simple as checking the labels on boxes and cans or as complex as following directions in a cookbook.

Snapshot of Development

Fine motor development is a major determinant of which cooking experiences are suitable for your grandchild. Since finger dexterity takes many years to develop, the toddler will need to use primarily whole hand and arm movements. As she gets older, she is able to do tasks that take more precise fine motor skills.

Since toddlers typically have short attention spans, short and simple recipes that can be eaten immediately work best. Older children can persist through a more complex recipe and find it easier to delay eating what they have made until it has cooked or cooled. As they get older, children also learn to appreciate the need for carefully following directions in order to end up with an edible product.

Tips for Cooking Experiences

Enhance the educational potential. Capitalize on opportunities to teach science, math, and reading concepts that arise as you cook. Encourage your grandchild to observe and talk about physical processes and changes that are occurring. Talk about all the bubbles and steam from the boiling water or how the apples are getting mushy as they cook. Point out how the strainer traps the macaroni but lets the water through. Count the ice cubes as you drop them in the gelatin. Check to see for how long and at what temperature to bake the cake. Decide what half a cup is and compare teaspoons with tablespoons. Figure out how to double a recipe or make only half. Point out the words on food packages, and read them together. Use recipes with illustrations and simple text. Then encourage your grandchild to "read" the directions. As you check each step in the written recipe, even nonreaders start to focus on the print and try to identify a few words.

Use resilient recipes. With all the potential recipes available, which should you choose when planning cooking experiences for your grandchild? You doubtless have your favorite recipes. Look them over to see which parts your grandchild can do. If the recipe is too fragile, takes a long time to prepare, or requires too many special skills, save it for when she is older. Much of the time, choose resilient recipes that are hard to mess up— ones in which the exact proportions are not critical, extra stirring is okay, and special techniques are not essential. If the French toast has too much milk or too little cinnamon, it still tastes good. Even if you stir and stir and stir the instant pudding, the texture and taste remain the same.

Keep it simple. Look for recipes that allow your grandchild to do most of the preparation. The goal is to let her work as independently as possible, while you serve as facilitator. She wants to be involved in doing, not just watching. If the task is too difficult or frustrating, you may end up doing most of the cooking, while she quickly losses interest and wanders off. Perhaps you can do the most difficult tasks, such as grating carrots or cubing meat, ahead of time.

Set clear guidelines. Since cooking is not a time for random experimenting, your grandchild must be willing to follow directions and accept your rules. Talk about these limits before you start. If this becomes a problem, put cooking on hold and substitute open-ended sensory or art experiences.

Organize for success. Big messes, injuries, or an inedible product are potential problems when you cook with your grandchild. The best defense is upfront organization. Supersize mixing bowls and measuring cups to minimize spills. Assemble all ingredients and utensils on a tray for quick access, so you never need to turn your back on her. It only takes a few seconds for her to add a cup of salt to the cookie dough or spill a gallon of milk.

Still, messes are bound to happen from time to time. There's no use crying over all that spilt milk or flour on the floor. Have sponges and towels readily available for quick cleanup. While the cake bakes, your grandchild can wash dishes and wipe off the table and chairs with a soapy sponge.

Pick the right time. When to cook? Probably not at 6:00 when everyone is hungry and in a hurry to eat. And probably not on Thanksgiving morning when you are rushing to get the turkey in the oven. I often choose a time after my grandchildren have eaten, so they can focus more on stirring the batter than licking the spoon. We still like to taste as we go, provided, of course, it contains no raw eggs. Slow down and remember that for your grandchild cooking may be the main event, while eating runs a distant second.

Look for impromptu opportunities. In addition to your carefully planned cooking experiences, do include your grandchild in spur-of-the-moment cooking opportunities. Look for safe and simple ways that she can participate. She can cut up a banana or cheese, break an orange into sections, whip the mashed potatoes, or stir the cheese and milk into the macaroni. When I was preparing pazole, Jenna sniffed the spices and liquid smoke, studied the can labels, and boldly sampled the hominy.

Make personalized portions. Some recipes lend themselves to each person assembling his or her version from prepared ingredients. Put out small bowls of each ingredient, and let everyone choose which to include on his or her customized portions. When I did this with tacos, I set out refried beans, grated cheese, meat sauce, diced tomatoes, shredded lettuce, sour cream, guacamole dip, salsa, and two types of taco shells. My grandchil-

Play It Safe: Careful supervision and realistic rules can minimize accidents. Putting food in or out of the oven should be your responsibility. Using a child-size table is safer than having her stand on a chair to reach the kitchen counter. An electric skillet on a low table allows easy observing at a safe distance. It's more stable than a hot plate. Since sharp knives are too dangerous for young children, substitute a wave slicer for cutting fruits, veggies, and cheese. It doesn't have a sharp edge and makes interesting designs.

Any time your grandchild is near a stove or cooking appliance, remind her about the potential dangers of burns, and stay on code-red alert. Everyone should wash their hands before starting to cook and after handling raw meat, poultry, or eggs. When close supervision is needed, limit to one grandchild at a time.

dren had at least as much fun creating their tacos as they did eating them. Honoring Jake's request to repeat this experience, the next week we made individual pizzas and fruit salads using this make-your-own approach.

Reach across the miles. Even though you live far from your grandchild, you can share cooking experiences with her. Send her care packages in the mail with items that travel well. Good choices are slightly soft, yet firm cookies, hard candies, firm-textured cakes, candied popcorn, and flavored nuts. Include the recipe and a personal note describing interesting or funny incidents that occurred while preparing it. For your older grandchild, send a mix-in-a-bag for cookies, brownies, or pancakes. Measure and mix together the dry ingredients and seal in an air-tight container. Enclose a step-by-step illustrated guide that your grandchild and a parent can use to complete the recipe.

Activities

Most of the recipes in this chapter are easy to prepare and are kid-pleasers that still rank high on nutrition. The three categories of recipes are:

- Healthy favorites
- Treats for special occasions
- Cute creations

Healthy favorites are nutritious recipes that children typically enjoy. Directions illustrate how to maximize your grandchild's participation in each step of the process. Treats for special occasions are easy-to-make versions of traditional recipes—great for including your grandchild in holiday and birthday preparations. Cute creations have special kid appeal. A salad resembling a rocket lets her imagination take flight. A licorice stick in witch's brew stirs fantasies of magical potions.

To expand your repertoire of children's recipes, look for children's cookbooks that have photographs of the finished product (e.g., *My First Cookbook*) and pictorial, step-by-step illustrations for your grandchild to follow (e.g., *Pretend Soup and Other Real Recipes*). For older children, *Cool Kids Cook* provides a variety of fun recipes with convenient spiral binding, easy-to-follow directions, and colorful illustrations. Also, check the many websites that feature child-friendly recipes (e.g., *www.allrecipes.com* and *www. recipe-source.com/misc/kids*).

Two-Year-Olds

Developmental Insights

I would wait until that second birthday before initiating food preparation experiences. Even then, with her short attention span and need for instant gratification, recipes with just a few ingredients and short preparation time work best. Since fine motor skills are in the early stages of development, look for tasks she can do with her whole hand: dropping strawberries in a blender, stirring gelatin into warm water or dumping sugar in a mixing bowl. With your assistance, she can spread peanut butter on toast, cut a banana, or pour milk into batter.

Cooking provides opportunities for sensory exploration. Have your grandchild smell the vanilla and cinnamon. Listen to the sound of popcorn or the whir of a blender. Before making a fruit salad, feel a prickly pineapple, a smooth apple, and a hairy kiwi. Taste a pinch of sugar, salt, butter, or lemon juice.

The autonomous 2-year-old may resist your guidance and want instead to add a whole box of salt or a quart of milk to the bowl. To minimize such problems, measure the ingredients ahead of time. If she craves greater freedom, let her do some pretend cooking. Set out small bowls of salt, flour, water, and dried rice. Provide measuring cups and spoons. Let her mix them together in a large bowl in whatever proportions she chooses. Or, take it outside where she can mix up a delicious concoction of sand, water, grass, and pebbles.

Healthy Favorites

Fruit and Veggie Scrub: When you are preparing apples, carrots, potatoes, or cucumbers, your grandchild can clean them for you. Put a little water in the sink, add a sponge or vegetable brush, and let her scrub away as long as she likes and dry them with a towel.

WHAT YOU NEED: *apples, carrots, potatoes, or cucumbers; water, sponge or vegetable brush, towel*

Sweet and Crunchy Toast: Cinnamon toast, an all-time favorite, is easy to prepare. Put sugar and cinnamon in a container with holes large enough for easy sprinkling. Tightly secure the top, and have your grandchild shake it until well mixed. Under your supervision, she can put bread in the toaster and push down the lever. Let her spread soft butter or margarine on the warm toast with a table knife and sprinkle on the cinnamon-sugar mixture.

WHAT YOU NEED: *2 tablespoons sugar*
1 tablespoon cinnamon
1 tablespoon butter
2 pieces of bread
Shaker, toaster, table knife

Whir Away: Make nutritious fruit smoothies with your grandchild's favorite fruit. She can put the milk, yogurt, and small pieces of fruit in the blender, put on the top, and, with your guidance, turn on the blender.

WHAT YOU NEED: *½ cup milk*
½ cup vanilla yogurt
½ cup fresh or frozen strawberries, blueberries, peaches, or bananas
Measuring cup, blender

Pretty Parfait: With just a few ingredients, easy stirring, and fast results, this is a sure winner for your toddler. She can mix together the milk and pudding with a wire whisk. For a parfait effect, layer the pudding and fruit in a clear plastic cup.

WHAT YOU NEED: *1 package instant pudding*
2 cups milk
Strawberries, pineapple tidbits, or blueberries
Bowl, whisk, clear plastic cups

My Mix: This trail mix is great for taking on picnics, walks, and car rides. Set out each ingredient in a separate bowl. Your grandchild can scoop her choice of ingredients into small zip-lock plastic bags.

WHAT YOU NEED: *Raisins*
Dried pineapple and banana chips
Peanuts or walnuts
Dried cereal, such as Cheerios or Chex
Pretzel sticks, broken in half
Small bowls, big spoon, zip-lock bags

Marshmallow Melt: After playing outside on a cold day, a mug of hot chocolate hits the spot. Warm a mug of milk in the microwave. Then your grandchild can put chocolate mix into the milk and stir until combined. Have her add a few miniature marshmallows and stir them as they melt.

WHAT YOU NEED: *1 cup of milk*
2 teaspoons chocolate mix
5 miniature marshmallows
Spoon, mug, microwave

No-Drip Frozen Treats: Avoid the messy dripping that too often plagues toddlers when they eat popsicles with this no-drip recipe. Combine the water and gelatin in blender. Let your grandchild add the yogurt and turn on the blender. Pour into a popsicle mold or small paper cups with a craft stick in each. Freeze until firm.

WHAT YOU NEED: *1 cup boiling water*
3 oz. package fruit-flavored gelatin
Cup of vanilla yogurt
Blender, measuring cup, popsicle mold or paper cups,
    craft sticks

Treats for Special Occasions

No-Bake Pumpkin Pie: This quick and easy pie is a great addition for a Halloween party or Thanksgiving dinner. Open the pumpkin pie can and pudding mix, and measure the milk. Your grandchild can mix them together. Pour into a graham cracker pie shell and chill.

WHAT YOU NEED: *1 16 oz. can pumpkin pie mix*
1 small package vanilla instant pudding
1 cup milk
Graham cracker pie shell
Measuring cup, bowl, spoon

Sweet Potato Bake: Here is a sweet potato recipe for Thanksgiving dinner that is simple enough for a toddler to make and sweet enough that she will ask for seconds. Put drained sweet potatoes in a large bowl and have your grandchild smash them with a potato masher. Melt butter in microwave and then have her mix in the other ingredients. Pour into the sweet potatoes and have her stir it together. After you put this mixture into a casserole dish, she can drop the marshmallows over the top. Warm in the oven at 325 degrees until the marshmallows begin to melt and brown slightly (about 35 minutes).

WHAT YOU NEED: *3 cups cooked sweet potatoes*
⅓ cup milk
3 tablespoons butter
¾ cup sugar
1 teaspoon vanilla
½ teaspoon salt
2 eggs
2 cups miniature marshmallows
Bowl, potato masher, measuring cup, microwave, casserole dish

Jack-O-Lantern Treats: This is a good recipe to do at Halloween. Color softened cream cheese with food coloring. Let your grandchild spread the cream cheese on a toasted English muffin and then create a Jack-o-lantern face with black olives. Add a celery slice on the top for a stem.

WHAT YOU NEED: *English muffin*
½ cup cream cheese
4 drops orange food coloring
¼ cup pitted black olives
One-inch slice of celery
Toaster, table knife

Cute Creations

Frogs on Logs: This nutritious cream cheese treat may inspire pretend play, especially if you chant and act out *Five Speckled Frogs.** Soften cream cheese by warming it briefly in the microwave, and then stir it until smooth and creamy. Let your grandchild use her fingers or a plastic knife to spread it on 6-inch stalks of celery and add five grapes to each.

WHAT YOU NEED: *2 stalks of celery*
2 tablespoons cream cheese
10 green grapes
Microwave, plastic knife

* Five speckled frogs sitting on a log
Eating some most delicious bugs.
One jumped into the pool,   *(Take one grape off.)*
Where it was nice and cool.
Now there are four speckled frogs.

Repeat this verse for four, three, two, one, and no speckled frogs.

Blast Off: Create a rocket ship that is posed to blast off into space. Place the banana in the middle of a pineapple ring. Secure with a toothpick. To represent the fiery takeoff, arrange a ring of red pepper slivers radiating out from the pineapple. After you do one, see if your grandchild wants to create her own rocket.

WHAT YOU NEED: *Half a banana, peeled*
                        Pineapple ring
                        Red pepper
                        Knife, toothpicks, plate

Fruity Faces: Your grandchild can create a face with food. Spoon yogurt into a small serving bowl and arrange fruit on a plate. Show her how to use grapes or blueberries for eyes and a nose and raisins or a wedge of kiwi for a mouth. Then encourage her to make a face in her bowl of yogurt.

WHAT YOU NEED: *½ cup plain or vanilla yogurt*
                        Grapes, blueberries, strawberries, raisins, or kiwi wedges
                        Small serving bowls

Three- and Four-Year-Olds

Developmental Insights

Your grandchild is ready for recipes with more ingredients and longer preparation time. Advances in fine motor abilities mean she can do many more tasks. Although you may still want to measure ingredients in advance, she can dump them in and do most of the stirring. With careful supervision, she can cut soft items with a table knife or wave slicer. She can even break eggs without too much mess if she cracks them on the bottom of a bowl.

She can grasp concrete science concepts and add many cooking terms to her rapidly expanding vocabulary. Think of all the possibilities just in making gelatin: *steam* from the *boiling* water, *dissolving* the mix, changing from a *liquid* to a *solid*. She may also be interested in books about food and gain much from a trip to a bakery or farmer's market.

Healthy Favorites

Creamy Frozen Pops: This nutritious frozen treat beats popsicles cold. Have your grandchild mix the juice and yogurt together with a whisk in a large measuring cup. Then she can pour it into small paper cups with a craft stick in each. Put a ½-inch banana slice in the bottom of the cup to hold the stick upright while freezing. Or you can cover each cup with a square of aluminum foil and punch the stick through a hole in the center.

WHAT YOU NEED: *⅓ cup concentrated orange juice*
1 cup vanilla yogurt
Banana or aluminum foil
Whisk, large measuring cup, knife, paper cups, craft sticks

Painted French Toast: French toast is a good choice for the young chef. The proportions need not be exact, it is quick to make, and liked by most children. Your grandchild can break the eggs by knocking them on the bottom of a large, shallow bowl. After beating the eggs slightly, she can add the milk and cinnamon and stir with a whisk. Then she can dip each slice of bread in the egg mixture and flip it over. You will need to put the bread in a hot skillet lightly coated with vegetable oil and brown on both sides.

To jazz it up a bit, reserve a small amount of the egg yolk in a small bowl and add a few drops of blue food coloring. Use a small paint brush to decorate the toast before grilling. My grandchildren like to write their initials on the toast or draw a face.

WHAT YOU NEED: *2 eggs*
½ cup milk
Pinch of cinnamon
4 slices of bread
Vegetable oil
Food coloring
Bowls, whisk, pancake turner, small paint brush

Cinnamon Applesauce: Observing the physical changes of the apples as they cook adds to the excitement of making applesauce. Start by having your grandchild wash the apples. For a smooth applesauce, peel the apples. Leave the peels on for a chunky and more nutritious alternative. After you core the apples, your grandchild can cut them up with a wave slicer, put them in a large sauce pan, cover with water, and cook until very soft, about

10–20 minutes. Mash with a potato masher. Stir in the sugar. Sprinkle cinnamon lightly over the applesauce before serving.

WHAT YOU NEED: *Four apples*
½ cup water
4 tablespoons sugar
1 teaspoon cinnamon
Apple corer, wave slicer, large sauce pan, fork, spoon,
   potato masher

The Best Blueberry Pancakes: This is my grandson's favorite breakfast. I take the easy way and use a mix. Measure the mix and water or milk and let your grandchild stir them together in a large mixing bowl. Use an electric skillet on a low table for safe and easy viewing. If you put the pancake mixture in a small pitcher, your grandchild can pour the mix into the skillet and add blueberries. She can observe the bubbles forming and see how you flip them over to brown the other side. We first tried this recipe after reading *Curious George Makes Pancakes*.

WHAT YOU NEED: *1 cup pancake mix*
¾ cup water or milk
½ cup fresh or frozen blueberries
Measuring cup, mixing bowl, electric skillet, pancake turner,
   pitcher

Grammy's Granola: This makes a nutritious breakfast cereal or snack. Your grandchild can mix the first six ingredients in a large bowl, then mix the honey, oil, and vanilla together and add to oatmeal mixture. You may need to help with the final mixing. Spray a cookie sheet with vegetable oil, and spread granola evenly over it. Bake in a 300-degree oven for 30 minutes, stirring occasionally. After it has cooled, your grandchild can add the raisins and walnuts. Store in an air-tight container.

WHAT YOU NEED: *4 cups uncooked oatmeal*
1 cup wheat germ
1 cup shredded coconut
1 cup sunflower seeds
1 cup powdered milk
4 teaspoons cinnamon
½ cup honey
½ cup vegetable oil
4 teaspoons vanilla
½ cup walnuts
1 cup raisins
Vegetable oil spray, cookie sheet, spoon, oven

Count-to-Ten Gelatin: Since my grandchildren like to eat what they make immediately, we solve the delay problem with gelatin by using this super quickset method. Measure 2 cups boiling water into a shallow bowl and let your grandchild add the flavored gelatin and stir until completely dissolved. Then count 10 ice cubes as she adds them to the gelatin and stir them until melted. Repeat a second time with 10 more ice cubes. Pour the gelatin into a large measuring cup and let her pour the gelatin into 10 small plastic cups. Count as she adds 10 blueberries to each cup. Put the cups in the refrigerator and set the timer for 10 minutes—just long enough to read a book or play a game of cards. Check the gelatin, and repeat for another 10 minutes if needed.

WHAT YOU NEED: *6 oz. package flavored gelatin*
2 cups boiling water
20 ice cubes
2 cups frozen blueberries
Bowl, spoon, measuring cup, plastic cups, timer

Creamy Fruit Salad: Introduce your grandchild to new fruits with this recipe. She can use a wave slicer to cut up the cheese and fruit and mix them together in a large bowl with the orange juice and yogurt.

WHAT YOU NEED: *Two pieces of stick cheese*
⅓ cup seedless grapes
½ banana
½ cup kiwi, mango, papaya, or tangelo
2 tablespoons concentrated orange juice
½ cup plain yogurt
Wave slicer, large bowl, spoon

Treats for Special Occasions

Fourth-of-July Pie: This makes a perfect dessert for a hot Independence Day celebration. Mix yogurt and whipped topping. Pour into graham cracker crust. Decorate the top with blueberries and strawberries. Sprinkle on colored sugar to simulate fireworks. Cover with foil and put in the freezer, but let it thaw slightly before serving.

WHAT YOU NEED: *16 oz. vanilla yogurt*
9 oz. softened whipped topping
½ cup blueberries
½ cup strawberries
Graham cracker crust
Mixing bowl, spoon, foil
Colored sugar

Holiday Cookies: Make cookie dough using a basic sugar cookie recipe. Or speed up the process by using ready-made, refrigerated cookie dough. Because mixing stiff dough and cutting out shapes is difficult for preschoolers, I usually do this part myself and then have my grandchildren help with decorating the cookies. For a simple frosting, your grandchild can stir together powdered sugar, water, and food coloring. She can apply the icing to the baked cookies with a table knife or small paintbrush and decorate with sugar sprinkles, cinnamon hearts, M&Ms, or dried cranberries.

WHAT YOU NEED: *Baked sugar cookies*
1 cup sifted powdered sugar
1 tablespoon water (enough to make it easy to spread)
A few drops of food coloring
Sugar sprinkles, cinnamon hearts, M&Ms, or dried cranberries
Mixing bowl, table knife or small paintbrush

Campfire Favorite: S'mores are a traditional, yummy treat for campouts. Roast marshmallows over a campfire until soft and lightly brown. Put four squares of chocolate on a graham cracker, add the marshmallow, and top with another graham cracker.

WHAT YOU NEED. *5 large marshmallows*
2 plain Hershey chocolate bars
10 graham cracker squares
Campfire, roasting sticks

Seasonal Sandwiches: Use cookie cutters to make sandwiches in holiday shapes—hearts for Valentine's Day, bells for Christmas, stars of David for Hanukkah, and pumpkins for Halloween. Soften cream cheese and add a few drops of food coloring in a traditional color for this holiday. Have your grandchild cut out the holiday shapes from sandwich bread and use a table knife to spread the cream cheese on them, making little open-faced sandwiches.

WHAT YOU NEED: *Bread*
Cream cheese
Food coloring
Holiday cookie cutters, table knife

Cute Creations

Sailboat Salad: This is one salad your grandchild will love to make and eat. Cut the cheese in half diagonally to make two right-angle triangles. Make a sail by pressing the two cheese triangles together around a large toothpick.

Anchor it into the deck—half of a canned pear or peach with concave side up. Top the toothpick with a miniature marshmallow. Float on a lettuce leaf. My 4-year-old granddaughter enjoyed making several sailboats but did need help with fastening the cheese on the toothpick.

WHAT YOU NEED: *Slices of processed cheese*
Canned peaches or pears
Miniature marshmallows
Lettuce leaves
Plate, toothpicks, knife

Tinker Toy Treats: Your grandchild can create dramatic, edible structures using pretzel sticks to connect marshmallows. Demonstrate how to push pretzel sticks deeply into marshmallows and use them to connect to each other in intricate ways. Use as a centerpiece for dinner, and then eat for dessert.

WHAT YOU NEED: *1 package marshmallows*
1 package pretzel sticks

Bird Nests: These are fun to make for Easter or a celebration of spring. Melt chocolate chips and butter or margarine in microwave. Using a large bowl, pour this mixture over chow mein noodles, and mix until well coated. Spray vegetable oil on several small paper bowls, and place generous spoonfuls of the mixture in each. While still warm, form into nests. Put in the freezer for ten minutes to harden. Gently remove from the bowl. Fill with jelly beans or chocolate eggs.

WHAT YOU NEED: *4 oz. chocolate chips*
2 tablespoons butter or margarine
5 oz. can chow mein noodles broken into small pieces
Jelly beans or chocolate eggs
Microwave, large bowl, vegetable oil spray, small bowls

Five- to Eight-Year-Olds

Developmental Insights

Your grandchild can now do much of the mixing, measuring, and cutting needed in preparing foods. You should still handle any hot foods, especially removing them from the oven.

Do encourage your grandchild to prepare main dishes, vegetables, breads, and beverages, not just desserts. Have her try out special family recipes and your simplified versions of those all-time children's favorites, like grilled cheese sandwiches, chili, tacos, or spaghetti. To increase her interest in preparing fruits and veggies, start with a trip to the store to select fresh ones from the produce department.

A children's cookbook with simple recipes, photos, and picture guides fosters independence and utilizes emerging reading skills. You could also create your own rebus recipe cards. Write a simplified version of a recipe on a file folder and draw pictures to replace some of the words in the directions. For example, draw pictures of the ingredients and indicate how much of each with pictures of measuring spoons or cups.

Healthy Favorites

Personal Pizza: Each of you can make a pizza with your personal preferences for toppings. Spray vegetable oil on 5-inch foil squares. Have your grandchild put a refrigerator biscuit on the foil and flatten it with her hand or a rolling pin. She can spoon on the pizza sauce, add her favorite toppings, and top with grated mozzarella cheese. Bake in 450-degree oven for about 10 minutes. My grandson made "monster faces" with green peppers and black olives.

WHAT YOU NEED: *1 can of refrigerator biscuits*
Small can pizza sauce
Grated mozzarella cheese
Pepperoni or hot dog slices
¼ cup chopped onion
¼ diced green pepper
¼ cup sliced mushrooms
Diced black olives
¼ cup pineapple tidbits
Vegetable oil spray, foil, rolling pin, spoon, oven

Carrot Coins: These carrots are sweet enough to tempt even your veggie-avoiding grandchild. After you have scraped the carrots, your grandchild can slice them into thin rounds. Cook carrots in ½ cup water about 15 minutes or until tender. Add orange juice, butter, brown sugar, and a pinch of salt. Simmer on low, stirring frequently until most of the liquid has disappeared.

WHAT YOU NEED: *4 carrots*
⅓ cup orange juice
2 tablespoons butter
2 tablespoons brown sugar
Pinch of salt
Knife, sauce pan, spoon

Apple Dipper: Apples and peanut butter are a winning combination. Simmer peanut butter, water, and honey in a sauce pan over low heat until blended, stirring constantly. Add vanilla and powdered milk. Cut up apple wedges to dip in the peanut butter mixture.

WHAT YOU NEED:
½ cup peanut butter
¼ cup water
¼ cup honey
½ teaspoon vanilla
2 tablespoons powdered milk
Measuring cup, spoon, sauce pan, knife or wave slicer

Apple Crisp: Easier than pie and just as tasty, serve it topped with a scoop of vanilla ice cream for a special dessert. Heat the oven to 375 degrees and grease a 9 × 9 pan. Peel the apples and core with apple corer. Mix together the apple slices with the lemon juice, raisins, flour, and cinnamon. Place the apple mixture in the greased pan and sprinkle the water over it. Mix together all the topping ingredients and press evenly over the apple mixture. Bake for 25 minutes.

WHAT YOU NEED:

Apple mixture:	*Topping:*
8 apples	*1½ cups rolled oats*
Juice of one lemon	*½ cup flour*
¾ cup raisins	*½ cup brown sugar*
2 tablespoons flour	*½ cup melted margarine or butter*
1 teaspoon cinnamon	*2 teaspoons cinnamon*
2 tablespoons water	*½ teaspoon salt*

Apple corer, knife, spoon, mixing bowls, 9 × 9 pan, oven

Mystery Muffins: Add a bit of amusement to muffin-making. Mix the dry ingredients together in a large bowl. In a separate bowl mix the eggs, milk, vanilla, and oil. Stir this mixture into the dry ingredients. Line muffin pan with cupcake liners. Fill each liner ⅔ full. Add one type of fruit to each. Bake 20 minutes at 375 degrees. Remove from the pan to cool. What fruit will you find hidden in your muffin? Take a bite to solve the mystery.

WHAT YOU NEED:
¾ cup whole wheat flour
¾ cup white flour
2 teaspoons baking powder
½ teaspoon baking soda
½ teaspoon salt
½ cup sugar

(continued)

> *2 eggs*
> *1 cup milk*
> *½ teaspoon vanilla*
> *4 tablespoons olive oil*
> *Blueberries and strawberries (fresh or frozen)*
> *Slices of banana and kiwi*
> *Mixing bowls, muffin pans, spoon, cupcake liner, oven*

Treats for Special Occasions

Latkes (Potato Pancakes): Celebrate Hanukkah with a traditional meal of latkes and applesauce. Peel, core, and coarsely grate the potatoes. Mix with a beaten egg and flour. Fry tablespoon-size pancakes in hot vegetable oil, browning on both sides. Serve topped with applesauce.

WHAT YOU NEED: *2 medium potatoes*
1 egg
¼ cup flour
¼ cup vegetable oil
Vegetable peeler, knife, spoon, frying pan

Witch's Brew: This is the perfect beverage for Halloween celebrations. Mix cranberry and apple juice in a large saucepan. Add a cinnamon stick and simmer for 10 minutes. After it cools, serve in clear plastic cups decorated with Halloween stickers and a licorice stick topped with a black gumdrop.

WHAT YOU NEED: *2 cups cranberry juice*
2 cups apple juice
1 cinnamon stick
4 licorice sticks
4 black gumdrops
Large sauce pan, clear plastic cups, Halloween stickers

Foolproof Fudge: Your grandchild may like to make candy for Valentine's Day gifts. Here is a recipe for fudge that is easy to make and guaranteed to taste delicious every time. In a large saucepan, combine evaporated milk, sugar, salt, and butter. Bring to a rolling boil over medium-low heat and cook, stirring constantly, for 5 minutes. Remove from heat; add chocolate chips and stir until melted. Quickly stir in marshmallow cream, vanilla, and walnuts. Pour into a buttered 8-inch square baking pan; spread to make an even layer. Let cool and refrigerate until firm (30–45 minutes). Cut into 1-inch squares, and store in the refrigerator.

WHAT YOU NEED: *5 oz. can evaporated milk*
1⅓ cups sugar
¼ teaspoon salt
¼ cup butter
6 oz. package semisweet chocolate chips
¾ cup marshmallow cream
1 teaspoon vanilla
½ cup chopped walnuts or pecans
Saucepan, measuring cup, spoon, 8-inch square pan, knife

Cute Creations

Snail Snacks: These tiny sandwiches are fun to make for an afternoon snack, served up with a glass of milk. Use a rolling pin to flatten a piece of bread. Spread with peanut butter or cream cheese. Roll it up like a jelly roll and slice into bit-size sandwiches. When I told Jake these were called pinwheel sandwiches, he replied that the swirls looked more like snails, so that became their new name.

WHAT YOU NEED: *2 oz. cream cheese or peanut butter*
2 slices of bread
Rolling pin, knife

Chocolate Spiders: Make these fun treats for a Halloween party. Melt chocolate in microwave for two minutes at 50% power, stirring after first minute. Stir in marshmallows, return to microwave, and heat on 50% power until melted. Mix until thoroughly blended. Drop by tablespoonfuls onto wax paper. Cut licorice into 2-inch pieces, cut each piece in half lengthwise, and press eight pieces into each mound for the legs. Use two M&Ms on each spider for eyes. Refrigerate about 20 minutes.

WHAT YOU NEED: *12 oz. semisweet chocolate chips*
1 cup miniature marshmallows
Black licorice sticks
Chocolate M&Ms
Microwave, glass mixing bowl, spoons, wax paper

Peanut Butter Bugs: Your grandchild can use this recipe to make all kinds of bugs. My grandson made Charlotte, her web, and a fly, while my granddaughter made a beetle and a bee. Use your hands to mix together the peanut butter, powdered milk, graham cracker crumbs, and honey. Then make 1-inch balls and roll in more graham cracker crumbs. Create bugs by adding pieces of chow mein noodle for antennae, raisins for eyes, and almonds for wings. Enrich the experience by providing pictures of bugs that your grandchild could make.

WHAT YOU NEED: *½ cup peanut butter*
½ cup powdered milk
½ cup graham cracker crumbs
½ cup honey
½ cup chow mein noodles
¼ cup raisins
¼ cup slivered almonds
Mixing bowl, pictures of bugs

10

Let's Celebrate

Launching Birthday and Holiday Traditions

"**W**hat are you going to be for Halloween?" asked Jake. I hadn't dressed up for Halloween in years, but his question got me thinking. I found a long, flowing dress in the back of my closet, bought some wings and a tiara,

Let's Grandparent: Activity Guide for Young Grandchildren, pages 161–189
Copyright © 2008 by Information Age Publishing

and with a wave of my magic wand became a fairy godmother. With my newfound magical powers and a trip to the party store we created an eerie haunted house, complete with jack-o-lanterns, cobwebs, and ghostly mist. On Halloween night I gave out treats, cast magic spells, surprised children with a talking goblin, and had more fun than anyone. All of which goes to show the magical power that grandchildren have. They granted me my wish: to experience this holiday with all my childhood pleasure.

Why Try It?

The awe and excitement that children experience during holiday and birthday celebrations is infectious. During these times, I feel especially blessed to have grandchildren. All those pleasant memories of holidays past come flooding back as I remember family traditions and delightful experiences.

Celebrating holidays with the extended family strengthens bonds by creating happy shared memories and a sense of continuity. Also, they are an appropriate venue for teaching religious traditions associated with holidays. Secular holidays, such as Valentine's Day and Thanksgiving, provide a golden opportunity to encourage expressions of gratitude, affection, and friendship

Doing holiday activities with your grandchild capitalizes on the inherent excitement generated by holidays. Even the reluctant artist, cook, or reader is lured into these activities when they have a holiday theme.

Snapshot of Development

Cognitive development plays a major role in how children understand holiday celebrations. Children under the age of 4 are not likely to have clear memories of previous holidays. An understanding of the historical and religious significance of holidays usually takes even longer. But even the youngest child can enjoy the general excitement and fun associated with celebrations.

Social development is a decisive factor in how your grandchild deals with the mix of family members typically brought together for holiday and birthday celebrations. Younger children usually need extra help in achieving positive social interactions with unfamiliar grown-ups and children, while older ones shift easily from sustained adult conversations to playing cooperatively with children of all ages.

Tips for Holiday and Birthday Celebrations

Enhance family traditions. When extended families get together, it's a chance to renew connections and values. These large gatherings bring home to grandchildren that their family includes grandparents, uncles, aunts, and cousins. Holiday rituals often play a central role in such celebrations. Traditions handed down for many generations provide continuity and shared memories. When a couple marries, it faces the challenge of blending the traditions of two families. Ideally, the result is enriching experiences for all, as each contributes their special rituals and memories. Everyone learns to sing both *Silent Night* and *I Have a Little Dreidel* along with *Jingle Bells* and *Frosty the Snowman,* and to enjoy the experience of new holiday foods.

Sometimes traditions start from a pleasant shared experience that the family resolves to repeat in subsequent years. Once you find the perfect spot for viewing fireworks on Independence Day, you go there every year. Or, you return each year to cut down a Christmas tree at a farm that gives children train rides.

Be proactive in solving potential problems. Expectations for fun and fellowship are high when extended families get together. But mixing together an excited, diverse family group can be a recipe for chaos. Children may become too noisy, bored, or overactive. Young children do best when they can move at their own unrushed pace. They need their regular routine and some quiet downtime. Younger children need consistent monitoring and quick intervention before little frustrations erupt into anger and open warfare.

Another potential problem is that holidays can set the stage for conflict and competition between grandparents, as they vie for the privilege of celebrating with their grandchildren. Both sets of grandparents may want grandchildren to be with them and feel hurt or left out if not the chosen ones. If families try to resolve this dilemma by including all grandparents, it may create other problems. An unhealthy competition for the attention and affection of grandchildren can surface. If one grandparent indulges grandchildren with expensive gifts, others may feel their more modest ones are inadequate. Even when competition is not an issue, having so many people together makes it harder to have sustained one-on-one time with a grandchild. My sister compared her feelings in this situation to those one has at a cocktail party where you see everyone but don't have a satisfying conversation with anyone. It may take some negotiating to come up with a solution acceptable to all. Some families alternate spending major holidays with each set of grandparents or celebrate a few days before or after the official holiday.

Include your grandchild in planning and preparation. Since a big part of holiday fun is the anticipation that goes along with the preparation, include your grandchild in preparing for the "big day." Older children can plan games and art projects and help with grocery shopping and cooking. Grandchildren of all ages can make decorations. Anything with holiday colors is a festive addition to the front door, mantle, or centerpiece for the table. Even for holidays that are not family-centered, it's fun to do a few holiday-related activities with your grandchild. Send him a handmade valentine or create noisemakers together for New Year's Eve.

Develop gift-giving rituals. Giving gifts is often a part of birthday and holiday celebrations. The following two chapters offer suggestions about what to give your grandchild and how to help him make gifts for others. Enhance the excitement and ceremony around the opening of gifts by developing special family rituals. For example, along with serving hot chocolate and eggnog on Christmas Eve, have your grandchild open a gift from you. Or let grandchildren take turns selecting a gift from under the tree to deliver to its recipient.

Plan *can-do* family activities. Plan a few simple activities to initiate at large family gatherings. If children are bouncing off the walls, start a game of croquet outside. If the toddlers are fighting over the one fire truck, set out a generous supply of play dough and invite them over to join you. Consider these activities as *can-dos*, not *must-dos*. Trying to do too much can be counterproductive. Plan both active and quiet activities and ones that children and grown-ups can do together. Outdoor options give the high energy and noise an acceptable outlet. Check the chapter on games or activities that can work effectively with mixed age groups. Plan a simple art activity that even the youngest grandchild can do. Also keep in mind that this time together is a great opportunity to share family history through storytelling, photo albums, and videos. Since even the grown-ups may get tired of sitting around the house, you might plan a visit to a mall to see holiday decorations or attend a community Easter egg hunt.

Have a special time with each grandchild. In the bustle of holiday preparations and large family gatherings it is easy to end up never really connecting with your grandchild. To avoid this pitfall, set as a priority to do something simple but special with each grandchild. Your 5-year-old granddaughter can help prepare her favorite dessert, while her 2-year-old brother will enjoy a leisurely stroll around the block to see all the holiday lights.

Spotlight the birthday child. Birthday celebrations are an opportunity to center special attention on one child. It need not involve an elaborate party or expensive gifts. Perhaps you can prepare his favorite dish for dinner or let him select the restaurant where the family will go. Valuing his uniqueness is the fundamental focus.

With all this focus on a brother or sister, don't neglect the feelings of younger siblings. Since it is hard to have all the gifts and attention focused on their sibling, you may want to give each grandchild a small gift to unwrap.

Activities for All Ages

It is fun to have a few special activities that your family repeats each holiday. You probably have some time-tested favorites. Looking for more ideas? Here are some to try.

Halloween

Enter if You Dare: Have your grandchild come to your house as the final stop when trick-or-treating. Bewitch him with hot witches' brew, apple dippers, and a ghost story. To set the mood, put up a few Halloween decorations—orange and black crepe paper streamers, a jack-o-lantern, a dangling skeleton, and a spider's web in the entry.

WHAT YOU NEED: *ingredients for witch's brew and apple dippers (in "Let's Cook"), Halloween decorations*

Special Treat: For the best of all treats, take your grandchild to a special Halloween event. You may be able to find a pumpkin patch open to the public that provides hay rides and a haunted house. Many communities sponsor special Halloween exhibits and activities through a library, museum, or zoo. Or tour a neighborhood that goes all out for Halloween with elaborate house decorations.

WHAT YOU NEED: *Halloween event*

Thanksgiving

Grateful Giggles: It is a tradition in many families to ask each person to say something for which that they are especially thankful during Thanksgiving dinner. For a change, ask each person to say something funny for which he or she is thankful: "I'm glad I dropped the pumpkin pie instead of the pecan pie, since it's my favorite," or "I'm thankful for my hearing aid, so I can turn down all the noise."

WHAT YOU NEED: *Thanksgiving dinner, a good imagination and sense of humor*

Mall Madness: Since Thanksgiving has become the official beginning of the holiday shopping season, take a trip to a mall to see decorations and do some browsing for Christmas or Hanukkah gift ideas.

WHAT YOU NEED: *shopping center*

Hanukkah

More Menorahs: The youngest child traditionally lights the menorah candles on each of the eight days of Hanukkah. You can have a "practice" earlier in the day with another menorah, and let each grandchild take a turn lighting the candles. Let them use a candle snuffer to put them out.

WHAT YOU NEED: *menorah, candles, matches*

Spin and Win: Organize a traditional dreidel game. Buy a dreidel and provide each player with a stack of pennies or gold-covered chocolate gelt (coins). Each player places one piece in the center of the circle (the pot). Then the first player spins the dreidel, chanting:

> *I have a little dreidel.*
> *I made it out of clay.*
> *And when it's dry and ready,*
> *Then with it I will play.*

If the dreidel has the Nun (N) facing upward, the player receives nothing from the pot. If it has the gimmel (G), he receives everything from the pot; if hay (H), he takes half of the pot; if shin (S), he must add two pennies to the pot. The game ends when one player wins all of the pennies or gelt.

WHAT YOU NEED: *dreidel; pennies or gold-covered chocolate gelt*

Songs and Stories: There are many musical recordings and storybooks available for children with Hanukkah themes. The best stories for young children are those that feature families celebrating Hanukkah in traditional ways.

WHAT YOU NEED: *Hanukkah storybooks and musical recordings*

Christmas

Town Tour: Take a walk around the neighborhood to see the Christmas lights or drive to neighborhoods that go all out with spectacular decorations. Suggest each person pick out his or her favorite decoration and take a photo of it.

WHAT YOU NEED: *camera, homes with Christmas decorations*

Christmas Caroling: Gather around the piano or guitar to sing Christmas songs. No musicians in the family? Play recorded songs and encourage everyone to sing along. Or join up with another family or two to serenade your neighbors.

WHAT YOU NEED: *Christmas songs; piano, guitar, or recording*

Trimming the Tree: Your family may enjoy trimming the tree together. It's best to set up the tree ahead of time and probably also add the lights. Then set out the other decorations and let everyone add a few. If you save homemade ones from previous years, it's a good opportunity to reminisce about past celebrations. Then you can put presents under the tree and try to guess what's inside each.

WHAT YOU NEED: *Christmas tree and stand, tree decorations, presents*

Christmas Game: Buy a board or card game with a Christmas theme. It could be dominoes or Bingo with holiday pictures or a Rudolph or Christmas Story game of Monopoly. Include even the youngest grandchild by teaming him up with a grown-up. If you store the game away along with the tree ornaments, it will be fresh and exciting when you bring it out the next year—one more family tradition to enjoy together.

WHAT YOU NEED: *Christmas game*

Stick It Up: Make a gigantic collage from the wrapping paper, ribbon, and cards left over from opening gifts. Tape a long piece of paper securely to a wall or table and encourage everyone to add items by using a glue stick. Or use contact paper to eliminate the need for glue.

WHAT YOU NEED: *used wrapping paper, ribbons, and cards; contact paper or glue stick, tape*

Valentine's Day

Hunt for Hearts: Buy candy hearts wrapped individually in foil or cellophane. Hide them in one room of the house. Hand each grandchild a bag and have a "hunt for hearts." Give the youngest grandchildren extra help by pointing to obvious ones. Afterward, suggest they share their hearts with people they love.

WHAT YOU NEED: *individually wrapped candy hearts, bags or baskets*

Easter

Easter Egg Hunt: For an Easter egg hunt, hide plastic eggs filled with candy, balloons, stickers, pennies, or small toys. To prevent older children from taking the lion's share while the youngest come out empty-handed, have each child look for eggs of only one color. Follow up with an Easter egg hunt in which your grandchild hides the eggs and the grown-ups have to find them.

The following story illustrates another advantage of plastic eggs. A few weeks after Easter, a foul smell permeated the house. We searched everywhere for the source. Jenna finally located it: the eggs she had hidden too well in a drawer. She told me later, "Those were not magnets; they were maggots!"

WHAT YOU NEED: *plastic eggs; candy, balloons, stickers, pennies, or small toys*

Signs of Spring: Celebrate the arrival of spring with a trip to a botanical garden or a hike on a nature trail. Look for spring flowers, budding trees and shrubs, returning robins, and rushing streams. Appoint a scribe to write down all the signs of spring that you observe.

WHAT YOU NEED: *botanical gardens or nature trail; paper and pencil*

Passover

Child-Friendly Version: Since the traditional Passover dinner is too long for most young children, you might want to try Grandma Karen's plan. She held a separate celebration the day before Passover for her preschool granddaughter and several other neighborhood children. She used a very simple script for the "service," mostly explaining why special Seder food items were served. She also followed the tradition of hiding the middle matzo, but she filled treat bags so that each child received a prize when they were found.

WHAT YOU NEED: *Seder plate and food items, treat bags filled with goodies*

Traditional Treat: Help your grandchild make and serve charoset, traditionally served during the Seder. It is a reminder of the mortar that was used in construction projects during the time the Jews were enslaved by the Egyptians. To make it, shred two medium apples. Then add ¼ cup finely chopped almonds, ¼ cup grape juice, and ½ tablespoon cinnamon. Allow to sit for 3–6 hours, until the juice is absorbed by the other ingredients. Serve on matzos.

WHAT YOU NEED: *apples, grater, almonds, grape juice, cinnamon, bowl, spoon, matzos*

Independence Day

Active and Outside: Take advantage of warm weather by planning plenty of active play outside. Balls, Frisbees, croquet, or badminton are fun for people of all ages. If you have a swimming pool, you can keep everyone busy and cool for much of the day. You need provide only floats, kickboards, water toys, sunscreen, and total supervision.

WHAT YOU NEED: *play equipment, open space or swimming pool*

Team Up to Hunt: For a more structured activity, have a scavenger hunt. Make a list of items—a rose, a pinecone, a no-parking sign—whatever is nearby. Send people off in groups of two or three to find the items. The group that locates the most items or completes the list first wins. The prize could be first choice for desserts or exemption from doing the dishes.

WHAT YOU NEED: *paper and pencils*

Fireworks: A fireworks display is typically the highlight of this holiday. Most communities set off impressive displays as soon as it gets dark. If you need to go early to get a good spot, bring along a picnic dinner and some games. Glow sticks (foot-long noodles that glow in various shades of color) are a fun and safe alternative to any personal fireworks.

WHAT YOU NEED: *fireworks display, car, glow sticks, picnic dinner, equipment for games*

Birthdays

Beautiful Balloons: This quick and easy technique adds sparkle to balloon decorations. Blow up and tie balloons. Sprinkle confetti or glitter in a tray. Rub balloons against clothing and have your grandchild roll in the tray. Static electricity attracts and holds the sparkly bits on the balloon for a surprisingly long time.

WHAT YOU NEED: *balloons, tray; confetti or glitter*

Birthday Hat: Make a cone-shaped hat for the guest of honor at his birthday party. Use a brightly colored 12 × 24-inch piece of construction paper. Fold in half and cut out a quarter-size circle. Open and have your grandchild decorate it with markers, sequins, glitter, or pom-poms. Then roll it into a cone and adjust to fit your grandchild's head size and tape it together. Or, instead of a cone hat, make a crown, as described in "Let's Pretend."

WHAT YOU NEED: *construction paper, scissors, markers, glue, tape; sequins, glitter, or pom-poms*

Made to Break: Make a papier-mache piñata with a balloon as a mold. (See directions for papier-mâché in the "Let's Make Art" chapter.) After you fill with candy and small toys, cover the hole with tape and decorate with crepe paper and streamers. Use a heavy string to suspend the piñata from a ceiling fan, light fixture, or tree branch. Then blindfold the birthday child and have him swing at the piñata with a plastic bat until it breaks. If you use it at a children's party, let each child take a turn trying to break it.

WHAT YOU NEED: *balloon, newspaper, flour, string, tape, crepe paper, candy, small toys, plastic bat*

Activities for Specific Ages

The previous section described activities to do with grandchildren of all ages when they are together at holiday celebrations. This section focuses on holiday and birthday activities targeted for specific ages. These are one-on-one activities to do with an individual child. The focus is on holidays most loved by children: Halloween, Thanksgiving, Hanukkah, Christmas, Valentine's Day, and Easter.

The First Year

Developmental Insights

Your grandchild may find all the people and commotion at family gatherings overwhelming. It helps to minimize the amount of stimulation and keep him as close as possible to his regular schedule. He may need time and space to warm up to you and any "strangers." He can watch from a safe distance until he decides to join the action.

Although your grandchild cannot yet make much sense of holiday happenings, you will appreciate his wide-eyed stare at holiday lights or his rambles through heaps of wrapping paper, toys, and boxes. Don't be surprised if he is more fascinated by the box and ribbons than the carefully selected gift inside. Capture those moments on camera for viewing in future years.

Halloween

Tigger Too: There are some adorable costumes for babies that are sure to bring out the oohs and aahs and cameras. There are even buntings for newborns. Coordinate the baby's costume with that of an older sibling. If big brother is going as Winnie the Pooh, then his baby brother could dress up as Tigger. If he is Peter Pan, little sister can be Tinker Bell. My pick for the cutest baby costume was a bumble bee outfit on a 6-month-old.

WHAT YOU NEED: *Halloween costume, camera*

Christmas/Hanukkah

Boxes Galore: After opening gifts, salvage an assortment of boxes that your grandchild can fit together, put things in, or crawl into. Hide a new toy or bunch of bows in a box, put on the lid, and suggest that he peek inside. Show him how to nest boxes of different sizes together.

WHAT YOU NEED: *empty boxes, toys, bows*

Decoration Exploration: Since looking is not enough, let your grandchild gently touch the Christmas tree and its ornaments when the lights are off and you are right there to guide his every move. This carefully supervised exploration also works for a menorah. He can feel the slippery candles and then watch from a distance as the candles are lit.

WHAT YOU NEED: *Christmas or Hanukkah decorations*

Valentine's Day

Gelatin Hearts: For a delightful sensory experience, make bright red gelatin hearts. Add 1 cup boiling water to a small package of cherry-flavored gelatin. (Do not add the usual cold water.) Pour into an 8 × 12-inch pan. Chill for several hours until firmly set. Dip the bottom of the pan in warm water, just long enough to melt it slightly. Use a heart-shaped cookie cutter to cut out gelatin hearts. Put on his highchair tray for your grandchild to touch and taste.

WHAT YOU NEED: *cherry gelatin, water, 8 × 12 inch pan, heart-shaped cookie cutter*

Easter

Bucket Basket: For your grandchild's first Easter, a large sand pail can double as the Easter basket. Fill it with a cuddly bunny, shovel, and plastic eggs.

WHAT YOU NEED: *large sand pail, stuffed animal, shovel, plastic eggs*

Shake-Rattle-Roll: Use brightly colored plastic eggs to make Easter rattles. Put a few pennies in one, beans in another, and rice in a third. Tape them securely shut. Let your grandchild shake, roll, and toss them about.

WHAT YOU NEED: *plastic eggs, pennies, beans, rice, tape*

One- and Two-Year-Olds

Developmental Insights

It is easy for young children to become overstimulated and tired during family celebrations. Do what you can to ensure that he maintains his normal routine, especially at nap time, and that he has the opportunity for some quiet time with you away from the noise and excitement of group activities. Although interested in being with other children at family gatherings, he is just beginning to learn how to play harmoniously with others. Expect pushing and hitting, grabbing toys, and protests of "It's mine!" Close supervision and quick intervention are needed.

When you want your grandchild to make a holiday decoration or gift, select process-oriented activities such as those described below. The simplest solution is to provide shapes and colors associated with the specific holiday and let him paint or color these. Glue them on paper in contrasting holiday colors for pleasing finished pictures.

On his first and second birthdays, your grandchild has little understanding of birthdays or parties, but he still can enjoy a balloon, a cake with candles, and a new toy. These early birthday parties are times for the family to commemorate a significant milestone in the life of this grandchild and to document it on camera for sharing later.

Halloween

Treat Bag: An older toddler may want to join his older siblings in trick-or-treating at a few houses. To make a treat bag, have him decorate a small paper bag with orange and black markers and Halloween stickers. Then securely fasten a handle made from a strip of heavy paper.

WHAT YOU NEED: *small paper bag, markers, Halloween stickers, tape, heavy paper*

Paint-a-Face: Since toddlers seldom want to wear masks, use face paint instead. It is easy to create a cat, clown, or princess face. If you do it in front of a mirror, your grandchild can see what he looks like and make suggestions. Make your own face paint by mixing 1 tablespoon cold cream, 1 tablespoon cornstarch, and 1 teaspoon water. Put this mixture in several bowls and add a few drops of food coloring to each. Apply with a makeup sponge or small paint brush.

WHAT YOU NEED: *cold cream, cornstarch, water, food coloring, bowls, paint brush or makeup sponge*

Pick a Pumpkin: Carry on the tradition of carving jack-o-lanterns each year. First, visit a pumpkin patch where your grandchild can select his very own pumpkin still on the vine. Talk about its color, shape, and texture. Have him pick it up to see how heavy it is.

To make a jack-o-lantern, cut a hole in the top and encourage him to scoop out the seeds. Assist him in drawing a face on the pumpkin with a black marker. Ask, "Where should we put the eyes? What about a mouth? Should he have a nose?" Then you can cut out what he has drawn and put a votive candle inside.

WHAT YOU NEED: *pumpkin patch, pumpkin, black marker, knife, votive candle*

Trick-or-Treat Jar: Your grandchild can help you decorate a candy container. He can put Halloween stickers all over the outside of a large plastic jar and fill it with candy. When spooks come knocking, he can hand out treats from the jar.

WHAT YOU NEED: *large plastic jar, Halloween stickers, tape, candy*

Thanksgiving

Colorful Creations: Your grandchild can add a burst of fall colors to the dinner table with quick and easy disposable placemats. He can decorate orange, red, and yellow construction paper with markers and Thanksgiving stickers.

WHAT YOU NEED: *construction paper, markers, Thanksgiving stickers*

Fall Findings: Take your grandchild on a walk to collect acorns, pinecones, and seed pods. To brighten them up, roll or dip in bowls of red, yellow, and orange tempera paint. Spread on a tray to dry. Then use in a centerpiece for the Thanksgiving table.

WHAT YOU NEED: *acorns, pinecones, and/or seed pods; tempera paint, bowls*

Hanukkah

Light a Candle: Make a felt menorah for your grandchild. Cut out nine candles, nine teardrop-shaped flames, and a menorah from felt. The menorah has nine candle holders, with the one in the middle being slightly higher than the others. A quick way to obtain a pattern for the menorah is from an online site for children's Hanukkah crafts. I found an easy one to trace on a coloring page for Hanukkah activities. Put the menorah on a flannel board and encourage your grandchild to place the nine candles and their flames in the candleholder, using one-on-one correspondence. He can pretend to light and blow out the candles as he adds and removes the flames.

WHAT YOU NEED: *felt, scissors, flannel board, pattern for menorah*

Star-of-David Prints: Make a Star-of-David stamp by cutting a six-pointed star out of a kitchen sponge. Your grandchild can dip it in blue or gold tempera paint and make prints on white construction paper.

WHAT YOU NEED: *sponge, tempera paint, paper*

What's Inside?: The object of this game is to guess what's inside a box. Show your grandchild some small objects associated with Hanukkah, such as a candle, dreidel, gelt, and Star-of-David. Have him hide his eyes while you put one item inside a shoe box and close the lid. Then see if he can guess which one is inside by holding and shaking it. Ask him: "Is it heavy? Does it rattle? Does it roll around?" Do the same thing with each of the other items.

WHAT YOU NEED: *shoe box, small Hanukkah items*

Christmas

Trim the Tree: For a simple but attractive decoration, help your grandchild make a Christmas tree from a large piece of green construction paper. To make the tree symmetrical, fold the paper in half the long way, draw a trunk and branches for one side of the tree, and then cut both sides at the same time. Put paste or glue in a small container along with a small pasting brush or Q-tip. Your grandchild can put dabs of glue on the tree and then attach pom-poms, sequins, beads, ribbon, and bits of wrapping paper.

WHAT YOU NEED: *green construction paper; pom-poms, sequins, beads, ribbon, wrapping paper*

Christmas Prints: Help your grandchild make a picture of holiday shapes using cookie cutters. Put a sponge in a saucer and saturate with red paint. Repeat with green paint. Your grandchild can press Christmas cookie cutters into a sponge and then print angel, star, tree, and bell shapes onto construction paper.

WHAT YOU NEED: *saucers, red and green tempera paint, Christmas cookie cutters, paper*

Valentine's Day

Play Dough Hearts: Make a batch of play dough using the basic play dough recipe in "Let's Do Art." Divide in half and color one part with a generous amount of red food coloring, while leaving the other half white. My granddaughter delighted in creating pink, her favorite color, when she mixed them together. Roll out the dough and then cut out hearts with a heart-shaped cookie cutter. As a final touch, decorate them with colored rice.

WHAT YOU NEED: *flour, salt, water, vegetable oil, red food coloring, heart-shaped cookie cutter, colored rice*

Heart to Heart: Cut out two identical hearts from nine-9 squares of heavy red or pink construction paper. Place one heart on top of the other, glue together, and punch holes around the perimeters of the two hearts. Thread a 45-inch white shoelace through one of the holes and tie a knot in the end to keep it from coming out. Show your grandchild how to weave the shoelace through the holes and then let him finish sewing the hearts together. Undo the lacing and he can do it over and over again.

WHAT YOU NEED: *heavy pink or red paper, hole punch, glue, scissors, long white shoelace*

Easter

Hide and Hunt: Do a simplified Easter egg hunt. Hide plastic eggs in obvious places. Then help your grandchild find them by pointing to them or giving verbal cues, for example, "Look on the piano" or "I see one under the chair."

WHAT YOU NEED: *plastic eggs*

Easter Egg Toss: Use an Easter basket and plastic eggs for a game of toss. Put the basket on the floor right in front of your grandchild. Demonstrate how to throw a plastic egg into the basket and then encourage him to try it. Cheer and clap each time it lands in the basket. Then make it more challenging by moving the basket a little farther away.

WHAT YOU NEED: *basket, plastic eggs*

Hop to It: Visit an "Easter bunny." Perhaps a friend has a pet rabbit, or you can find a petting zoo with rabbits brought in especially for this season. Before you go, look at realistic pictures of rabbits and talk about their special features—long ears, whiskers, strong hind legs, and fluffy tails. On the visit, let your grandchild pet the rabbit and touch its ears and tail, but discourage him from picking it up, as he may get scratched.

WHAT YOU NEED: *rabbit, pictures of rabbits*

Easy Eggs: When dying Easter eggs with toddlers, simple and safe are priorities. Prepare a half dozen hard-boiled eggs ahead of time. Use an egg dying kit with tablets that dissolve in cold water, because they allow your grandchild safely to drop in the tablets and stir without concern about burning himself with hot water. Use sturdy coffee mugs for holding each of the primary colors and a big slotted spoon for scooping them out.

WHAT YOU NEED: *hard-boiled eggs, egg dying kit, water, coffee mugs, slotted spoon*

New Beginnings: Since spring and Easter are times to celebrate new beginnings, take your grandchild to see new baby animals. You may be able to observe and touch a lamb, calf, chick, or duckling at a petting zoo or farm.

WHAT YOU NEED: *baby animals, petting zoo or farm*

Passover

Match and Name: Make a Seder plate from a large paper plate. Cut out pictures of the traditional foods that go on a Seder plate. Make a duplicate set of the food items. Supermarket flyers, magazines, or clipart are good sources for these pictures. Your grandchild can match the food items with those on the plate and learn their names.

WHAT YOU NEED: *large paper plate, pictures of Seder foods, glue, scissors*

Three- and Four-Year-Olds

Developmental Insights

Your grandchild begins to have memories of past celebrations and to look forward to holidays with great anticipation. To enhance this budding memory for past events, bring out photos and videos of earlier holidays and talk about what you did. Preschoolers often become interested in making decorations and gifts for holidays. Keep the projects simple and open-ended. It is the process, not the product, that gives them the most satisfaction.

Expect a change in your grandchild's birthday expectations when he becomes a preschooler. My granddaughter was quite satisfied with a simple party with mostly family and one friend on her third birthday. All that changed when her fourth birthday rolled around. She was very clear that she wanted a princess party with many friends, games, party favors, cake, and presents. You may want to have a family-only party on a different day from the party with friends. Your grandchild will appreciate the extra attention and extension of his special day.

Halloween

Five Little Pumpkins: Cut out five pumpkins about 2 inches tall from orange felt. Use a black permanent marker to add a face on each and a green marker to color the stem. Use your pumpkins to act out the fingerplay below. Line up the pumpkins and point to each as you say the first part of the rhyme. On the last line make all the pumpkins roll away.

Five little pumpkins sitting on a gate.

The first one said, "Oh, my, it's getting late!"
The second one said, "There are witches in the air."
The third one said, "But we don't care."
The fourth one said, "Let's run, let's run!"
The fifth one said, "It's Halloween fun!"

Then Woooooo went the wind
And OUT went the light.

And five little pumpkins rolled out of sight.

WHAT YOU NEED: *orange felt, black and green markers*

Paste-A-Face: Decorate the house with jack-o-lanterns, black cats, and monsters made from construction paper. To make a jack-o-lantern cut a pumpkin shape from orange construction paper. From black paper cut out two circles for eyes, a triangle for a nose, and a jagged mouth. Have your grandchild paste these on the pumpkin. To make the face of a black cat cut out a large black circle from construction paper. Your grandchild can paste on black triangles for ears, green circles for eyes, a tiny pink triangle for a nose, and thin black strips for whiskers. The older preschooler may like to create a monster face as well. Provide an oval shape and let him add his choice of details. If you want to use them as window decorations, suggest making faces on both sides and then tape them in the window.

WHAT YOU NEED: *construction paper, scissors, paste, markers, tape*

Ghost Hunt: Tell this simple ghost story that invites active participation. It's a Halloween version of the traditional story/game of "Going on a Bear Hunt."

We're going on a ghost hunt	
Going to find us a big scary ghost.	*(Tap hands on lap to imitate walking.)*
What's that I see ahead?	*(Put hand to forehead and stare intently ahead.)*
Looks like tall, wavy grass.	
Can't go over it, can't go under it.	
Can't go around it.	
We'll have to go through it.	
Swishy, swashy, swishy, swashy.	*(Rub hands together to make swishing sound.)*

Repeat, inserting the following:

It's a deep, wide river.	
Splash, splotch, splash, splotch.	*(Make swimming motions with arms.)*
It's a deep, dark forest.	*(Walk slowly with outstretched arms.)*
Stamble, trip, stamble, trip	
It's an old haunted house.	
Tiptoe, tiptoe	*(Walk on tiptoes.)*
It's some steep, creaky stairs.	
Creak, crack, creak, crack.	*(Lift legs in slow climbing motion.)*
It's sticky, dusty spider webs.	
Sticky, icky, sticky, icky.	*(Brush webs away with arms.)*
It's a dirty, old chest.	
Squeak, squawk, squeak, squawk.	*(Turn the knob. Open the lid.)*
It's white. It floats. It wails.	
It's a ghost!!!	*(Pretend to run back quickly through each place and into your own house, where you shut and lock the door.)*

We made it.
No more ghost hunts tonight!

WHAT YOU NEED: *A dark, cozy corner, words and actions to "Going on a Ghost Hunt"*

Make A Mask: A dinner-size white paper plate makes a great Halloween mask. Ahead of time make a simple model with the eyes cut out and other features drawn on with a marker. To make a mask for your grandchild, hold a plate over his face and mark the best location for the eye holes. Cut them out, punch holes on either side of the plate, and attach a ribbon for tying. He can glue on yarn for hair and a nose, ears, and mouth cut from construction paper, and then add details—such as eyebrows, teeth, or rosy cheeks—with colored markers. He can make a cat or rabbit by adding ears cut from construction paper and whiskers made from black pipe cleaners.

WHAT YOU NEED: *large white paper plates, scissors, ribbon, hole punch; yarn, pipe cleaners, markers, construction paper, tape*

Black Cat or Bat?: Take your grandchild to a store with a wide selection of Halloween costumes and decorations, such as a party supply store. Walk slowly up and down the aisles, discussing what you see. Then let him pick one or two items to buy. When my granddaughter was 3, I was surprised by her choice of a large, scary bat, and even more by her decision to hang it upside down at the bottom of her bed!

WHAT YOU NEED: *store with Halloween supplies*

Thanksgiving

Handy Turkey: An easy way for your grandchild to draw a turkey is for you to trace around his hand with his fingers spread widely apart. The thumb becomes the head while the fingers are the tail feathers of the turkey. He can color the tail feathers and add eyes, legs, and feet with markers or crayons.

WHAT YOU NEED: *paper, markers or crayons*

The Disappearing Dinner: Collect 5–10 pictures of foods that you are having for Thanksgiving dinner. Cut them from magazines or use clipart. Display them one at a time on the table, naming and describing interesting facts about each as you do. Have your grandchild close his eyes while you remove one. After he has a chance to look carefully at the remaining items, see if he can tell which one is missing. Replace it and do the same for the other items.

WHAT YOU NEED: *pictures of Thanksgiving food*

Hanukkah

Star-Studded Collage: Cut out two equilateral triangles from blue construction paper. Have your grandchild glue one on a large piece of gold paper and then invert and glue the other triangle on top of it. To make a collage, add four or five more stars to the paper.

WHAT YOU NEED: *gold and blue construction paper, glue*

Whirl and Rest: This is a simple chant that has easy-to-act-out motions. Twirl around on the first two lines and then stretch out quietly on the floor for the last two lines.

> I am a blue dreidel wound up tight!
> I whirl and whirl with all my might!
> And now the whirls are out of me.
> So I'll rest quietly as can be!

WHAT YOU NEED: *words to the chant*

Handprint Menorah: It is easy to create a menorah with just your hands and some paint. Help your grandchild paint his palm blue and his fingers and thumbs white. Then make a handprint on black construction paper, making sure all his fingers and thumb are facing straight up. Repeat with his other hand, but let the thumb print overlap with the first thumb print. The overlapping thumbs are the Shamesh and the other fingerprints are the eight candles in the menorah. Dip a finger tip into yellow paint and press above each candle to create flames.

WHAT YOU NEED: *yellow, white, and blue tempera paint, paint brushes, piece of black construction paper*

Loops and Links: For a simple project, make paper chains in the traditional Hanukah colors of blue and white. Make chains with white and blue 1 × 4-inch construction paper strips. Start by making a loop fastened with tape. Put the next strip through this loop, fasten it, and continue until you have made a long chain. Grandma Karen did this with her granddaughter and then hung them decoratively around the room.

WHAT YOU NEED: *blue and white construction paper, scissors, tape*

Christmas

Visit to Santa Claus: Take your grandchild to a department store or mall to see Santa Claus. Try to go at a time when you don't have to wait in a long line. Before you go, rehearse sitting on Santa's lap and telling him what you want for Christmas. You will doubtless want to purchase a photo as a memento of this occasion.

WHAT YOU NEED: *mall or other location where Santa is stationed*

Sing Along: Teach your grandchild to sing a favorite children's Christmas song, such as *Frosty the Snowman* or *Rudolph the Red-Nosed Reindeer*. Buy both a recording of the song and a book that illustrates the story. After you have played the recording and read the book several times, see if your grandchild wants to sing along with you and the recording.

WHAT YOU NEED: *recording and book of Christmas song*

Glitter and Gold: Pinecones can make simple, but attractive ornaments for the Christmas tree. Your grandchild can paint small pinecones with gold tempera paint and roll them in glitter while still wet. Then tie a piece of yarn around the pinecone and hang on the tree.

WHAT YOU NEED: *pinecones, gold tempera paint, glitter, yarn*

Red and Green Chains: Complete your Christmas tree with a long, colorful paper chain. Make chains with red and green 1 × 4-inch construction paper strips. Start by making a loop fastened with tape. Put the next strip through this loop, fasten it, and continue until you have made a long chain to drape around the tree.

WHAT YOU NEED: *red and green construction paper, scissors, tape*

Candy Cane Creations: Make candy canes to hang on the tree with large tube-shaped pasta, such as penne or ziti. Paint half of the pieces red and the other half white. After they are dry, alternate stringing red and white pieces on a 12-inch white pipe cleaner. Fold up each end of pipe cleaner to secure the pieces. Bend in a candy cane shape and add a red bow at the bottom.

WHAT YOU NEED: *tube-shaped pasta, red and white tempera paint, white pipe cleaner, red ribbon*

Valentine's Day

Simple Valentines: To make valentines for your grandchild to decorate, cut out large heart shapes from pink, red, and white construction paper by folding the paper in half and cutting both sides of the heart at the same time. Your grandchild can glue on glitter, doilies, silver foil, ribbon, and little precut hearts.

WHAT YOU NEED: *red, white, and pink paper, glue, glitter, doilies, silver foil, ribbon*

Valentine Box: A homemade valentine box is fun to make. Since Valentine exchanges are a common practice in preschools, your grandchild can use it for carrying valentines to and from school. First cut red, white, and pink tissue paper into 2 × 2-inch squares. Have him use a small brush to spread glue on the box and lid and then cover it completely with overlapping tissue squares. Add more glue as needed to attach all edges of the tissue paper. Complete by gluing a few heart shapes made from construction paper to the lid.

WHAT YOU NEED: *shoebox, red, white, and pink tissue paper, small brush, glue, paper*

Special Delivery: Help your grandchild prepare valentines for a few friends or relatives. For those who live close by, make a personal home delivery. Take the rest to the post office and drop in the mail box. While there, look for mail trucks and explain how the valentines will get from the post office to the recipient's house.

WHAT YOU NEED: *valentines, addresses; post office*

Five Little Valentines: Cut out five valentines from 4-inch squares of red or pink paper. Paste one onto a doily. Draw a face on another. Write "I love you" on one and "I do too" on another. On the fifth valentine, draw a face and attach thin strips of paper for arms and legs. Store the valentines and a copy of the fingerplay in a zip-lock bag. Then take them out one at a time, line them up, and present this fingerplay:

Five little valentines were having a race.	*(Point to the row of valentines.)*
The first one was frilly with lace.	*(Point to valentine with the doily.)*
The second one had a funny face.	*(Point to valentine with face.)*
The third one said, "I love you."	*(Point to one with these words.)*
The fourth one said, "I do too."	*(Point to one with these words.)*
The fifth valentine was sly as a fox.	*(Point to one with arms and legs.)*
He ran the fastest to the valentine box.	*(Place in your grandchild's hand.)*

WHAT YOU NEED: *pink or red paper, scissors, glue, marker, doily, zip-lock bag, words to fingerplay*

Easter

Eggs Deluxe: Have your grandchild help with each step in dyeing Easter eggs. He can count out the eggs into a saucepan and cover with cold water, watch for the water to boil, turn off the heat, and set a timer for the 15 minutes that the eggs need to remain in the hot water. After the eggs have cooled, peel one egg and compare to a raw egg that you crack in a bowl.

You can make your own dye by adding ¼ teaspoon food coloring and 1 teaspoon vinegar to 1 cup hot water. Make cups of red, blue, and yellow dye. Experiment with dipping eggs in multiple colors to create green, purple, or orange eggs. Next dye each half of an egg a different color by submerging only half of the egg in the dye and then turning it over to do the other half in another color. To create a marbling effect, add a teaspoon of vegetable oil to dye. If your grandchild draws a design or writes his initials on eggs with a white crayon before dying them, he will delight in seeing them emerge on the colored eggs.

WHAT YOU NEED: *eggs, food coloring, water, vinegar, cups, spoons, vegetable oil*

With All the Frills upon It: Make fancy Easter bonnets from paper plates. Punch a hole on opposite sides of a paper plate and attach a ribbon on each side to tie under the chin. Your grandchild can decorate the plates with feathers, rickrack, fabric scraps, glitter, crepe paper, and yarn.

WHAT YOU NEED: *paper plates, hole punch, ribbon; feathers, rickrack, fabric scraps, glitter, crepe paper, yarn*

Little Bunny: With all the talk about the Easter bunny, it's a good time to teach this simple fingerplay about a bunny:

Here's a little bunny with ears so funny.	*(Hold up pointer and index fingers.)*
And here's a little hole in the ground.	*(Make a circle with thumb and index finger.)*
When a noise he hears,	*(Clap hands.)*
He picks up his ears,	*(Hold up pointer and index fingers.)*
And jumps in the hole in the ground.	*(Put two fingers in hole made with fingers on other hand.)*

WHAT YOU NEED: *words to fingerplay*

Passover

Matzo Collage: Let your grandchild break matzos into small pieces and then glue the broken pieces on a large piece of heavy construction paper in an interesting design. Talk about how matzo is an important part of the Passover celebration.

WHAT YOU NEED: *matzos, heavy construction paper, glue*

Making Matzo Song: Sing these words to the tune of "Row, Row, Row Your Boat," as you do the hand motions.

Roll, roll, roll your dough.	*(One hand palm up, other hand above it, palm down making circular motions.)*
Make it nice and round.	*(Make a circle with fingers.)*
Make it flat.	*(Slap palms together.)*
Poke lots of holes	*(One hand palm up; with fingers on the other hand pretend to poke holes in it.)*
And bake it till it's brown.	*(Both palms up, touching on sides, move forward, as if putting a tray in the oven.)*

WHAT YOU NEED: *words and motions for song*

Five- to Eight-Year-Olds

Developmental Insights

At family gatherings your grandchild has the social skills to join in grown-up conversations and to adapt his play to the abilities and interests of younger children. He may enjoy the role of caregiver for younger children or that of assistant chef.

With his growing ability to understand historical events and diverse cultural and religious customs, this is a good time to teach him about holiday celebrations in other cultures and religions and about the historical significance of holidays. An excellent source for in-depth information is the book series *A World of Holidays*. Each book illustrates with colorful photographs the history of a specific holiday and how it is celebrated in different parts of the world.

Your grandchild's birthday can be an occasion to do something special with only him. Find an outing associated with his special interests, perhaps a soccer game or a ballet performance. Or take him out to dinner and have an uninterrupted, one-on-one conversation. One grandmother with a number of grandchildren takes each one out to his or her favorite restaurant as a birthday treat.

Halloween

On a Dark and Gloomy Halloween Night: To set the mood for telling a round-robin ghost story turn the lights down low and play some eerie music. Begin with a story-starter such as, "On a dark and gloomy Halloween night just like tonight, two children went out trick-or-treating." Take turns adding a few sentences to the story. Use sound effects, such as tapping a stick or rattling foil.

WHAT YOU NEED: *foil, stick, darkened room, story-starter*

Miniature Spiders: Make a little spider from just one 12-inch black pipe cleaner. Cut it into five pieces of equal length. After placing four pieces side by side, twist the fifth piece around the middle of the other four pieces several times to hold them tightly together. Spread out the legs to complete your spider.

WHAT YOU NEED: *12 inch black pipe cleaner, scissors*

Mighty Spiders: To make a much larger spider, wrap black yarn around a 1-inch Styrofoam ball until it is totally covered, tucking in the end. Then cut four 12-inch pipe cleaners in half and stick four pieces into each side of the ball for legs. Glue on two yellow pom-poms for eyes. Purchase spider webbing where Halloween decorations are sold and place your miniature and mighty spiders in it.

WHAT YOU NEED: *1-inch Styrofoam ball, black yarn, black pip cleaners, pom-poms, scissors, spider webbing*

Create a Costume: Help your grandchild create original costumes from scarves, hats, and other items you have on hand. Take him to a thrift store to search for interesting possibilities and reasonable prices. *The Halloween*

Costume Book is an inexpensive paperback that provides directions for 60 easy-to-make costumes, such as how to make a simple cape or a dinosaur tail. *Super-Simple Creative Costumes* provides patterns and directions for costumes and accessories, including box and sandwich board styles.

WHAT YOU NEED: *scarves, hats, and other clothing items*

Jack-O-Lantern or Black Cat: Make Halloween decorations with papier-mâché. A simple way to make the paste is to mix equal parts of flour and water and then add more water until it has the consistency of thick glue. Tear newspaper into strips about 1 inch wide by 6 inches long. Use an inflated balloon as a mold. Dip newspaper strips into the paste and spread over the balloon, covering it completely. Hang the balloon from a string over the kitchen counter to make it easier to add the strips on the bottom. Leave it hanging up to dry overnight. If you want to hang up your finished decoration, leave the string on the balloon.

To make a jack-o-lantern, paint the balloon orange and glue on eyes, nose, and mouth cut from black construction paper. A cylinder from green construction paper attached to the top serves as the stem. To make a black cat, paint the balloon black and glue on ears, eyes, nose, and mouth cut from construction paper, plus whiskers from black pipe cleaners.

WHAT YOU NEED: *newspaper, balloons, string, tempera paint, glue, construction paper, pipe cleaners, scissors*

Thanksgiving

Nifty Names: Your grandchild can make unique place cards for each dinner guest. Purchase colorful 3 × 5-inch index cards or cut from heavy construction paper. Fold in half the long way and print each dinner guest's name on a card. Trace over each letter with glitter glue. To complete the decorations glue on a few pom-poms, sequins, or brightly colored feathers.

WHAT YOU NEED: *index cards or heavy construction paper, pencil, glitter glue, feathers, pom-poms, or sequins*

Food for Feasting: Have your grandchild make a collage of traditional Thanksgiving foods. Search through magazines for pictures of a roasted turkey, pumpkin pie, green beans, sweet potatoes, or other food items that your family typically eats on Thanksgiving. He can cut out and paste these on a large piece of construction paper. Help him write a label beside each item and then display his collage in the dining room.

WHAT YOU NEED: *magazines with pictures of food, paste, construction paper, markers, scissors*

Hanukkah

Make-and-Bake Menorah: Make a batch of make-and-bake play dough (recipe in "Let's Make Art" chapter). Roll out nine cylinders about the size of your thumb for the candleholders. Secure these to a 9 × 1-inch rectangular base by wetting the surfaces with water. Place small birthday candle holders in the top of each cylinder. Put it in the oven for an hour at 200 degrees. When it is completely dry, paint it and add birthday candles.

WHAT YOU NEED: *water, flour, salt, mixing bowl, craft stick, pencil, birthday candle holders and candles, tempera paint*

Star of David: Glue three craft sticks together to form a triangle. Repeat with three more craft sticks. Overlay the two triangles and glue together to make a six-pointed star. Paint the star blue on both sides and add glitter while still wet. When it is dry, hang it from a string in a window or on a doorknob.

WHAT YOU NEED: *craft sticks, glue, blue tempera paint, glitter, string*

Collecting Coins: A tzedakah box is a place to save money that you plan to give to a charity. It isn't an activity directly linked to Hanukkah, but many families encourage children to put some of their gift money from Hanukkah in the box. Grandma Karen gave her preschool granddaughter a box and then gave her quarters on each day of Hanukkah, some to keep and some for the box. At the end of the holiday her granddaughter gave the money to a charity for children.

You can purchase a tzedakah box for your grandchild or help him make his own. Look through your recycled jars and cans and ask him to pick his favorite. He can decorate it with paint, stickers, or tissue paper, creating a unique tzedakah box.

WHAT YOU NEED: *jar or can, coins; glue, paint, stickers or tissue paper*

Christmas

Multicolored Bulbs: Make interesting paper ornaments to hang on the Christmas tree. Your grandchild can cut out 3-inch circles in two or three colors and then make half a dozen holes in each with a single hole punch. The next step is to glue two circles of different colors together. The contrasting colors show through the holes for an interesting effect. To hang on the tree, punch a hole in the top and add a ribbon loop.

WHAT YOU NEED: *construction paper, scissors, single-hole punch, paste, ribbon*

Snowflakes: Make snowflakes from 2- to 4-inch squares of lightweight white paper. Fold it in half twice and then fold again to make a triangle. Next, cut out snips on all three sides and unfold. My grandson liked to use a single-hole punch to add to the design. Glue on some silver glitter to make them sparkle. Tape the snowflakes to a window or hang on the Christmas tree.

WHAT YOU NEED: *white paper, single-hole punch, scissors, glitter, tape*

Sparkly Spirals: This is an easy ornament to make for the Christmas tree. Start with a red, green, or silver circle that is 4 inches in diameter. Glue glitter on both sides of the circle. Then, starting on the outside edge, cut a half-inch wide spiral round and round into the center of the circle. Punch a hole in the center of the spiral and attach a loop of ribbon for hanging on the tree.

WHAT YOU NEED: *construction paper, glue, glitter, scissors, ribbon*

Shopping Spree: Take your grandchild to the mall to shop for gifts and enjoy the holiday decorations. Help him select some small gift items for his parents and siblings. Before you go, discuss how much he can spend and what he wants to buy for each person.

WHAT YOU NEED: *shopping center*

Valentine's Day

Sweets for Sweethearts: Make a batch of foolproof fudge to give to family and friends. (See recipe for foolproof fudge in the "Let's Cook" chapter.) Put pieces of fudge on plastic disposable pink plates and wrap with pink tissue paper and ribbon.

WHAT YOU NEED: *foolproof fudge, disposable pink plates, pink tissue paper, ribbon*

Treat a Friend: Let your grandchild select a good friend to join you for a special treat. It could be a trip to the ice cream parlor for a sundae or to the discovery museum. He can enclose the invitation in a homemade valentine, labeling it *a special treat for a special friend.*

WHAT YOU NEED: *valentine, pencil, envelope, special activity*

Flowers for Friends: Visit a florist shop to observe special floral arrangements for Valentine's Day and see how many flowers your grandchild can identify. Explain that yellow roses are traditionally associated with friendship, and let him buy one for a special friend. Then go with him to deliver it along with a homemade valentine.

WHAT YOU NEED: *florist shop, valentine*

Heart Basket: A little heart-shaped basket filled with valentine candies makes a pretty gift. Fold one of the bottom corners of an envelope in half. With the corner of the envelope serving as the point of the heart, cut a semi-circle for the rounded top. When opened, it makes a heart-shaped container. Add a handle by securing a 12-inch pipe cleaner through the holes punched on both sides of the heart and tie a pink bow on the top. Then your grandchild can decorate the basket with markers, stars, valentine stickers, or sequins. Line the basket with pink tissue paper and fill with candy hearts.

WHAT YOU NEED: *large envelope, pipe cleaner, single-hole punch, scissors, bow, tissue paper; stars, valentine stickers, or sequins.*

Easter

Eggs in a Nest: Your grandchild will enjoy making and playing with a bird nest filled with eggs. Pour a quarter cup of glue into a margarine tub and add brown paint to the glue. Then break 1 cup uncooked spaghetti noodles into small pieces to make about a cup and mix into the glue. If it is too dry, add a bit more glue; if it is too wet, more spaghetti. Press the mixture around the sides and bottom of the tub to form a nest and remove the nest when it is completely dry. Make small eggs from foil; rub each with glue and wrap with blue tissue paper. Line the nest with colorful feathers before placing the eggs in it.

WHAT YOU NEED: *glue, margarine tub, brown paint, spaghetti noodles, foil, blue tissue paper, colorful feathers*

Easter Egg Tree: If you are looking for an attractive decoration, this admittedly more involved project is a sure winner. First, search the neighborhood for a small branch that has fallen off a tree. Use pebbles and plaster of Paris to anchor it upright in a coffee can. After it has hardened, paint the tree and glue construction paper around the can. Finally, cut out pastel-colored eggs from construction paper, decorate with glitter, punch a hole at the top of each, and add a yarn loop for hanging on the tree branches.

WHAT YOU NEED: *small branch from tree, pebbles, plaster of Paris, coffee can, tempera paint, construction paper, glitter, hole punch, yarn*

Passover

Seder Plate: Collect pictures of Passover foods from supermarket flyers or magazines. Cut these out into 2-inch circles. Have your grandchild glue these around the border of a large paper plate and write the name under each item. This is a good opportunity to talk about the meaning of each of the items and why they are eaten during the Passover dinner.

WHAT YOU NEED: *pictures of Passover foods, scissors, glue, marker, large paper plate*

$$11$$

Let's Give Gifts

Giving the Right Gift at the Right Time

Bubbling with barely contained excitement, Jake caressed the brightly wrapped present and emphatically declared, "I just can't wait!" Granddad relented and let him open his birthday gift one day early, because, to tell

Let's Grandparent: Activity Guide for Young Grandchildren, pages 191–205
Copyright © 2008 by Information Age Publishing
All rights of reproduction in any form reserved.

191

you the truth, he couldn't wait either. Ever since spying a race car doing loops on a motorized track at the toy store, he had been anticipating all the exhilarating races he would share with his grandson.

Why Try It?

Gift-giving is definitely high on the list of grandparenting pleasures. Of course, we want to give an especially memorable gift on birthdays and holidays, but don't overlook that impromptu gift given at just the right time. When watching your grandchild for the weekend, a gift brought out at the right moment may distract her from missing her parents or be a remedy for boredom. On long family trips, everyone appreciates a travel package with simple lightweight items: sticker books, games with magnetic boards, crayons, or a handheld computer game with earphones. For the long-distance grandparent, a gift lets your grandchild know you are thinking of her. When you visit, it's a pleasant way to renew the relationship. And any time is the right time when you find that doll she has been longing for, the science kit to encourage her new interest in nature, or the game to strengthen her developing math skills. The "right time" for 18-month-old Emerson came one morning when his fascination with the vacuum cleaner ended up in a cloud of smoke and fire, enough to burn a hole in the rug and put the sweeper permanently out of commission. That was the day I found a toy vacuum cleaner, complete with authentic sounds and no fire hazard.

Besides the mutual pleasure experienced by you and your grandchild, carefully chosen gifts also can broaden your grandchild's interests and strengthen her developing skills. Giving a 3-year-old a tricycle gives her the opportunity to master this new skill, while giving a 7-year-old a book-publishing kit may stimulate a desire to write many of her own stories. You may sometimes want to give a gift that challenges your grandchild to develop a new interest. When I gave Jenna a simple sewing machine for her 7th birthday, she became an enthusiastic seamstress, making many gifts for all her family and friends.

Snapshot of Development

A cognitive understanding of the meaning of gifts develops gradually as your grandchild comes to appreciate the giver's point of view. During his first few years, my grandson wanted nothing to do with unwrapping packages, and not until he was 3 did he have any sense of ownership about gifts he received. It took this long for him to realize that this new truck belonged to him, and his older brother needed to ask him before playing with it.

Don't be too disappointed if your grandchild does not express enthu- siastic appreciation of the gift you invested so much time and money to obtain. It takes a combination of teaching and a conceptual grasp of gift- giving before she masters proper etiquette when receiving a gift. Only then will she remember to thank the gift-giver wholeheartedly and graciously accept a gift that she doesn't particularly want.

Tips for Buying Gifts

You play too. My focus in this chapter is upon gifts that you and your grand- child can use together. When you choose a gift, consider how you can use it with her. If you buy a board game, teach her how to play it. Take a baby doll for a walk around the block with a new doll stroller. Bring out the new family of plastic ducks the next time you give her a bath.

Consider a gift that includes an outing together, like tickets for a theme park, ball game, or children's play for you to attend together. It could be a membership to the zoo or discovery museum and a promise to take her there soon. Or it could be those ballet or gymnastics lessons she has been yearning for and "coupons" for your chauffeur services. Wrap a book about Sleeping Beauty along with the ballet tickets or a set of zoo animals and photo-filled brochure with your zoo membership.

With some extra determination and imagination long-distance grand- parents can still give gifts that create shared experiences. Give her a camera and plan a regular photo exchange. Or send a tape-recorder, along with the first installment of a recorded story. With a package of art supplies, request a few of her masterpieces. Send subscriptions to a children's magazine to both you and your grandchild, and then talk about the articles during your weekly phone conversations. To share the pleasure that your grandchild experiences when she receives your gift, ask her parents to take a photo of her using it. She can include the photo in her thank-you note.

Give little surprise gifts. Try some inexpensive, impromptu gifts that suggest an activity to do together. It is amazing how much fun a dollar gift can bring: a bag of balloons, markers, a deck of cards, a bottle of bubble solution, a packet of seeds, or a set of jacks. You can make a sculpture with a package of pipe cleaners, build ramps for marbles, or go for a walk with a pinwheel. Grandma Susan frequently takes her grandchildren to the dollar store where they have the extra fun of choosing what to buy. Long-distance grandparents can send these little gifts in the mail along with a message about how to use the item. "Have the seeds sprouted yet?" or "Did you make some big bubbles?" are good conversation-starters for the next phone call.

Limit the loot. Giving too many gifts can boomerang. We don't want our grandchildren to become overly materialistic or assume we will always bring a gift when we visit or return from a trip. We want them to greet us at the door with a big hello hug, not "What did you bring me?"

On birthdays and holidays an overabundance of gifts may overwhelm your grandchild. She may quickly tear through a pile of packages only to ask dejectedly, "What else?" One solution is to spread out gifts over several days, so that she can play with each item immediately. Hanukkah, with its eight days of gift-giving, provides a good model. You might want to give your gifts on Christmas Eve or at a separate birthday celebration. Then you and your grandchild will have plenty of time to focus on playing together with this one gift.

Buy the basics. I often face the dilemma of whether to give my grandchildren what they want or what I believe is a more appropriate choice. Appeals to buy the newest toys and games bombard our grandchildren. They look so much fun in the TV ads and all their friends are getting them. It's hard to totally ignore the media hype and kid pressure. But fads fade fast, and motorized toys that run the show, while our grandchild is relegated to the passive observer, quickly become candidates for the discard pile. Instead, choose toys with staying power, these have multiple uses, encourage imagination, and sustain long-term interest.

Foster your values. When selecting toys, ask yourself what play they will encourage. Will they foster the learning and values you want for your grandchild? Does the toy encourage passive observation or active and varied participation? The battery-operated dancing ballerina is fun to watch a few times, but the tutu may encourage many sessions of creative dancing and pretending. Do you want to encourage prosocial play with the doctor's kit or aggressive play with the space weapons set? If you want to foster specific skills and concepts, look for a toy designed for doing a specific task in a prescribed way, for example, a puzzle, board game, or stacking cone. If you want to foster creativity, choose toys, such as blocks, Legos, or art supplies, that are open-ended in how to use them.

Resolve the girl toy/boy toy dilemma. Toys marketed specifically for either boys or girls become increasingly evident during the preschool and school-age years. Peruse a toy department and you will find a girls' section with dolls, dishes, frilly costumes, and makeup kits, while vehicles, action figures, and weapons are featured for boys. Do you want to foster or discourage this gender-typing? I want my grandchildren to develop all their abilities and to feel free to pursue personal interests, even if they are not in line with traditional stereotypes. I also want them to have a positive gender identity. I don't have an easy answer for this dilemma. Still, it's good to make a thoughtful decision about buying gender-typed toys. When possible, I look for toys intended for both girls and boys, such as art supplies, books, puzzles, and manipulatives.

Whether you choose to foster or discourage this gender-typing, peer pressure and the desire for gender identity will likely win the day with your young grandchild. They did when I took my 4-year-old granddaughter shopping to select a toy. As she browsed through the toy department, she asked repeatedly, "Is this a girl toy?" and firmly rejected any that hinted at being "for boys." She preferred any item that was pink or had a girl pictured on the box. Being the indulgent grandmother, I bought her the cute little purse that she wanted, even though she had several at home.

Be a savvy shopper. Where to shop? Large toy stores with their many options can be alluring, but overwhelming. Should you select those prominently displayed items with the hefty price tags? How can you choose which of the 101 available board games is the right one for your grandchild? For best results, have some definite ideas in mind before stepping inside the store.

Do expand your options beyond traditional toy departments. Craft stores have art supplies and kits for creative projects. Bookstores offer a wide selection of classic and popular children's books. Museum gift shops often have books, games, and kits with art, science, or nature themes. Electronics stores typically carry a wide selection of children's computer programs and video games and DVDs. For sturdy items with high educational value, you can't beat teachers' stores. Or shop online, using sites that specialize in children's toys. My favorites are Sensational Beginnings (*www.sensationalbeginnings.com*), Constructive Playthings (*www.constplay.com*), and Museum Tour (*www.museumtour.com*).

Match gift to age and interests. How can you decide whether a gift is age-appropriate? Toy manufacturers often include a recommended age range, along with cautions about potential choking hazards for infants and toddlers. The activities described throughout this book include many suggestions for toys and materials suitable for each age level. The following sections provide a quick review of age-appropriate suggestions.

Also consider your grandchild's special interests and skills. With her passion for ballet, Jenna cherished the ballerina doll complete with tutu and ballet slippers. The electric train for his 7th birthday upgraded Jake's enduring interest in trains.

Talk with your grandchild about what he would like. Older children are quite proficient at generating specific suggestions. With younger children, browse through a toy catalog together to get ideas about their interests.

Gift Ideas

Sections for each age are grouped according to the primary type of play they encourage. *Manipulative play* fosters fine motor development and eye–hand coordination. *Active play* uses the whole body, especially the large muscles. *Creative play* includes sensory exploration and artistic expression. *Pretend play* stimulates role-playing and imagination. *Educational play* fosters cognitive and academic skills. Specific recommendations for each type of play are included.

Birth to Six Months

Baby Gear: Arriving with nothing but a healthy cry, your 7-pound grandchild wastes no time in demanding tons of supplies. Not just clothes, blankets, and diapers, she also craves big-ticket items—a crib, stroller, car seat, baby carrier, bassinet, and rocking chair. You will probably want to celebrate this new arrival with a special gift. Especially if this is the first child, parents appreciate help with one of the many major purchases needed. Since new parents usually have definite ideas about what they want, do get their input before buying.

    Sensory Stimulation: Even newborns enjoy new sights and sounds. They see best when objects are 8–10 inches away and have bold outlines in sharply contrasting colors. They tune into music and novel sounds. A soft lullaby can lull a fussy baby to sleep.

- **A tape recorder or CD player** can provide music for play or sleep time.
- **A wind-up or pull-down musical toy,** enclosed in a plush teddy bear or bunny, provides tactile, visual, and auditory stimulation.
- **Musical mobiles** combine a spinning visual display with musical selections. With many themes available, you are sure to find one that matches your interests or the nursery decor. Look for one that has bright colors and high contrast. Figures should face downward for better viewing by your grandchild.
- **A nonbreakable mirror** lets your grandchild look at her favorite image—the human face. By 3 months, she will be smiling at her own reflection.

Manipulative Play: Soon your grandchild becomes actively engaged in touching, mouthing, and grasping objects. Since everything is sure to end up in her mouth, make sure there are no small parts that can come off and cause a choking hazard. Random movements become more deliberate as she tries to reproduce interesting sights and sounds.

- **An activity mat** in contrasting colors and textures and securely attached toys provides interesting things to do and see during floor time. Those with kicking-activated sights and sounds foster early cause-and-effect learning. Those with toys hanging from overhead arches encourage reaching and batting.
- **Small toys to shake and hold** also encourage reaching and grasping. Use lightweight rattles, squeaky toys, and teething rings as you interact with your new grandchild.

Six Months to One Year

Manipulative Play: Once your grandchild can sit up, her toy needs change. Toys that encourage her to use her arms and hands are especially appropriate. She uses two hands to bang toys together or passes a toy from one hand to the other. Select ones sturdy enough to withstand the rigors of vigorous banging on the floor or being hurled from great heights. Consider these toys as props for you to use when playing games with your grandchild.

- **A few simple water toys** make bath time more fun. Good additions are a floating duck family or toys with suction cups that stay attached to the bottom of the tub.
- **Blocks** for stacking and knocking down are best in a soft vinyl or fabric. Some make sounds when squeezed and have colorful patterns on each side.
- First **huggables** need to be chosen with great care. The cute teddy bear with the beady eyes and metal wind-up knob can be double trouble. Look for ones that can be thrown into the washing machine and have no removable, hard, or sharp parts. Since it may become your grandchild's constant companion, invest in one made for the long haul. The best size is one that your grandchild can easily carry wherever she goes.
- **Board books**, made of heavy cardboard, can withstand all the rough treatment that your grandchild dishes out. Those with a single object on each page are best for point-and-say "reading," while touch-and-feel books encourage active exploration.

Active Play: Between 9 and 12 months of age, your grandchild begins to crawl, stand up, and cruise, walking sideways as she holds on to furniture. Toys and equipment that strengthen her legs and utilize newfound mobility are good additions.

- **Rolling toys** come into their own. She will delight in pushing her car or any toy with wheels across the room. Do stick with ones designed specifically with infants and toddlers in mind, those that have no small and potentially detachable parts.
- **Balls** are great for encouraging social interaction. A big, soft, lightweight ball is easiest for your grandchild to catch and roll.
- **A stationary activity center** lets your grandchild easily sit, stand, or bounce. Most come with toys attached and a tray space to hold snacks and drinks. It's good exercise for those developing leg muscles and a safe place to keep her busy for short periods. Stationary models are much safer than walkers. Even though infants delight in the great mobility that walkers provide, the U.S. Consumer Product Safety Commission warns of the dangers inherent in even those with new safety features.

One- and Two-Year-Olds

Manipulative Play: Your toddler likes toys that make things happen. She wants dials to turn, buttons to push, lids to open and shut, containers to fill and dump, and objects to stack. She typically uses her whole hand to perform tasks, so to avoid unnecessary frustration, select simple toys that she can operate with minimal assistance.

- **The classic pounding board** with a hammer that knocks balls or pegs through the holes illustrates a toy especially well suited for a toddler. She can readily master the motor skills needed to produce striking results.
- **Stacking and nesting toys** teach eye–hand coordination and size and number concepts. At first, your grandchild may only take apart and knock down what you have put together, but eventually she will begin to stack and nest them herself. An all-time favorite stacking toy is plastic "doughnuts" that fit over a center post.
- **Large cardboard blocks** are a good choice for older toddlers. They are a good investment, for your grandchild will enjoy playing with them for many years.

- **Puzzles** develop spatial awareness and fine motor skills. Begin with wooden, knobbed puzzles with a separate inlay for each piece. Then, progress to those with 5–10 interlocking pieces that fit in a tray.

Active Play: Is your toddler grandchild always full of energy and constantly on the go? Her first hesitant steps soon turn into running and climbing everywhere. Toys that safely let her exercise developing motor skills are good choices.

- A child who is just beginning to walk often likes the stability provided by a **sturdy push toy**. Consider such classics as the popcorn popper push toy or one that plays music. After your grandchild becomes more sure-footed, she may like **pull toys** as well. Wooden pull toys with wide bases are sturdy and stable enough for rough play. A small, lightweight wagon is one pull toy that she will use long past the toddler years.
- Redirect her penchant for climbing everywhere on everything, with a **low-to-the-ground climber** designed specifically for toddlers. Resist the urge to buy larger playground equipment that "she can grow into." There are both indoor and outdoor versions, most with wide steps, a slide, and crawl-through space.
- Soon she will like **ride-on wheeled toys** that she propels with her feet. The four- wheeled models provide more stability than those with only three. Save the pedal models for when she is 3.

Creative Play: Toddlers never tire of playing in water and sand. With careful supervision, they can explore simple art materials. They also like to move to music and experiment with sounds and rhythms. The right equipment makes it easier to provide many such sensory and artistic experiences.

- **A water table**, essentially a large tub on legs with a drain in the bottom, makes water play easy to provide. Some have sections for both water and sand. Others have waterways for floating toys. Add a bucket, sieve set, and waterwheel for many hours of fun.
- During warm summer weather, **a kiddy pool and sprinkler** are good choices. Some inflatable pools come with added features, such as slides or water sprays.
- **Supplies for painting and drawing** include tempera paint, painting cups, large brushes, a waterproof apron, washable markers and an easel.
- **A large whiteboard** works well for drawing with markers and is easy to wipe off for reuse.

■ **A child-size table and chairs** provide a good place to do art and sensory experiences. Look for ones with sturdy legs and washable surfaces.

Pretend Play: Toddlers like to try out grown-up roles. To foster this budding pretend play, look for toys to use for imitating typical family themes.

■ **Baby dolls and stuffed animals** are favorites for both boys and girls. Skip the ones that walk and talk, and, instead, opt for those that are simple, soft, and indestructible. Accessories for taking care of a baby include a stroller, cradle, bottle, and blankets.
■ Augment your grandchild's pretend cooking with a set of **toy dishes, pots and pans, plastic food, and a shopping cart.**
■ **Cars, trucks, planes, and trains** come in many styles and sizes. Look for sturdy construction and no small, easily detachable parts. Ones with passengers to load and unload are often popular.

Educational Play: Toys, books, and games can be a vehicle for learning colors, shapes, numbers, and letters, but do skip those with structured lessons on academic skills.

■ Early exposure to entertaining **books** is the best way to lay a foundation for future academic success. Look for books with fun features. Pop-up books have dramatic three-dimensional expansions. Lift-the-flap books invite active participation in opening and closing each flap.
■ Some **computer programs**, particularly those with interactive story formats, are appropriate for older toddlers. Actively participating with your grandchild enhances the social and educational value.
■ Along with their primary benefit as manipulative toys, **puzzles and shape sorters** can be a handy way to teach the names of shapes and colors.

Three- and Four-Year-Olds

Manipulative Play: Manipulative toys develop fine motor skills, problem solving, and creativity. Open-ended construction sets sustain interest with their multiple possibilities. Give your grandchild plenty of time to experiment with her own designs. Although she may identify what she has built as an airplane, spaceship, or skyscraper, don't rush her to make the models shown on the package. She will get to this in her own good time.

- **Wooden unit blocks** are a pricey but long-term investment. These come in many lengths and shapes. Your grandchild will get significantly more use out of a larger set that permits more elaborate constructions. To enhance pretend play, add sets of small vehicles, people, and animals to use with the castles, corrals, and highways that she builds.
- **Plastic interlocking building sets** provide easy, open-ended construction. Sets with larger pieces are best for beginners.
- For older preschoolers add variety to manipulative play with **Tinker Toys, Lincoln Logs, a gear set, or a marble run** with multiple construction options.
- Preschoolers soon move beyond one-piece wooden **puzzles** to those with 10–20 pieces that fit into a tray and to floor puzzles with large, interlocking pieces.

Active Play: Toys and equipment for active play develop coordination, balance, and large muscle strength. They encourage preschoolers to get the vigorous, whole body exercise they want and need.

- Preschoolers are ready for **wheeled toys with pedals**. The right-size trike is one she can get on and off without assistance. Or select from the many kiddy car models with pedals.
- **Backyard climbers and gym sets** come in many styles and prices. Wood, metal, or plastic? Each has its pros and cons. Consider aesthetics, price, and maintenance in making your decision. What features to include? Options include slides, ladders, bridges, towers, crawl-through spaces, swings, cargo nets, and rock-climbing walls. Some encourage imaginative play by incorporating a playhouse or hideout.

Creative Play: Your preschool grandchild can explore sound, rhythm, and movement with musical instruments. Art supplies encourage artistic expression. For an attractive gift presentation, display in a large straw basket or carrying case.

- **Basic art supplies** include scissors, colored construction paper, tempera paint, fingerpaint, paint brushes, crayons, washable markers, play dough, and glue.

- **A kid-friendly tape recorder or CD player** puts your grandchild in charge of selecting and playing music. She will probably want to sing along and move to the music. Along with **recordings** specifically for children, provide her with music of many different styles and tempos. A good introduction to classical music is the *Classical Kids* series.

- **A toy piano** lets your grandchild create her own music. With a set of **percussion instruments** she can experiment with sounds, tempo, and rhythm.

Pretend Play: During these prime pretend play years, toys that stimulate your grandchild's imagination are bound to be favorites. The pretend games of older preschoolers can have complex storylines and include fantasy as well as realistic roles.

- Both boys and girls enjoy playing with **dolls**. There are now many multicultural dolls available to reflect our national diversity. Look for an easy-to-dress baby doll that has several outfits or a waterproof doll for water play.

- A **kitchen center** with stove, sink, and refrigerator encourages extensive pretend cooking. A sink with a removable basin makes it easy to add water play.

- Preschoolers often expand grown-up roles to include a doctor, veterinarian, police officer, astronaut, firefighter, chef, or construction worker. You can buy **costumes, hats, and kits with accessories for community helpers**. For example, a doctor's kit would typically include a stethoscope, syringe, blood pressure cuff, and other medical supplies.

- All kinds and sizes of **vehicles** inspire imaginative play. With a dump truck and bulldozer in the sandbox, your grandchild can engineer major road constructions. Wooden train sets become more complex as you add new bridges, tunnels, roundhouses, and other accessories.

- **Mini-pretend settings** are another option. The all-time favorite, **a doll house**, comes in many plastic and wooden models. Preschoolers find that simple accessories and an open floor plan make for ease in handling. Be sure to include a family of dolls to live in the house. Introduce a new pretend theme with a castle, parking garage, or pirate ship. A **floor mat** with a farm scene or city roads encourages many hours of pretend play. Add a set of **animals or small cars** when you roll out the mat.

Educational Play: Simple games and puzzles are a fun way to learn colors and shapes, recognize letters and numerals, and practice counting. Even though your grandchild is the brightest on the block, resist the urge to buy ever more advanced educational toys. Good ones build on skills that she has begun to master. Technology can add pizzazz to literacy experiences and skills mastery, but let your first criteria in selecting tech toys be that it is fun.

- Select **board games that are based on chance**, not skill, and have a few simple rules. These are easy to modify for cooperative play and lenient rule enforcement. Classic board games, such as *Candyland, Chutes and Ladders,* and *Hi Ho! Cherry-O,* provide ample practice in math skills. Updated versions may have the extra appeal of popular licensed characters. Games, such as *Concentration* and *Lotto,* foster memory and vocabulary development.
- **Picture books and subscriptions to children's magazines,** such as *Humpty Dumpty's Magazine* or *Ladybug,* are the best way to foster literacy. It's worth investing in quality hardback books, for your grandchild will want to read her favorites over and over.
- **DVDs, videos, and CD-ROMs featuring storybook classics** are another avenue to quality literature. Expand the literacy experience with a book version of the story.
- Many preschoolers enjoy **electronic books,** such as LeapPad, because they can click on objects and make things happen. They are a fun way to learn basic concepts and are easy to take along when traveling.
- **Computer games** can entertain your preschooler while teaching reading and math skills. For best results, play along with your grandchild, keep the screen time brief, and follow up with real objects that she can manipulate.

Five- to Eight-Year-Olds

Manipulative Play: Your grandchild's advances in dexterity and conceptual thinking mean she can handle more difficult manipulative toys. Encourage your granddaughter, as well as your grandson, to play with these toys.

- **Construction sets,** such as Legos, magnetic sets, and Tinker Toys, continue to be good choices. Your grandchild may like to make more realistic objects that she can play with, such as spaceships and machines. She is better able to follow directions and to utilize pictures of models included with the manipulative toys, so sets designed to make a specific item are now appropriate.

▪ Your grandchild may like the challenge of **puzzles with 25 or more pieces.** These puzzles lend themselves to a cooperative effort with you and your grandchild.

▪ What about **video game systems**? I really can't recommend them. They do improve fine motor skills and reaction times, but they can become so addictive that they take too much time away from more valuable types of play, and they often have aggressive themes.

Active Play: Your grandchild is able to master more complex gross motor skills. There is typically a shift toward team sports and lessons for teaching specific physical skills.

▪ Give your grandchild **sports equipment** to practice her favorite team sport at home. Buy scaled-down but solid sports equipment, such as a T-ball set, baseball glove, bat and ball, basketball and hoop, or soccer ball and goal.

▪ Many kindergartners are ready for a **bicycle** with training wheels. Skip the gears and handbrakes. Learning how to balance is challenge enough. The right size is one she can easily straddle without adult assistance.

▪ Consider equipment for active play that your grandchild can do on her own, such as a **jump rope, scooter, snorkeling mask, sled, skates, or hopscotch mat.**

▪ Give a gift of **gymnastics, swimming, or martial arts lessons.**

Creative Play: Your grandchild will probably become more interested in the finished product. She may be ready to concentrate on mastering a new art or craft.

▪ Some **crafts kits** are appropriate for young children, such as simple jewelry-making or sewing kits. One advantage is that the kits include everything needed to complete the project: materials, tools, and directions.

▪ Encourage early carpentry efforts with a **woodworking kit** for making a bird feeder or treasure chest and a **tool box** with real but child-size tools.

- **Enhance basic art supplies** with clay and modeling tools or a good-quality set of painting supplies.

Pretend Play: A good way to keep your grandchild's imagination active is to enrich her current fantasy interests with new toys and props.

- Your granddaughter may especially like **dolls** such as Barbie or American Girl, which have many **outfits and accessories**.
- Your grandson may like to pretend through **action figures and their many accessories**.
- **Elaborate costumes** for pirates, knights, princesses, and other fantasy characters can enhance imaginative play.
- **A set of puppets and a stage** will encourage your grandchild to create and act out her own stories.

Educational Play: Toys and games can entertain even as they support school learning.

- **Science equipment**, such as a microscope, binoculars, ant farm, or rock tumbler, tweaks curiosity and provides concrete learning experiences.
- **Board games that add an element of strategy** enhance thinking ability. Examples are such classics as *Clue, Chinese Checkers*, and *Parcheesi.*
- Teach geography through a **globe or puzzle of the United States.**
- Encourage writing with a **book-publishing kit** that allows your grandchild to create a professionally finished book (e.g., *IlluStory*).
- Encourage reading with a **magazine subscription** that taps into her special interests (e.g., *Ranger Rick, National Geographic Kids* or *Sports Illustrated for Kids*).

For more gift ideas consult the most recent annual edition of *Oppenheim Toy Portfolio: The Best Toys, Books, DVDs, and Music for Kids.* This book summarizes the findings of an independent consumer group that tests new toys, books, and technology for children, describes the pros and cons of specific products, and provides a list of award-winning products. Another practical guide is *Toy Tips: A Parent's Essential Guide to Smart Toy Choices.* Based on many years of independent consumer-focused research, it is a practical guide for selecting appropriate toys.

12

Let's Make Gifts

Creating Hats, Hearts, and Handprints

In the glow of Christmas anticipation, my grandchildren and I worked diligently to make candle holders as gifts. We went through five pounds of plaster of Paris, a box of votive candles, and too many jewels, stones, and beads to count. We used the tissue paper we had decorated with Christmas

Let's Grandparent: Activity Guide for Young Grandchildren, pages 207–217

trees, bells, and stars to wrap each gift. Although it took Jenna 15 minutes and a half roll of tape to wrap one package, her reward was a great sense of satisfaction and Jake's "You're a great wrapper!" I also received an unexpected reward on Christmas morning. When I asked Jake what he wanted to open first, he exclaimed, "The gifts we made!" and then enthusiastically delivered a gift to each of the assembled grown-ups. The jewels did glimmer in the candlelight as they lit up our Christmas dinner table, just as Jake had predicted. They also lit up my hope for nurturing positive social attitudes in my grandchildren.

Why Try It?

Sometimes the focus is so much on what gifts to give our grandchild that we neglect the other side of the coin, teaching the pleasure of giving. Encouraging your grandchild to make gifts for others is an excellent way to do this. When he makes a gift and delivers it to its enthusiastic recipient, he has the double pleasure of creating the gift and then receiving kudos for his thoughtfulness and productive work.

Snapshot of Development

Understanding what gift-giving is all about slowly develops during your grandchild's early years. No amount of urging would get my toddler grandson to show any interest in making or giving gifts, but when he turned 3 he surprised me by putting a lump of play dough and a painting in a box for his mother's birthday. Without quite understanding its significance, he was imitating his older sister, who had worked for several days making and wrapping a gift. At 6 she was able to understand what her mother would like and how much pleasure she would feel in receiving this gift. She had developed a mature theory of mind, in which she could take the perspective of another person and appreciate what he or she might be thinking and feeling.

Another hurdle to overcome when making gifts with your grandchild is producing a pleasing finished product. Young children are primarily interested in doing the activity, not making something that looks good. This is all well and good when doing art or using exploratory materials, but you will doubtless have some vested interest in making a gift moderately appealing.

A third hurdle is that the precise fine motor development of fingers and hands takes many years to develop. Even though your grandchild may know what he wants to make, he may have trouble executing it.

With all these developmental roadblocks, wouldn't it just be better to wait until your grandchild is school-age before attempting to make gifts? Easier, yes, but then he would miss out on some rewarding early opportunities for prosocial learning.

Tips for Making Gifts

Limit alternatives. While your grandchild may be able to generate excellent gift ideas for other children, he may have a hard time coming up with appropriate grown-up gifts. He thinks more in terms of what he would like instead of the grown-up's interests. One solution is to let him choose between a few clearly defined alternatives. He can pick out a coffee cup or plate to paint for his father. He can choose between placemats or a potted plant for his mother.

Balance process and product. How do you overcome the dilemma of having your process-oriented grandchild produce a pleasing final product? You have to balance his desire to have fun in the here and now with your desire to end up with a presentable final product. Choose a project that gives him some latitude to explore the materials and try to resist any impulse to take over and redo his efforts. When he is done, you can add some finishing touches, perhaps a frame or extra glue to hold it securely together, but let it remain his project.

Provide a model. It often helps to provide a visual image of what he is trying to make. This is not so that he can make a carbon copy, but to give him a better understanding of his goal. A picture on a kit or photo in a book can serve this purpose. Or you could make a simple model. While making it, you may also discover how to head off potential problems or ways to enrich the project.

Give technical assistance. Your grandchild may know what he wants to do but not have the fine motor skills to carry it out. You can provide technical assistance without interfering with his creative choices. You are there to thread the needle, hold the wooden pieces in place until the glue dries, or securely clamp the pieces of the earrings together. You may also need to guide him through each step in the directions and encourage him to stay on task until it is completed.

Enhance with frills and fanfare. The gift-giving process needn't stop once the gift is made. Your grandchild can decorate wrapping paper and help wrap the gift. Provide ample tape, stick-on bows, and large nametags, and then stand by to assist as needed. Suggest making a card to accompany the gift. Remind him that although he can display the package he has wrapped, he should keep the contents secret. Then make a big production out of presenting the gift.

Activities

The following sections include ideas for gifts to make for both grown-ups and children. Some are super simple, while others require special materials and your help to complete successfully.

The First Three Years

Developmental Insights

Of course, an infant has no concept of gift-giving, and even the 2-year-old, with his egocentric view of the world, has at best a foggy notion of what it means to make and give a gift. But don't let this deter you from making a memento of your grandchild's earliest years to give to his appreciative parents.

Gifts to Make

Many Moods: Surround a copy of your grandchild's birth announcement with a collage of photos depicting many moods: a smile of recognition, an angry cry, wide-eyed surprise, and the contentment of sleep. Set in an attractive frame for hanging in the nursery.

WHAT YOU NEED: *birth announcement, baby photos, glue, frame*

First Impressions: Capture your grandchild's tiny handprints in plaster of Paris. With 10-month-old Emerson, I did one hand and one foot. For the best finished product, use a kit that comes with a mold, plaster of Paris, paints, and step-by-step directions. It is important to measure the water and plaster carefully and check frequently until the consistency is just right. I strongly recommend that a second adult help you when you place your grandchild's hands in the plaster. After the plaster dries, remove from mold and decorate with paint.

WHAT YOU NEED: *mold, plaster of Paris, water, paint, brush, washcloth and towel*

Hands Down: Create an attractive painting from your grandchild's handprints. Put a sponge in a saucer and saturate with tempera paint. Prepare separate sponges for two or three colors. Have your grandchild press his hand into the paint and then place it carefully on the paper. Continue until you like the overall effect. Follow up by supplying another piece of paper that he can paint however much he pleases, with no concern about muddying colors or smearing the prints. Mount the handprint picture on poster board and frame.

WHAT YOU NEED: *paper, saucers, sponges, tempera paint, poster board, frame*

Painted Shells: Use your grandchild's interest in painting objects to create an attractive seashell display. He can paint shells collected at the beach or bought at a craft store. To display his shells, arrange them in a small box lined with foil or tissue paper.

WHAT YOU NEED: *tempera paint, brushes, seashells, box, foil or tissue paper*

Big Bugs: Turn stones your grandchild has painted into cute paper weights. Have your grandchild paint round stones in bright colors. Glue on goggle eyes and pipe cleaner antennae to create big bugs. For best results, use a glue gun.

WHAT YOU NEED: *round stones, tempera paint, brushes, glue, scissors, goggle eyes, pipe cleaner, glue gun*

Three- and Four-Year-Olds

Developmental Insights

Focus early gift-giving efforts on those for your grandchild's parents. He can show his affection and gratitude toward them by making a special gift. They will enjoy whatever he makes. Even if it is lopsided or the paint smeared, they will be appropriately pleased and complimentary.

Projects should take into account your grandchild's limitations in fine motor skills and stay within his comfort zone. Those that can be completed fairly quickly in one sitting are good choices. To accomplish this, do some of the work ahead of time, such as selecting appropriate photos or cutting out shapes. Keep in mind that he may be primarily interested in doing the activity, not the final product. Let him have fun and then add a few finishing touches.

When giving gifts, preschoolers often reveal their immature theory of the mind. They assume that others know what they know. *Secret* and *surprise* are difficult concepts to grasp. As a result, Jenna could say to her mother, "I made you a necklace. I'm going to wrap it up, so it will be a surprise."

Gifts to Make

Treasure Chest: Your grandchild can create a unique storage box from family photos. Cut photos into small circles, ovals, triangles, and squares. Have him glue them all over the top and sides of a large shoe box.

WHAT YOU NEED: *shoe box, family photos, scissors, glue*

Photo Mats: To make memorable placemats, cut brightly colored poster board into 12 × 16-inch rectangles. Have your grandchild cut family photos into interesting shapes and glue on the poster board. On the back, he can draw a picture with colorful markers. Cover with clear contact paper, leaving a 1-inch margin beyond the poster board to keep out moisture. If you do this each year and then put out a set on a special family occasion, it will generate animated discussion about past events and how much everyone has changed.

WHAT YOU NEED: *poster board, photos, markers, contact paper, scissors*

Sweet and Pretty: Help your grandchild make several kinds of cookies. One could be a sugar cookie with colors and decorations to match the holiday. He can decorate the outside and top of a shoe box or plastic container with tempera paint. Line the container with foil, and fill with cookies.

WHAT YOU NEED: *cookies, shoe box or plastic container, paint, foil*

Mosaic Candle holder: To make a decorative candle holder, mix plaster of Paris and water together as directed on the package. Pour mixture into a small, shallow plastic or paper bowl. Anchor a candle in the plaster. Then have your grandchild push shiny, brightly colored beads, stones, buttons, or glass jewels into the plaster. Let it dry thoroughly before removing from the bowl. Since the plaster dries quickly, select items to use before mixing the plaster.

WHAT YOU NEED: *plaster of Paris, water, shallow bowls, candles, beads, stones, buttons, or glass beads*

Silly Soap: Soap-making kits come with blocks of soap, molds, and scents. Children's versions often include such odious items as metal spiders or worms to put in the soap. Your grandchild can cut up the soap and select the mold, scent, and item to add. When my grandchildren did this, Jake added a tiny car to his soap, while Jenna added glitter. Then melt the soap in the microwave, pour in the mold, and cool briefly in the freezer.

WHAT YOU NEED: *soap-making kit, small plastic or metal objects, microwave oven*

Jewelry in a Jiffy: A quick and easy method to make jewelry is with long pipe cleaners and beads with large holes. Your grandchild can easily string these on the pipe cleaners and then twist the ends together. One pipe cleaner makes a nice bracelet. To make a necklace, twist two or three pipe cleaners together before adding the beads.

WHAT YOU NEED: *pipe cleaners, beads*

Glitter and Glow: These easy-to-make candles sparkle in the glow of their own light. In no time at all, your grandchild can make one for each of the grown-ups on his list. Spread glitter or sequins on a paper plate. Dilute white glue with a little water in a paper cup. He can use a small brush to spread the glue all over a pillar candle and then roll it in the glitter or sequins until it is completely covered. Let it dry overnight before wrapping.

WHAT YOU NEED: *pillar candles, glitter or sequins, brush, glue, paper cup, paper plate*

Beautiful Blossoms: A flowering plant is a welcome addition to any windowsill or patio. Purchase small terracotta or Styrofoam gardening pots. Have your grandchild paint the pots in several bright colors and tie a ribbon around the pot when it is dry. He can fill the pots with potting soil and then plant several marigolds, daisies, or petunias in each pot. Suggest that he water his flowers and put them in a sunny spot. Just before he gives his flower gift, help him wrap it in tissue paper and add a big bow on the top.

WHAT YOU NEED: *gardening pots, paint, brushes, ribbon, potting soil, flowering plants, tissue paper, bows*

Original Wrap: Decorate paper to use for wrapping gifts. Tissue paper works best. Saturate several sponges with tempera paint, using traditional holiday colors. Then use a cookie cutter to stamp holiday shapes on the paper. Or cut a sponge into an interesting shape for making prints.

WHAT YOU NEED: *tissue paper, sponges, tempera paint, cookie cutters*

Five- to Eight-Year-Olds

Developmental Insights

Your grandchild will want to expand his gift-making to include his teacher, grandparents, siblings, and best friends. His more mature theory of mind means he can take the perspective of another person and figure out what would be an appropriate gift. He enjoys working secretively on a gift and anticipates the recipient's surprise and pleasure.

He has the fine motor skills to attempt more difficult projects and is goal-directed enough to choose projects that require several work sessions. He wants an attractive finished product and may be critical of his own efforts if it does not measure up to his standards. He may want you to help him make improvements and may need your encouragement to persist until he has completed his gift.

Gifts to Make

Mini-Magnets: Small magnets are great for holding pictures or notes on the refrigerator. Buy small magnets at a craft store. Cut out 2-inch circles from white cardboard. Have your grandchild decorate each with a brightly colored drawing and glue a magnet on the back of each. Another option is to glue a magnet to a clip-type clothespin and decorate it with sequins, glitter, and beads. The clip is useful for holding drawings and messages.

WHAT YOU NEED: *small magnets, cardboard, scissors, markers, glue; clip-type clothespin and sequins, glitter, or beads*

Designer Digs: It is fun to create a personalized T-shirt with fabric paint. Start with a white or pastel shirt. Encourage your grandchild to make a draft of the design on paper first, because there is no removing the paint once applied to the fabric. He can write a family member or friend's name or a short message and then draw a few pictures around the words. This becomes his guide as he paints on the shirt. Put a piece of cardboard inside the shirt to prevent the paint from bleeding through to the other side. And be sure to have him wear a smock to protect his clothing. After the front is dry, turn it over and let him paint on the back. Another time, use fabric paint to decorate a canvas bag or wide-brimmed fabric hat.

WHAT YOU NEED: *T-shirt, canvas bag, or hat; fabric paint, brushes, cardboard*

Personal Plate: Ceramic items decorated by your grandchild make long-lasting keepsakes. In a make-it-yourself ceramics store, such as *Color Me Mine*, your grandchild can select a plate, mug, or figurine to paint. The firing and glazing produces brilliant colors, guaranteeing an aesthetically pleasing final product. An alternative, available in craft stores, is a kit that includes permanent markers and a plate or cup to decorate. These require no firing but the paint is not as durable.

WHAT YOU NEED: *kit for decorating plate or cup or make-it-yourself ceramic store*

Hands on the Wall: To make a wall hanging that features your grandchild's handprint, mix plaster of Paris with water according to directions on the package and pour into a saucer. Help your grandchild place his hand into the plaster and slowly remove it, palm first. Use a pencil to make a hole through the plaster for hanging. Have him etch his name and the date under the handprint with a large toothpick. He may like to sketch small figures around the handprint as well. When it is completely dry, he can paint it with tempera paint.

WHAT YOU NEED: *plaster of Paris, saucer, mixing bowl, spoon, toothpick, tempera paint*

Frame a Masterpiece: When your grandchild has created an especially interesting picture, suggest that he set it off with a frame to give as a gift. First glue the picture on poster board. Then have him glue craft sticks around the borders and decorate with paint and glitter.

WHAT YOU NEED: *grandchild's picture, poster board, craft sticks, paint, glitter*

Gumdrops Galore: This attractive Christmas tree ornament is fun and easy to make. Push toothpicks through a large marshmallow, leaving a short piece of toothpick on each side. To completely cover the marshmallow, use eight toothpicks on the sides and four on the top/bottom. Put a gum drop on each end. Tie a thin ribbon around it and hang on the tree.

WHAT YOU NEED: *toothpicks, gumdrops, marshmallows, ribbon*

Rubber Band Board: Making a rubber band board is a great gift for another child. Have your grandchild pound nails halfway into a 1-foot square piece of plywood. After the board is covered with nails, provide rubber bands of various colors and sizes to stretch and crisscross between nails in interesting designs and patterns.

WHAT YOU NEED: *hammer, nails, rubber bands, square of plywood*

Beautiful Beads: Jewelry-making kits include materials for earrings, necklaces, pendants, and bracelets. Ones with alphabet beads are especially nice, because your grandchild can spell out the recipient's name and an affectionate *I love you* or *My best friend.*

WHAT YOU NEED: *jewelry-making kit, small pliers*

Personalized Stationery: Parents are sure to enjoy stationery designed by their child. To make letter-size stationery, help your grandchild select an interesting font and type the recipient's name on the top of a full sheet of paper. Then he can draw tiny pictures along the sides and bottom of the page. For the avid cyclist, bikes could race all around the edges. The gardener's stationery could have a flower garden along the bottom margin and vines running up the sides. Use a color printer to make copies on quality stationery paper.

To make note cards, use 8 × 5-inch index cards. Fold in half to make a 4 × 5 rectangle. Your grandchild can draw a picture on this. You can either open it up and make copies or have him continue to make original drawings on additional cards. Purchase envelopes to match the stationery, tie together with ribbon, and place in a clear plastic bag.

WHAT YOU NEED: *paper, computer, printer, markers, index cards, ribbon,*
                 plastic bag

Picture Puzzles: Your grandchild can make puzzles for friends and siblings. Cut a 6-inch square from a file folder. Have your grandchild use brightly colored markers to draw a picture that covers the entire area. Another way to make the puzzle is to use a large photo or magazine picture. Paste this to a file folder, being sure to spread the paste evenly over the entire surface. Make a border around the outside edges with a marker. Then cut the picture into nine 2-inch squares. Your grandchild may want to cut his puzzle into many zigzag pieces, similar to ready-made puzzles, but this can make putting it together quite frustrating, because the pieces do not interlock. Make a puzzle board from another 6-inch square cut from a file folder and draw a grid dividing it into nine 2-inch squares. The border and the board make it easier to put the puzzle together. Put the board and the pieces in a plastic zip-lock bag.

WHAT YOU NEED: *file folder, markers, scissors, plastic zip-lock bag; paste, photo or magazine picture*

Unique Board Game: Your grandchild can create an original board game to give to another child. Using a file folder as the board makes it easy to store. Use poster board if you want to make it larger. Show him how to make a zigzag or spiral path and subdivide it into squares. To determine moves, use ready-made dice or make a large die by gluing a picture or color on each side of a wooden block. Another option is to make a spinner. Cut out a 6 × 6-inch square from poster board and divide it into four to eight sections, putting a symbol or color in each section. Cut out an arrow from the poster board, push a brad through it, and attach it to the center of the spinner.

Select a theme that interests your grandchild. It could be kitties trying to get back to their mother or an astronaut headed for the moon. Or, it could be overcoming the many detours and hurdles along the road to Grandma's house, like flat tires, motion sickness, bathroom stops, running out of gas, or a stop for ice cream, and then use small cars to move along the road. Since my grandchildren were Winnie the Pooh fans, we made our trail using Pooh stickers and drew a big honey pot at the end of the trail. Each section on the spinner had a different Winnie the Pooh character. If the spinner landed on Tigger, that player moved up the trail to the next Tigger picture.

WHAT YOU NEED: *file folder or poster board, markers; stickers, dice, block, glue, brad*

Stitch It: Craft stores have needlework kits with simple instructions and all the materials needed to make an attractive gift. Most are too difficult for kindergartners, but with assistance, your grandchild may be able to use some of them. Simple sewing kits, featuring precut animal shapes, oversized needles, and precut holes, turned out to be an excellent first sewing experience for my grandchildren. They worked diligently on these projects and prized the stuffed animals they made, which made great gifts for their little brother.

WHAT YOU NEED: *simple sewing kit*

The Finishing Touch: Make unique nametags for your gifts, such as these that Grandma Susan and her granddaughter made. Using 2 × 3-inch index cards, they punched a hole in one corner and looped ribbon through it for fastening. Then they wrote the name on the card and glued on a few buttons. As a final touch, they pasted on words like *Celebrate* or *Season's Greetings* cut from magazines or greeting cards.

WHAT YOU NEED: *index cards, ribbon, glue, buttons, magazines or greeting cards*

Spin in the Wind: Pinwheels are fun to give to another child. Cut out a 5-inch square from lightweight paper. Origami squares are precut and have interesting patterns. Cut a diagonal line from each corner to ½ inch of center. Fold the outside corner of each flap into the center of the square and hold in place with tape. Place a straight pin through the paper and tape, and then attach it to a plastic straw. Bend the pin down with pliers and place tape over the sharp end. Be sure to leave the pinwheel loose enough so it can move freely. Test it out by blowing on it.

WHAT YOU NEED: *lightweight paper, scissors, straight pin, tape, plastic straw, pliers*

A Book Just for You: Your grandchild can create a book especially designed for the recipient. It could be a picture book of cars, trucks, and trains for his younger brother, a story about the big fish that got away for Granddad who loves to fish, a story about when Mommy was a track star, or the trip to the circus with Dad. Include a page dedicating the book to this person and add a brief explanation about why it is especially appropriate for him or her. Full-size sheets of typing paper give your grandchild plenty of room to draw a picture and write a sentence or two on each page. Don't bind the pages together in a book format until your grandchild is satisfied with each page. For a nice finishing touch, take it to an office store to get a clear plastic cover with coil binding.

WHAT YOU NEED: *pencils, markers, or crayons; paper; clear plastic cover with coil binding*

Conclusion

Let's Look Ahead
Expanding Options

"Two-four-six-eight. Who do we eliminate?" chanted three boys in the back seat of my car. Then with great glee they shouted, "Girls!" "Girls!" All for the benefit of their sisters and the male bonding experience. "But," mused Jake, "we can't eliminate my grandmother, 'cause she spoils me!"

Let's Grandparent: Activity Guide for Young Grandchildren, pages 219–221
Copyright © 2008 by Information Age Publishing
All rights of reproduction in any form reserved.

I hope that this book has shown you how to "spoil" your grandchild with quality time, fun activities, and in-depth understanding. Then your grandchild will also affirm that you "can't be eliminated" because you are such a great source of fun and affection. Let's review the tools this book has provided for making this happen.

First, you now have at your disposable a **solid understanding of child development**. You know how children learn and what grandparents can do to foster optimal development. Along with the added pleasure it brings to grandkid-watching, this knowledge has practical applications. The seemingly mysterious quirks and inconsistencies in a grandchild's behavior now make sense. You understand why your formerly friendly 10-month-old grandchild suddenly screams when you approach, why your 2-year-old granddaughter refuses to wear a pretty new outfit, or why your 4-year-old suddenly begins struggling to get her words out. Equipped with this understanding, you can better come up with effective solutions. You appreciate the need for selecting activities based on your grandchild's developmental level. Instead of a trial-and-error approach, you use your knowledge base to select appropriate, successful experiences. You take the 2-year-old to the neighborhood playground, not the mall. You give the 3-year-old play dough and the 5-year-old clay.

Second, you have a **repertoire of fun and educational activities** to enjoy with your grandchild. Each chapter focused on a different type of activity. The wide range of choices encourages you to select those that especially appeal to you. If you don't like to cook, you choose a card game or art project. If you aren't up for a major outing today, perhaps curling up together with a good book will fill the bill. You have developed a repertoire of Old Faithful activities. You keep these materials available for spontaneous use and repeat them frequently. Sometimes, for the excitement of something new, you plan a special activity from the New Twists section. You use the age categories for activities as general guidelines, for you have found that your grandchild often asks for and enjoys repeating previous experiences. You have found ways to lure your grandchild into trying many types of activities, for you want him to become a well-rounded person.

Third, you have an arsenal of **simple how-to tips** to help you prepare a setting in which you can interact effectively with your grandchild. You bridge the gap between child development theories and activities, as you apply theories in real-life situations. You know what to say to a 3-year-old as she is drawing or how much help to give a 5-year-old with a cooking project. In each chapter, I explored the benefits of different activities and tried to give preemptive solutions to potential problems.

I hope these activities have inspired you to come up with your own original ideas. I encourage you to share your original activities, experiences, recommendations, and anecdotes with other grandparents. You can do this on the *Let's Grandparent* website (letsgrandparent.com) or e-mail me at *joanevaughan@yahoo.com.* Along with sharing experiences, the website provides a forum for discussing grandparenting issues. It also has suggestions for fun things to do with grandchildren and links to websites with games for children and with information for grandparents. Visit this site often and become actively engaged with us in our discussion and sharing.

My plan is to include authentic, meaningful material obtained from this website forum in future books in the *Let's Grandparent* series. Books planned for this series are:

- *Let's Grandparent: Activity Guide for School-Age Grandchildren.* This book will provide guidelines for and examples of meaningful activities to do with grandchildren between 7 and 12 years old. It will focus on how to enrich academic learning and how to take successful extended trips together.
- *Let's Grandparent: Activity Guide for Teenage Grandchildren.* This book will help grandparents negotiate meaningful relationships with their grandchildren through those sometimes difficult adolescent years. It will focus on effective communications strategies, supporting the grandchild's special interests, and understanding common concerns and stresses faced by today's teenagers.
- *Let's Grandparent: Activity Guide for Grandchildren with Special Needs.* This book will serve as a guide for grandparents who have a grandchild with special needs. It will focus on adapting activities for a special needs grandchild and the importance of a positive attitude. It will discuss children with Down syndrome, autism, attention-deficit hyperactivity disorder, learning disabilities, hearing and visual impairment, and physical disabilities.
- *Let's Grandparent: Grandparents' Favorite Activities.* This will be a collection of grandparents' all-time favorite activities to do with their grandchildren. For each activity there will be information about the grandparent who submitted the activity, an anecdote that describes his or her experience in doing it, and a detailed explanation for carrying it out.

Index of Activities

Let's Do Art

One- and Two-Year-Olds

Three- and Four-Year-Olds

Let's Grandparent: Activity Guide for Young Grandchildren, pages 223–236

Copyright © 2008 by Information Age Publishing
223

Let's Talk

Let's Read and Write

Five- to Eight-Year-Olds

Let's Go

The First Year

One- and Two-Year-Olds

Three- and Four-Year-Olds

Five- to Eight-Year-Olds

Let's Explore

Let's Play Games

Let's Pretend

Let's Cook

Three- and Four-Year-Olds

Five- to Eight-Year-Olds

Let's Celebrate

Activities for All Ages

Three- and Four-Year-Olds

Five- to Eight-Year-Olds

Let's Make Gifts

The First Three Years

References

Ainsworth, Mary. (1993). Attachment as related to mother–infant interaction. *Advances in Infancy Research, 8,* 1–50.

Arthur's Computer Adventure. (2000). Fremont, CA: Learning Company.

Astroth, Sue. (2007). *Super-Simple Creative Costume.* Lafayette, CA: C&T Publishing.

Baby Einstein Company. (2001). *Baby Van Gogh.* Burbank, CA: Buena Vista Home Entertainment.

Bailey, Debbie. (1999). *Let's Pretend.* Toronto: Annick Press.

Barton, Byron. (1991). *The Three Bears.* New York: HarperCollins.

Bemelmans, Ludwig. (1967). *Madeline.* New York: Viking Press.

Brown, Marc. (1980). *Finger Rhymes.* New York: Dutton.

Brown, Marc. (1983–2007). *Arthur* series. New York: Random House.

Brown, Marc. (1985). *Hand Rhymes.* New York: Dutton.

Brown, Margaret Wise. (1947). *Goodnight Moon.* New York: Harper.

Burton, Virginia Lee. (1939). *Mike Mulligan and His Steam Shovel.* Boston: Houghton Mifflin.

Classical Kids series. (2002–2006). Stonington, ME: School Productions.

Cole, Joanna. (1995–2003). *The Magic School Bus* series. New York: Scholastic.

Cole, Joanna, and Stephanie Calmenson. (1991). *The Eentsy, Weentsy Spider: Fingerplays and Action Rhymes.* New York: Morrow Junior Books.

Crews, Donald. (1993). *Freight Train.* New York: Mulberry Books.

Cromwell, Liz, Dixie Hibner, and John Faitel. (1983). *Finger Frolics: Fingerplays for Young Children.* Livonia, MI: Partner Press.

Let's Grandparent: Activity Guide for Young Grandchildren, pages 237–239
Copyright © 2008 by Information Age Publishing

Cromwell, Liz, Dixie Hibner, and John Faitel. (1997). *Finger Frolics 2.* Livonia, MI: Partner Press.

Degen, Bruce. (1995). *Jamberry.* New York: HarperFestival.

Doggett, Bill, and Thomas Heinser. (1993). *Make Believe: A Book of Costume and Fantasy.* Palo Alto, CA: Klutz Press.

Eastman, Philip D. (1961). *Go, Dog, Go!* New York: Beginner Books.

Erikson, Erik. (1963). *Childhood and Society.* New York: Norton.

Ferguson, Don. (1996). *Disney's Aladdin.* San Francisco: Mouse Works, Inc.

Gardner, Howard. (1993). *Frames of Mind: The Theory of Multiple Intelligences.* New York: Basic Books.

Hay, Donna. (2004). *Cool Kids Cook.* New York: William Morrow.

Hill, Eric. (2000). *Where's Spot?* New York: Putnam.

Hoban, Tana. (1972). *Push, Pull, Empty, Full: A Book of Opposites.* New York: Macmillan.

Hoban, Tana. (1984). Is *It Rough? Is it Smooth? Is It Shiny?* New York: Greenwillow Books.

Holt, David. (1996). *Stellaluna.* Fremont, CA: Learning Company.

Humpty Dumpty's Magazine. Indianapolis, IN: Children's Better Health Institute.

Jumbo Box of Storybook Classics (DVDs). New York: Scholastic Video Collection.

Katzen, Mollie, and Ann Henderson. (1994). *Pretend Soup and Other Real Recipes: A Cookbook for Preschooler and Up.* Berkeley, CA: Tricycle Press.

Kimmel, Eric. (1993). *The Gingerbread Man.* New York: Holiday House.

Krauss, Ruth. (1993). *The Carrot Seed.* New York: HarperFestival.

Kunhardt, Dorothy. (1940). *Pat the bunny.* New York: Golden/Western.

Ladybug. Cricket Magazine Group. Peterborough, NH: Carus Publishing.

Lipson, Eden Ross. (2000). *The New York Times Parent's Guide to the Best Books for Children.* New York: Three Rivers Press.

Lobel, Arnold. (1970). *Frog and Toad Treasury: Three Books.* New York: HarperCollins.

Martin, Bill. (1983). *Brown Bear, Brown Bear, What Do You See?* New York: Holt, Rinehart, and Winston.

Maslen, Bobby Lynn. (2000). *Bob Books First!* New York: Scholastic.

Mayer, Mercer. (1968). *There's a Nightmare in My Closet.* New York: Dial Press.

Montroll, John. (1992). *Easy Origami.* New York: Dover.

National Geographic Kids. Washington, DC: National Geographic Society.

Oppenheim, Joanne, and Stephanie Oppenheim. (2007). *Oppenheim Toy Portfolio.* New York: Oppenheim Toy Portfolio, Inc.

Piaget, Jean. (1952). *The Origins of Intelligence in Children.* New York: International Universities Press.

Portis, Antoinette. (2006). *Not A Box.* New York: HarperCollins.

Printed in the United States
137687LV00003B/22/P

Ranger Rick. Reston, VA: National Wildlife Federation.

Rey, Hans Augusto. (1941). *Curious George.* Boston: Houghton Mifflin.

Rey, H. A. (1998). *Curious George Makes Pancakes.* Boston: Houghton Mifflin.

Rosen, Michael. (1997). *We're Going on a Bear Hunt.* New York: Little Simon.

Rowling, J.K. (1998–2008). *Harry Potter* series. New York: Scholastic.

Scarry, Richard. (1979). *What Do People Do All Day?* New York: Random House.

Seuss, Dr. (1957). *The Cat in the Hat.* Boston: Random House.

Seuss, Dr. (2001). *The Cat in the Hat* [CD-ROM]. Fremont, CA: Learning Company.

Seuss, Dr. (2001). *Green Eggs and Ham* [CD-ROM]. Fremont, CA: Learning Company.

Shannon, David. (1998). *No, David!* Leon: Editorial Everest.

Sobol, Donald. (1975–2007). *Encyclopedia Brown* series. New York: Dutton Children's Books.

Steig, William. (2005). *Sylvester and the Magic Pebble.* New York: Simon & Schuster Books for Young Readers.

Stevenson, Robert Louis. (1998). *A Child's Garden of Verses.* New York: Morrow.

Szymanski, Marianne, and Ellen Neuborne. (2004). *Toy Tips: A Parent's Essential Guide to Smart Toy Choices.* San Francisco: Jossey-Bass.

Temko, Florence. (1996). *Planes and Other Flying Things.* Brookfield, CT: Millbrook Press.

Thornton, Katharine. (1994). *The Halloween Costume Book.* New York: Berkley Books.

Waddell, Martin. (1996). *The Owl Babies.* Cambridge, MA: Candlewick Press.

Wade, Barrie. (2003). *The Three Billy Goats Gruff.* Minneapolis, MN: Picture Window Books.

Watson, N. Cameron. (1990). *The Little Pigs' Puppet Book.* Boston: Little, Brown.

Wells, Rosemary. (1996). *My very first Mother Goose.* Cambridge, MA: Candlewick Press.

Wilkes, Angela. (1989). *My First Cookbook.* New York: Random House.

A World of Holidays series. (1997–1999). Austin, TX: Raintree Steck-Vaughn.

Wright Group. (2004). *The Story Box.* New York: McGraw-Hill.